To Emily,

Chapter 5 is dedicated to you.

All my love,
Mark
x.

STATISTICAL DATA SCIENCE

Other World Scientific Titles by the Author

*Methods and Models in Statistics: In Honour of
Professor John Nelder, FRS*
edited by Niall Adams, Martin Crowder, David J Hand and
David Stephens
ISBN: 978-1-86094-463-5

Data Analysis for Network Cyber-Security
edited by Niall Adams and Nicholas Heard
ISBN: 978-1-78326-374-5

Dynamic Networks and Cyber-Security
edited by Niall Adams and Nick Heard
ISBN: 978-1-78634-074-0

STATISTICAL DATA SCIENCE

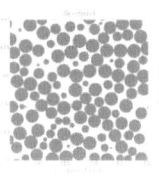

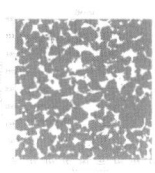

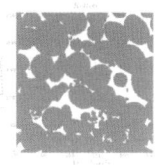

Editors

Niall Adams
Edward Cohen

Imperial College London, UK

World Scientific

NEW JERSEY · LONDON · SINGAPORE · BEIJING · SHANGHAI · HONG KONG · TAIPEI · CHENNAI · TOKYO

Published by

World Scientific Publishing Europe Ltd.
57 Shelton Street, Covent Garden, London WC2H 9HE
Head office: 5 Toh Tuck Link, Singapore 596224
USA office: 27 Warren Street, Suite 401-402, Hackensack, NJ 07601

Library of Congress Cataloging-in-Publication Data
Names: Adams, Niall M., 1968– editor. | Cohen, Ed (Statistician), editor.
Title: Statistical data science / edited by Niall Adams (Imperial College London, UK),
　　Ed Cohen (Imperial College London, UK).
Description: New Jersey : World Scientific, 2018. | Includes bibliographical references.
Identifiers: LCCN 2018010673 | ISBN 9781786345394 (hc : alk. paper)
Subjects: LCSH: Data mining. | Mathematical statistics.
Classification: LCC QA76.9.D343 S68455 | DDC 006.3/12--dc23
LC record available at https://lccn.loc.gov/2018010673

British Library Cataloguing-in-Publication Data
A catalogue record for this book is available from the British Library.

Copyright © 2018 by World Scientific Publishing Europe Ltd.

All rights reserved. This book, or parts thereof, may not be reproduced in any form or by any means, electronic or mechanical, including photocopying, recording or any information storage and retrieval system now known or to be invented, without written permission from the Publisher.

For photocopying of material in this volume, please pay a copying fee through the Copyright Clearance Center, Inc., 222 Rosewood Drive, Danvers, MA 01923, USA. In this case permission to photocopy is not required from the publisher.

For any available supplementary material, please visit
http://www.worldscientific.com/worldscibooks/10.1142/Q0159#t=suppl

Desk Editors: V. Vishnu Mohan/Jennifer Brough/Koe Shi Ying

Typeset by Stallion Press
Email: enquiries@stallionpress.com

Printed in Singapore

Preface

This volume is a collection of papers related to the conference "Statistical Data Science" held in July 2017 at both Imperial College London and Winton's[a] head office in London. The conference was organised jointly by two groups at Imperial College, the Department of Mathematics and the Data Science Institute, and Winton.

We are grateful to acknowledge very generous support from Winton, The Alan Turing Institute,[b] Mentat Innovations,[c] The Heilbronn Institute for Mathematical Research,[d] the Royal Statistical Society[e] and World Scientific.[f] Support from these organisation resulted in a remarkably successful conference, which attracted close to one hundred delegates from both industry and academia.

The conference was convened to explore synergies between Statistics and Data Science, specifically

> "Data science is an emerging discipline, fuelled by continuing advances in technology for data acquisition, storage and curation. Data Science is fundamentally inter-disciplinary, covering computer science and machine learning, mathematics and statistics, and domain knowledge from application areas. The role of statistics in this emerging discipline is unclear. This conference will feature invited and contributed papers exploring

---

[a] http://www.winton.com
[b] http://www.turing.ac.uk
[c] http://ment.at
[d] http://www.turing.ac.uk
[e] http://www.rss.ac.uk
[f] http://worldscientific.com

the nature of the relationship between statistics and data science, suggesting state-of-the-art reasoning from both areas, and developing a synergistic path forward."

The conference consisted of invited talks from eminent speakers, and contributed papers and talks. This collection consists of papers from both invited speakers and contributors.

The papers in this volume represent an eclectic mix of topics, perhaps consistent with the ethos of Data Science. The papers range across discussion about the relationship between the disciplines, fundamental aspects of statistical reasoning, and a diverse range of applications.

In Chapter 1, Oxbury asks the challenging question "Does data science need statistics?," a question central to the theme of the conference. Framing this question around the recruitment needs of a large organisation, a number of challenges are raised for the statistical community.

Kuffner and Young, in Chapter 2, discuss a number of deep statistical issues that arise in modern data science applications. They suggest that so-called "conditionality principles" are central to achieving valid statistical inference in data science.

The issue of performance assessment for classification methods is discussed by Hand in Chapter 3. It is shown that many familiar performance assessment methods are shown to have serious deficiencies. While some alleviation can be possible, Hand concludes that deeper thinking in the definition of the problems, and hence assessment measures, is required.

In Chapter 4, Edwards and Leslie use the example of the selection of elements for a webpage to a user to illustrate issues of accuracy and diversity in decision making. The concept of diversity is thoroughly described, and methods for finding an appropriate level of diversity are discussed.

Issues related to Bayesian model selection are reviewed by Briers in Chapter 5. In considering the issues, a new density estimation procedure is introduced, which exploits the output structure of the Markov Chain Monte Carlo procedures frequently used for Bayesian computations.

Briol and Girolami provide a concise introduction to the emerging field of "probabilistic numerics" in Chapter 6, and argue for its importance in the field of data science. At the core of the argument is the role of handling uncertainty in large-scale data science exercises.

Contributed papers included an impressive variety of both applications and methodologies. Meagher *et al.* consider the challenging problem of reconstructing the ancestral reconstruction of bat echolocation calls, in

Chapter 7. Using sophisticated phylogenetic methods based on Gaussian processes, a preliminary analysis suggest that such construction is feasible.

Mosser *et al.* consider the reconstruction of three-dimensional porous media in Chapter 8. Statistical approaches, incorporating physical knowledge and constrained to lower order moments are contrasted with methods based on generative adversarial networks. Arguments are made for the synthesis of the approaches.

Vollmer *et al.* also consider issues of uncertainty quantification, in the context of seismic onset detection, in Chapter 9. A particular emphasis is placed on uncertainty quantification for supporting and improving human decision making.

In Chapter 10, Abbot *et al.* consider the challenges of combining statistics and data science in the context of the UK government. These challenges are explored through two case studies; the first related to the production of official statistics, and the second related to using open source software to enhance document publication.

Finally, in Chapter 11, Araki and Akaho discuss issues of dimension reduction for spatio-temporal data, illustrating with the example of ozone concentration. A new method based on a spatially continuous dynamic factor model is detailed and shown to have desirable properties.

This collection of papers represents an eclectic mixture, similar to the character of the conference, and indeed to the character of data science.

Niall Adams and Edward Cohen

September 2017

Contents

Preface		v
1.	Does Data Science Need Statistics? *William Oxbury*	1
2.	Principled Statistical Inference in Data Science *Todd A. Kuffner and G. Alastair Young*	21
3.	Evaluating Statistical and Machine Learning Supervised Classification Methods *David J. Hand*	37
4.	Diversity as a Response to User Preference Uncertainty *James Edwards and David Leslie*	55
5.	*L*-kernel Density Estimation for Bayesian Model Selection *Mark Briers*	69
6.	Bayesian Numerical Methods as a Case Study for Statistical Data Science *François-Xavier Briol and Mark Girolami*	99

7.	Phylogenetic Gaussian Processes for Bat Echolocation	111
	J. P. Meagher, T. Damoulas, K. E. Jones and M. Girolami	
8.	Reconstruction of Three-Dimensional Porous Media: Statistical or Deep Learning Approach?	125
	Lukas Mosser, Thomas Le Blévec and Olivier Dubrule	
9.	Using Data-Driven Uncertainty Quantification to Support Decision Making	141
	Charlie Vollmer, Matt Peterson, David J. Stracuzzi and Maximillian G. Chen	
10.	Blending Data Science and Statistics across Government	155
	Owen Abbott, Philip Lee, Matthew Upson, Matthew Gregory and Dawn Duhaney	
11.	Dynamic Factor Modelling with Spatially Multi-scale Structures for Spatio-temporal Data	167
	Takamitsu Araki and Shotaro Akaho	
Index		181

Chapter 1

Does Data Science Need Statistics?

William Oxbury

Government Communications Headquarters, Cheltenham, UK

With modern cloud services offering elastic storage and compute, anyone with an online account can train models on data and can extract insights, visualisations and predictions. So for organisations with data scientific requirements, a question arises whether to hire statisticians or whether to focus on hiring computer scientists and developers. In this chapter, at the *Statistical Data Science* conference, we sketched some of our experience with data science in GCHQ, explored a few examples of analyses where pitfalls can arise from a naive application of tools, and we drew attention to some challenges for the statistical community.

1. Introduction

The title of this chapter is perhaps tongue-in-cheek, but it has a serious intent. The barrier to entry to 'doing data science' — for example, to training and deploying machine learning models — is getting lower. There is a wealth of packages across numerous high-level programming languages, especially Python and R, for numerical analysis, statistical modelling and machine learning. There are many accessible and high-quality blogs and online training materials. Above all, public cloud services such as Microsoft's Azure and Amazon Web Services offer low-cost, scalable storage and elastic compute for rapid experimentation and deployment of data models.

So to refine the question of the title: does the practice of data science require (mathematical) statistics? What is the right skill set, and where in that skill set does statistics sit? These are important questions for businesses and organisations who need to recruit for data processing and modelling requirements.

One can start with definitions. The phrase 'data science' is currently used to mean a variety of distinct activities: these include data mining, data cleaning and indexing, web application development, dashboard visualisation, web scraping and data pipelining as well as machine learning and modelling. Clearly not all of these activities require mathematical statistics.

2. Breiman's Two Cultures

At the turn of the century, Leo Breiman in a much-quoted paper (Breiman, 2001) articulated the difference of approach to data modelling between the statistics and computer science communities. Suppose that a random variable y that we would like to understand depends in some way on some other variables x:

$$y \longleftarrow \boxed{\text{nature}} \longleftarrow x. \tag{1}$$

In practice, it is usually the case that x is cheap to observe but that y is difficult or expensive and so we would like to infer it from observing x.

The mathematical statistics approach, according to Breiman, is to model what is going on inside the 'nature' box. We try to fit observed (x, y)-data to a mathematical model of the process that we can then use mathematics to understand. (And we see some great examples of this in this conference.) Breiman calls this approach *generative* modelling.

The computer science approach, on the other hand, rather than trying to understand nature, is to seek to emulate it algorithmically. That is, we design a family of algorithms (such as random forests or neural networks) and then use our observed (x, y)-data to minimise, over this family, a loss function that compares the data to the algorithmic output. Breiman calls this approach *predictive* modelling.

Breiman argued that while traditional generative models may be more interpretable, they often perform worse on predictive power, which is the strength of 'machine learning' predictive models. In business applications, it is usually predictive power that matters.

With advances in computing power and with available training data, predictive models are now dominant on benchmark machine learning problems across image, speech and text. Public cloud services have made learning of predictive models cheap and accessible.

3. Data Science at GCHQ

What are the data science applications that GCHQ cares about?

GCHQ's business is intelligence and security. On the intelligence side, we process data collected under warrant from electronic communications or from devices at rest. We process this data in order to derive intelligence under requirements from other government offices for purposes of countering terrorism, organised crime, threats from cyber attack and threats from hostile state actors.

A convenient mental map of the process, and of the role played by data science in it, is given by the OSI 7-layer communications model (Tannenbaum, 2012). This model delegates the various engineering functions and services that are needed in end-to-end communication to different layers of the processing stack. These layers also correspond to the tasks that are needed in reading communications. For a reader who is not the intended recipient of the communication — on a link which might be in the core of the internet or might be in a hostile overseas location — these tasks can be challenging.

At the lowest layer the task is to extract bits from some physical channel. This can require signal separation in low signal-to-noise environments, diagnosis of modulation schemes in use and figuring out things like frequency and time-division multiplexing.

At the next layer the data frame structure of the bit stream has to be worked out, and error correction decoded and removed. This is a challenging task for channels where bandwidth is at a premium and complex compositions of coding schemes with techniques such as puncturing and interleaving are in use.

At the network layer one is faced with routing and path prediction. At the transport and session layers one is faced with protocol analysis and end-to-end session reconstruction. Often there are challenges of encryption, anonymisation services, proxies and missing collection. Often, if processing at one layer is hard or infeasible, inference needs to be made from features observable in lower layers.

At the presentation and application layers we have tasks of file format analysis, diagnosis of compression schemes in use, and content reconstruction. In order to triage and search content, and to enable discovery of signals needed by intelligence analysis, we need to bring to bear tools of graph analysis, text mining, image processing, speech recognition and so on.

Coupled with problems of inference and discovery in data, we have challenges of high data rates and volumes. This leads to a need for streaming algorithms, probabilistic counts and approximations and scalable architectures. GCHQ was an early adopter of map-reduce processing on commodity clusters. In 2015 we released Gaffer (GCHQ, 2015) — a horizontally scalable distributed graph store designed for streaming ingest onto statistical summary data structures together with efficient local search — as our first open source project.

There has been much speculation about what covert reasons GCHQ may have for releasing Gaffer. But the reasons are not hard to find: open source projects are the most robust and trusted because they are tested against the widest community; and they grow exactly in proportion to the value placed in them by that community. Data science is an open source game, and, where sensitivities allow, participating in that game is the only way to keep on top of it.

On the security side, GCHQ's National Cyber Security Centre (NCSC) has been set up to help protect UK critical services from cyber attacks, to manage major incidents and to improve the underlying security of the UK Internet through technological improvement and public engagement.

Cyber security is a fertile testing ground for the development of data science platforms and algorithms. It is also a domain that presents some hard challenges: of high-speed processing and data summarisation, and of fused inference across many unsynchronised sources — packet capture, flow data, system logs, host metrics, knowledge sources, source code, malware analyses and so on.

NCSC's stated aim includes demonstrating across government what we recommend to others. The vision is a fundamentally evidence-based and data-driven approach to active cyber defence for the UK is set out in Ian Levy's 2016 blog:

> "This needs data, evidence and most importantly peer review."
> (Levy, 2016)

'Threatomatic', as this vision is dubbed (Fig. 1.1), seeks to automate active responses to threats based on a full range of information sources: email and domain reputation data, industry and service provider threat information, BGP (internet routing) monitoring, incident management logs and GCHQ-derived intelligence.

In collaboration with industry and academic partners, we have taken the first steps towards realising the threatomatic vision. It has data mining and data science at its core.

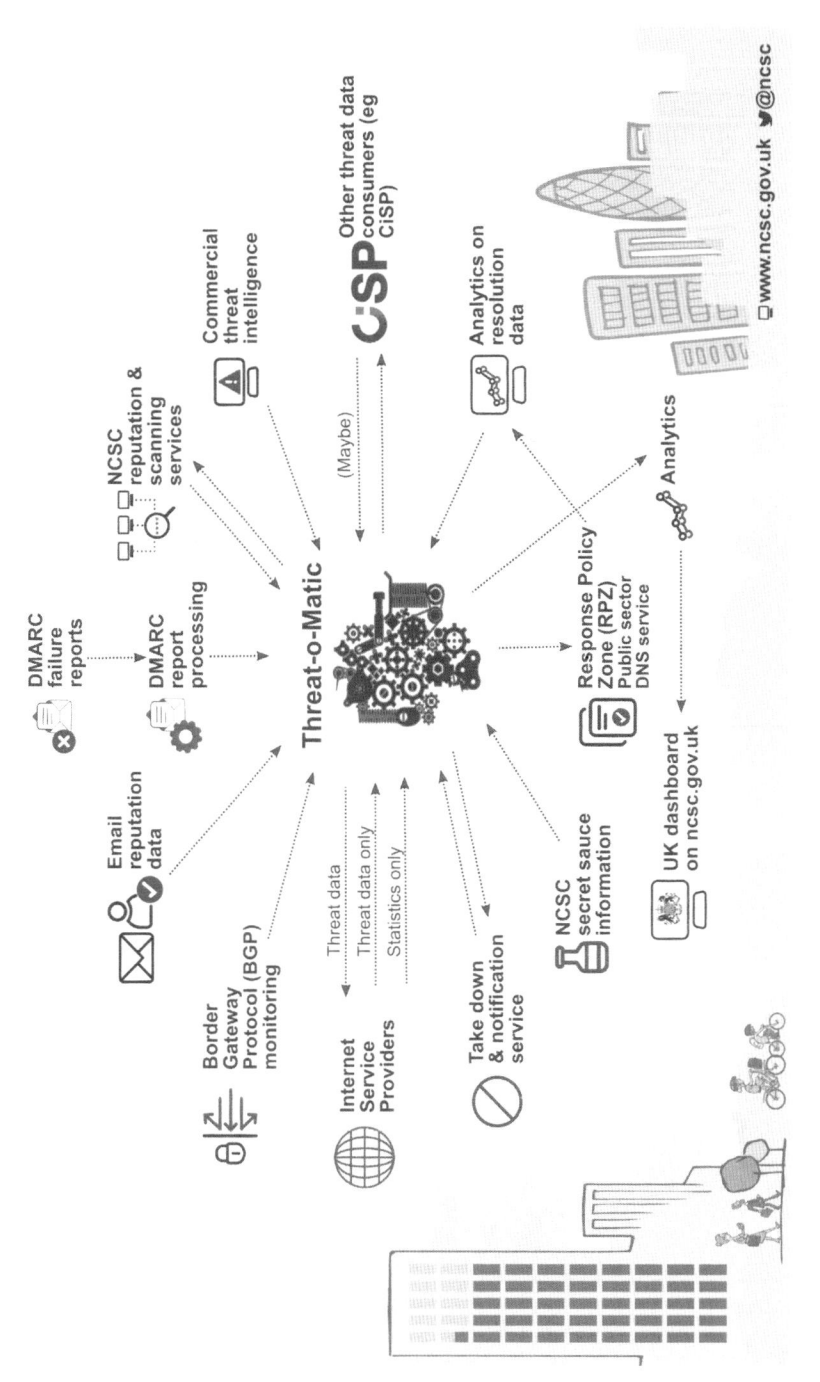

Fig. 1.1. National Cyber Security Centre's 'threatomatic' vision for full-spectrum data processing and automatic response to cyber threats.

4. Data Mining End to End

For GCHQ, as for other users of data processing and data mining technologies, the model of (1) is by itself insufficient. Our task is not only about the modelling step, but also about the questions: what is x? How should x be represented? What y are we really interested in for the problems we need to solve? How should y be interpreted?

This point of view was elegantly expressed by David Donoho in his Tukey centennial talk (Donoho, 2015). Donoho identifies six tasks, or 'divisions', in the data mining process:

(1) data exploration and preparation,
(2) data representation and transformation,
(3) computing with data,
(4) data modelling,
(5) presentation and visualisation,
(6) science about data science.

Of these tasks, only (4) is represented by the two cultures described by Breiman: data modelling may be generative or predictive, but all the residual data mining and analysis tasks are required for both. However, the approaches taken to tasks (1, 2, 3, 5) may be quite different depending on the approach taken to (4).

I will return to task (6) in the next section. For the moment, I would like to give some examples of the earlier tasks which for me illustrate the general need for at least a statistical 'mindset' throughout the process.

Let us start with task (1): the initial exploratory data analysis and data cleaning task. My example is around a public dataset released by Los Alamos National Labs in 2015 (Kent, 2015, 2016). This dataset consists of two months of anonymised cyber data from a Los Alamos network consisting of netflow records, DNS queries, Windows process events and authentication events.

The example I want to give here is on synchronisation of the time-stamp field across (three of) these four datasets.[a] Clearly, any analysis of the network should join the datasets, and we need to know that time-stamps have the same chronological meaning across all of them.

---

[a] For simplicity I consider only the netflow, DNS and Windows processes here. It turns out that the authentications data are synchronised to the Windows processes.

Figure 1.2 is an initial time series view (of raw event counts) of three of the datasets, for the first 15 days of the collection. A weekly cycle is clearly visible for the processes and the flows, which look well synchronised. This structure is slightly less obvious for the DNS. A more informative view, on the other hand, is obtained by looking at pairwise lagged correlations among the three series. In Fig. 1.3, the top two plots present correlations with lag ranging from zero to one week. The top plot uses Pearson (linear) correlation and the middle plot uses Spearman (rank) correlation. Both plots immediately give us a clear view of the daily (and even hourly) periodicity in the data — including the DNS — that is not visible in the original time series.

Time-stamp synchronisation would correspond to the maximum correlations occurring at lag zero. This is approximately the case, but not exactly. This is shown in the bottom plot, in which the Spearman cross-correlation is zoomed in close to zero. We find discrepancies of +20 and −60 minutes for the flows and DNS respectively with respect to the Windows process time-stamps (presumably corresponding to differences in collection start-times).

I give this example, partly because I'm not aware of this feature of the Los Alamos data having been observed elsewhere,[b] but also to illustrate the need for a statistical approach and mindset in the initial exploratory analysis — Donoho's task (1).

Tasks (2) and (5), data transformation, presentation, visualisation — representation of x and representation of y, if you like — likewise generally require care and statistical thinking. They are especially characterised by variance in the various choices that can be made: of mathematical transformation, vector representation, dimensional reduction and so on. We consider this issue — of dependence on ad hoc choices — next.

5. The Science in Data Science

Donoho's task (6), 'science about data science' is perhaps the most interesting. The key observation is that many choices are involved in the analysis tasks (1–5), and that these choices all provide a source of variance in the final outputs, inferences and conclusions. Variance in these outputs can arise from: naturally occurring variance in the process being modelled,

---

[b]Kent (2015) discusses time skew — inaccuracies in the reported time-stamp that can arise for various reasons within each dataset, but does not consider the time-stamp correlation between datasets.

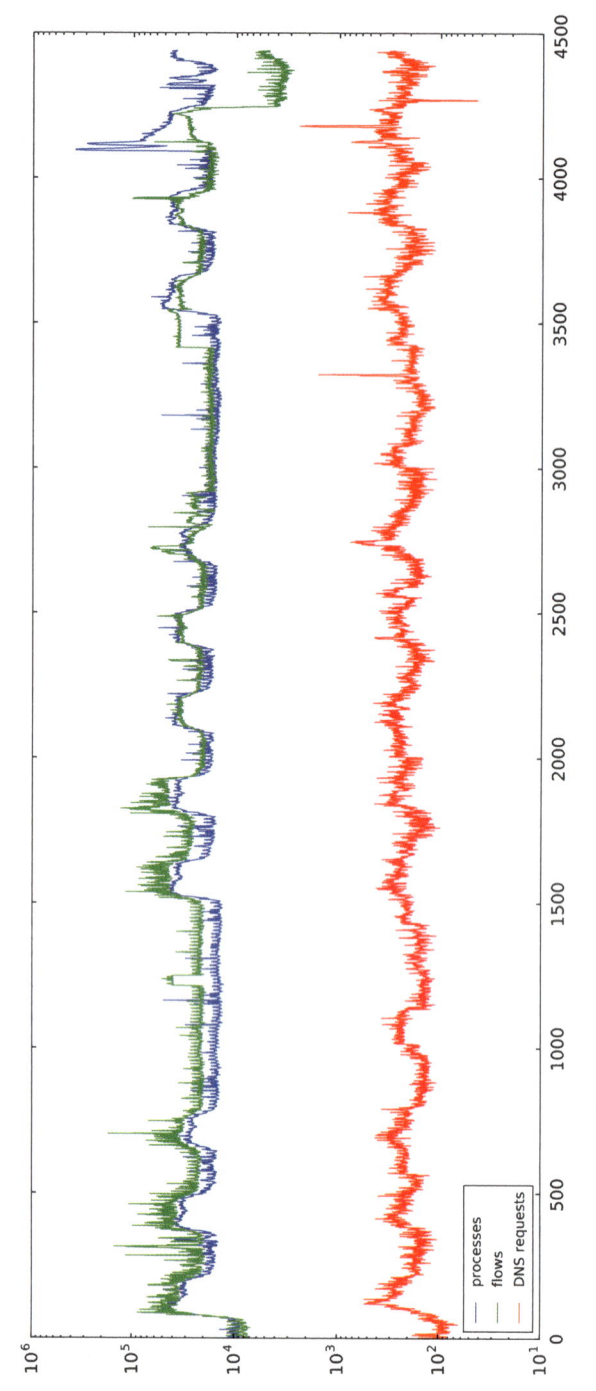

Fig. 1.2. Time series of event counts for the first 15 days of the Los Alamos cyber data (5-minute bins).

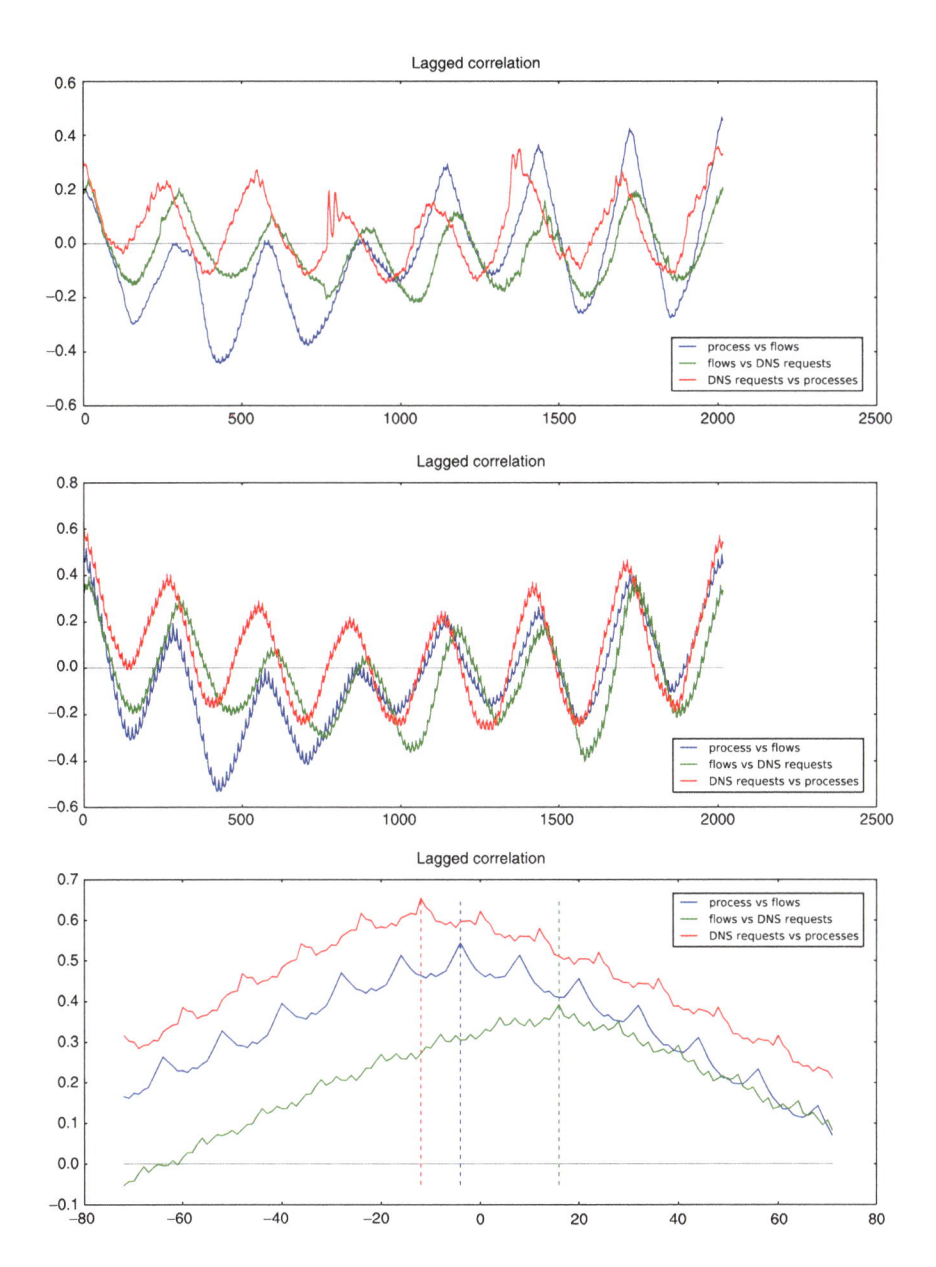

Fig. 1.3. Time stamp mis-synchronisation in the Los Alamos data (5-minute bins).

variance in the data sample used to train the model, from decisions made in the data cleaning and preparation processes — how the data is binned, how missing values are handled and so on — from choices of vector representation, normalisation, dimensional-reduction and so on, from choice of modelling algorithm, ensemble method, hyper-parameters, neural network architecture, and from choice of inference procedure and probabilistic interpretations.

By a 'science about data science', Donoho means a principled statistical study of these effects, via a combination of scientific experiment and mathematical reasoning. He points to interesting meta-analyses of this sort in the literature, comparing parallel work on a single problem (e.g. in bio-medical studies) by independent research teams applying different methodologies on different datasets — and often arriving at very different conclusions.

This seems very pertinent to data mining and analysis that we do within GCHQ. As mentioned in the previous section, many modelling applications make use of data representations in which choices of dimension and normalisation are often heuristic or ad hoc. The examples below only scratch the surface of this issue. They have to do with probabilistic interpretation of model outputs — but they will lead me, in the next section, to two key challenges of data modelling.

Let us begin with a standard classification problem: MNIST handwritten digits (LeCun *et al.*, 2015). Suppose we train a logistic regression using stochastic gradient descent (SGD). Then we get, for each input test image, a soft-max output which is a non-negative vector over the classes summing to 1. How good is this soft-max as a probability estimate?

Figure 1.4 shows the result of calibrating the model on test data. That is, across all test images and all soft-max units per input, we count the proportion of 'hits' on the class represented by that unit. We then plot this proportion (the empirical probability) against soft-max bins (the estimated probability). We would like, for good probability estimates, to see the profile line up along the main diagonal.

In the case of logistic regression, we see a substantial under-estimation for soft-max values above about 30%, and over-estimation for values below this threshold. But we can correct for that by using the observed profile to transform soft-max outputs to corrected probability estimates. (This is called Platt scaling (Platt, 1999; Caruana and Niculescu-Mizil, 2005).)

On the other hand, one can ask how robust this scaling is under randomness arising from the order in which the training data is visited during

Fig. 1.4. Calibration profile (below) for soft-max outputs from logistic regression on MNIST digits (some examples above).

the SGD. If we train on the same training data and calibrate against the same test data, how much variation we will see in the apparent calibration?

The answer is shown in Fig. 1.5 (top), in which the experiment is performed many times and the variance in the calibration is plotted. It turns out that this variance is small, and we can expect a good estimate via Platt scaling. (It would be interesting to have a theoretical statement to this effect: I don't know if such a result, and an analytical form of the curve in Fig. 1.5, exists.)

On the other hand, if we perform an identical experiment for a multilayer perceptron — a neural network with three hidden layers, and 10-way soft-max output as for the logistic regression — then we see a different picture. For a higher classification success rate (from 87% for the logistic regression to 98%) we pay the penalty of greater variance in the calibration profile. The 'deep' neural network is a take-it-or-leave-it algorithm: we get a good point classifier, but no useful probability estimates.

(Recent work on Bayesian neural networks — see Yurin Gal's thesis (Gal, 2016) for example — does address soft-max uncertainty. It is not clear whether this will lead to well-calibrated probability estimates from deep learning models.)

Why are probability estimates as outputs important? If we want point classifications from scenarios with low-entropy probability distributions (less uncertainty), it may not be important. But if the information available has inherently higher entropy (more uncertainty) then point classifications are less usable. In this case, a reliable probability estimate might be used to inform follow-on processing, via resource allocation that anticipates possible outcomes, for example.

Finally on this topic, it seems that recurrent neural networks (RNNs) have a better calibration behaviour. This statement is only on the basis of experience, however — I do not know of a theoretical explanation.

Figure 1.6 illustrates this. Synthetic sequence data has been generated from a hidden Markov model (HMM) outputting alphabetic characters, and with 15 internal states. A training sequence and a test sequence are generated. An RNN (with two hidden layers and Long Short-Term Memory (LSTM) units is trained on the training sequence, using some rate of dropout for regularisation. Calibration of the resulting model (i.e. of its soft-max outputs) is then evaluated on the test sequence.

The grey lines in Fig. 1.6 show the resulting calibration at different values of the dropout. Blue is the best (at dropout $\sim 5\%$). For comparison, the red line is calibration of probability estimates computed analytically assuming knowledge of the HMM parameters.

As one last example of variance affecting the results of analyses, consider ROC curves.[c] Among most machine learning practitioners, religious

---

[c] 'Receiver Operator Characteristic': in which we plot the rate of true positives found by a classification model in a test dataset against the rate of false positives returned by the model.

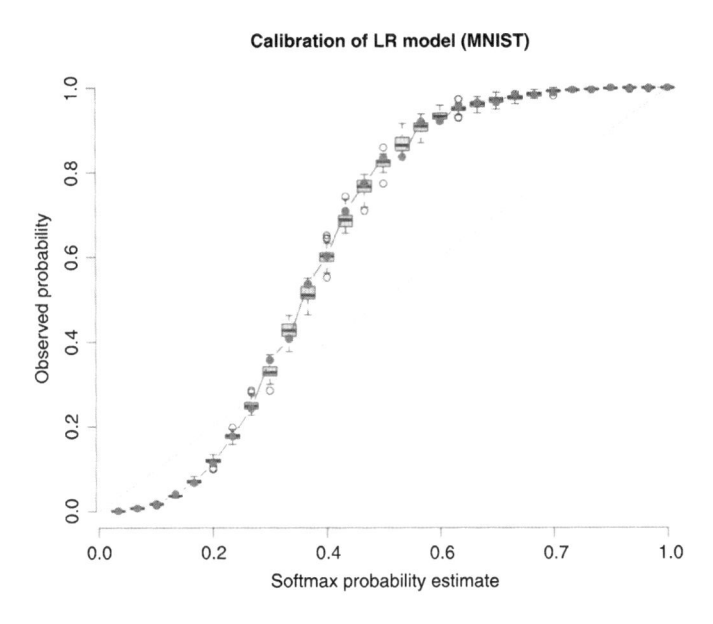

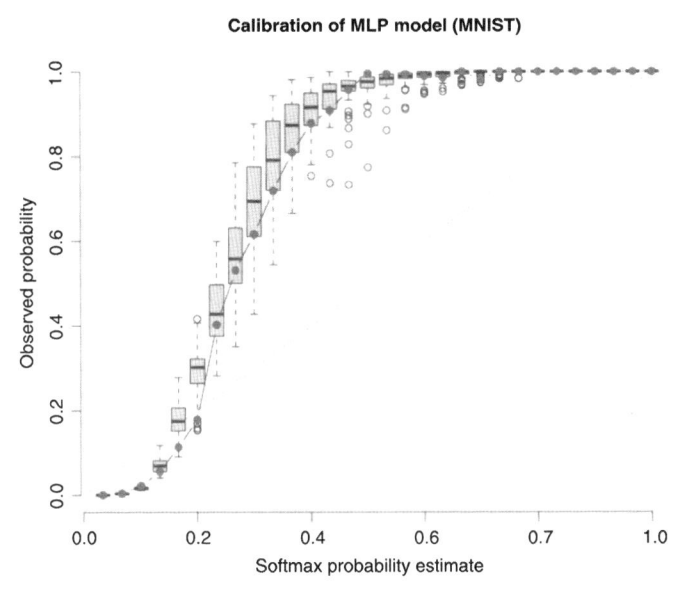

Fig. 1.5. Variance in the calibration profile on MNIST data for logistic regression (above) versus a 3-hidden-layer neural network (below).

Calibration of RNN model (HMM-generated data)

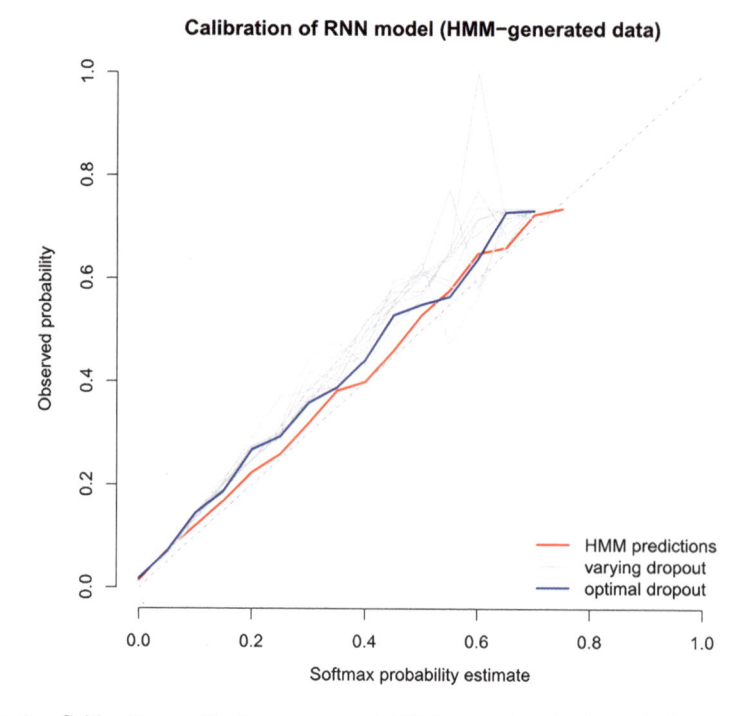

Fig. 1.6. Calibration profile for a recurrent LSTM network trained on Markov-generated data, as a function of dropout used for training.

observance is given to the authority of the ROC curve (and AUC, the area under this curve) as a measure of performance of a classification model. But of course, the ROC curve depends on both the training data used to construct the model and the test data used to measure true and false positive rates. It is a point estimate of a ROC distribution.

Figure 1.7 shows an example. On a 2-class (Gaussian mixture) population we have fitted a logistic regression classifier to a training data sample and evaluated the ROC curve on a test data sample. Then we have repeated this many times to view the distribution of ROC curves (with a subsample shown in blue). This variation occurs *for a single problem, in a single population, using a single modelling method, with fixed parameters*. It is clear that the sampling variance should be taken into account when using ROC and AUC as performance measures. (See also the paper by David Hand in this volume.)

In general, it is desirable to account as far as possible for variation arising from sampling, parameters and so on, to leave an analysis that is as

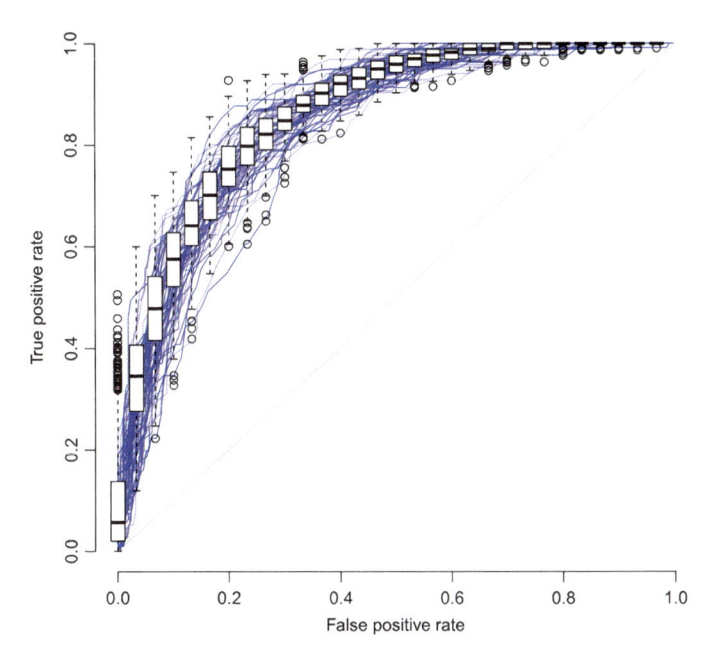

Fig. 1.7. The distribution of ROC curves for logistic regression models of a single 2-class population. In each case we use a different sample of training and test data.

independent of ad hoc choices. In practice, that is seldom feasible and we make many choices, preferences and accidents of experience or availability into our analyses. This issue has long been understood by the statistical community — since, for example, John Ioannidis's 2005 study '*Why most published research findings are false*' (Ioannidis, 2005).[d]

So to what extent can we have authoritative trust in our analytic outputs?

6. Two Challenges

In recent years we have seen spectacular progress made in applications of machine learning, and especially of deep learning (LeCun *et al.*, 2015) and deep reinforcement learning (Mnih *et al.*, 2015), to computer vision and

---

[d]Ioannidis addresses poor statistical design and poor inference from p-values. But machine learning is not immune to poor design!

multimedia processing, natural language understanding, recommendation systems and personalisation, game playing and decision-making. This has given rise — understandably — to great excitement about the future potential of artificial intelligence (The Royal Society, 2017).

In GCHQ we tend to be suspicious people. We note that many of today's applications are consumer-facing, are centred around advertising, recommendation and social networks, and are designed to increase revenue from engagement with users of Internet services. But when machine learning and data science are applied in safety-critical applications such as smart cities, transportation networks and autonomous vehicles, energy and utility grids or cyber security, then we need to be pretty sure they do what we expect them to do. The considerations of the previous section suggest that this level of trust is not yet present in machine learning-based systems.

When do predictive models not behave as intended? Aside from 'natural' causes — drift or change in the data distribution, inadequate data sampling for training, errors of design or implementation, and so on — there has been a great deal of recent interest in misbehaviour due to adversarial attacks. A predictive model can be intentionally 'poisoned'. That is, suppose a model has been trained to predict class labels, and we regard that model as fixed. The same methods that were used to train the model (search in the model parameter space) can be used to construct input data points that fool it (search in data input space).

This idea has been demonstrated in various ways: learning images that fool a deep neural network starting from random pixel vectors (Nguyen *et al.*, 2015), or starting from specific images of known classes and bounding pixel variation (Szegedy *et al.*, 2013). Learning the poisoning input data is an optimisation problem, and has been demonstrated with gradient descent, genetic algorithms and other methods.

Generative adversarial networks (Goodfellow *et al.*, 2014) take this idea a step further and estimate generative models via simultaneous training of competing models with opposing objective functions, one to generate (in the sense of (1)), the other to discriminate. This idea has even been applied to learning cryptographic strategies (Abadi and Andersen, 2016).

These considerations pose a serious challenge to the use of predictive models in safety-critical applications. The situation is analogous to cryptography, in which trust is based on analysis of the mathematical foundations of the algorithms in use and the attacks they admit. A similar approach is needed to machine learning pipelines and their vulnerabilities:

Challenge 1: *How do we build assurance, trust and transparency into machine learning systems and into end-to-end data processing and decision-making pipelines?*

We can equally frame the question of trust (a security notion) as confidence (a statistical notion). If we ask for guarantees on data processing pipelines, we would expect these to take the form of confidence bounds or probabilistic error bounds. Proving such bounds requires mathematical analysis. In the absence of proof, we should at least ask for probability estimates that are verifiable, in the sense of the calibration discussion of Sec. 5, in real time. But verification is a form of training and requires some form of training signal.

The second challenge we raise is to quantify the cost of training, to understand how to minimise this cost, and make online verification with error bounds a practical proposition. Namely, the cost of training a predictive model consists of the cost of preparing training data plus the cost of compute to learn the model. Typically it is dominated by the former because it entails evaluation of variables (e.g. class labels) that require some element of human input. Is it sometimes feasible to trade off more compute for less variable evaluation?

Minimising the cost of variable evaluation is the business of *active learning* (Settles, 2012). This involves targeting data points intelligently on the basis of global structure in the training data. Effectively, active learning combines an expensive supervised training signal with a cheaper, unsupervised, training signal derived from information in the data such as cluster separation, manifold approximation and so on. Can one formalise and extend the use of this signal?

Here is a toy example to illustrate the point.[e] Suppose we are asked for a classifier of handwritten digits (Fig. 1.4) but with the rules slightly changed: given N training images, we are allowed only $n \ll N$ supervised class labels. In return, we are given information that the N training images appear in a sequence derived from a language model that we are given, or are able to estimate.

---

[e] Details on this example will appear elsewhere.

In this situation, an EM or Viterbi-type algorithm (on a suitable transform of pixel space to make the classes closer to Gaussian) can be used to derive probability estimates for the classes (up to permutation) of all N training images. These estimates serve as an unsupervised component of the training signal that can be combined with the 'hard' training signal from the supervised data subset.

For this example, we can ask to quantify the trade-off between the hard and soft training signals (possibly under different active learning strategies). For example, how do we map the cost of entropy in the language model to information bits in the hard training signal?

Challenge 2: *Can one quantify the cost of training signal for tracking and updating of data modelling processes? Can generative statistical models be used to derive 'soft' training signal for trade-off against 'hard' training signal, and what are the principles for optimising such a trade-off?*

To return to the title of this paper: it does not need to be stated that the business of analysing and utilising data is fundamentally the business of statistics. But this is especially the case where we need transparency and trust in heuristic predictive models for application to safety-critical systems. I cannot do better than conclude by quoting Donoho (2015):

> "Information technology skills are certainly at a premium in the research we have just covered. However, scientific understanding and statistical insight are firmly in the driver's seat."

References

Abadi, M. and Andersen, D. G. (2016). Learning to protect communications with adversarial neural cryptography, preprint, arXiv:1610.06918.

Breiman, L. (2001). Statistical modeling: The two cultures, *Statist. Sci.* **16**, 3, pp. 199–231.

Caruana, R. and Niculescu-Mizil, A. (2005). Predicting good probabilities with supervised learning, in *Proc. ICML'05*, doi:10.1145/1102351.1102430.

Donoho, D. (2015). 50 years of data science, in *Tukey Centennial Workshop*, Princeton, NJ.

Gal, Y. (2016). *Uncertainty in Deep Learning*, Ph.D. thesis, University of Cambridge.

GCHQ (2015). Gaffer — a large-scale entity and relation database supporting aggregation of properties, https://github.com/gchq/Gaffer.

Goodfellow, I., Pouget-Abadie, J., Mirza, M., Xu, B., Warde-Farley, D., Ozair, S., Courville, A. and Bengio, Y. (2014). Generative adversarial nets, in *Advances in Neural Information Processing Systems*, pp. 2672–2680.

Ioannidis, J. P. (2005). Why most published research findings are false, *PLoS Med.* **2**, 8, p. e124.

Kent, A. (2015). Comprehensive, multi-source cyber-security events, http://csr.lanl.gov/data/cyber1/.

Kent, A. (2016). Cybersecurity data sources for dynamic network research, Chapter 2, in *Dynamic Network in cybersecurity*, World Scientific, pp. 37–66.

LeCun, Y., Bengio, Y. and Hinton, G. (2015). Deep learning, *Nature* **521**, 7553, pp. 436–444.

Le Cun, Y., Cortes, C. and Burges, C. (2015). The MNIST database of handwritten digits, http://yann.lecun.com/exdb/mnist/.

Levy, I. (2016). Active cyber defence — tackling cyber attacks on the UK, https://www.ncsc.gov.uk/blog-post/active-cyber-defence-tackling-cyber-attacks-uk.

Mnih, V. *et al.* (2015). Human-level control through deep reinforcement learning, *Nature* **518**, 7540, pp. 529–533.

Nguyen, A., Yosinski, J. and Clune, J. (2015). Deep neural networks are easily fooled: high confidence predictions for unrecognizable images, in *Proc. IEEE Conf. Computer Vision and Pattern Recognition*, pp. 427–436.

Platt, J. (1999). Probabilistic outputs for support vector machines and comparisons to regularized likelihood methods, *Adv. Large Margin Classifiers* **10**, 3, pp. 61–74.

Settles, B. (2012). Active learning, *Synth. Lect. Artif. Intell. Mach. Learn.* **6**, 1, pp. 1–114.

Szegedy, C., Zaremba, W., Sutskever, I., Bruna, J., Erhan, D., Goodfellow, I. and Fergus, R. (2013). Intriguing properties of neural networks, preprint arXiv:1312.6199.

Tannenbaum, A. (2012). *Computer Networks*, 4th edn., Prentice-Hall.

The Royal Society (2017). Machine learning: The power and promise of computers that learn by example, https://royalsociety.org/topics-policy/projects/machine-learning/.

Chapter 2

Principled Statistical Inference in Data Science

Todd A. Kuffner[*,‡] and G. Alastair Young[†,§]

[*]*Department of Mathematics, Washington University in St. Louis, St. Louis, MO 63130, USA*

[†]*Department of Mathematics, Imperial College London, London SW7 2AZ, UK*

[‡]*kuffner@wustl.edu*
[§]*alastair.young@imperial.ac.uk*

We discuss the challenges of principled statistical inference in modern data science. Conditionality principles are argued as key to achieving valid statistical inference, in particular when this is performed after selecting a model from sample data itself.

1. Introduction

In recent times, even prominent figures in statistics have come to doubt the importance of foundational principles for data analysis.

> "If a statistical analysis is clearly shown to be effective at answering the questions of interest, it gains nothing from being described as principled." (Speed, 2016)

The above statement was made by Terry Speed in the September 2016 *IMS Bulletin*. It is our primary purpose in this chapter to refute Professor Speed's assertion! We argue that a principled approach to inference in the data science context is essential, to avoid erroneous conclusions, in particular invalid statements about significance.

We will be concerned here with statistical inference, specifically calculation and interpretation of p-values and construction of confidence intervals.

While the greater part of the data science literature is concerned with prediction rather than inference, we believe that our focus is justified for two solid reasons. In many circumstances, such, say, as microarray studies, we are interested in identifying significant 'features', such as genes linked to particular forms of cancer, as well as the identity and strength of evidence. Further, the current reproducibility crisis in science demands that attention be paid to the formal repeated sampling properties of inferential methods.

2. Key Principles

The key notions which should drive consideration of methods of statistical inference are: validity, whether a claimed criterion or assumption is satisfied, regardless of the true unknown state of nature; and, relevance, whether the analysis performed is actually relevant to the particular data sample under study.

It is most appropriate to consider the notion of validity in the context of procedures motivated by the principle of error control. Then, a valid statistical procedure is one for which the probability is small that the procedure has a higher error rate than stated. For example, the random set $\mathcal{C}_{1-\alpha}$ is an (approximately) valid $(1-\alpha)$ confidence set for a parameter θ if $\Pr(\theta \notin \mathcal{C}_{1-\alpha}) = \alpha + \epsilon$ for some very small (negligible) ϵ, whatever the true value of θ.

Relevance is achieved by adherence to what we term the 'Fisherian proposition' (Fisher, 1925, 1934). This advocates appropriate conditioning of the hypothetical data samples that are the basis of non-Bayesian statistics. Specifically, the Conditionality Principle, formally described below, would maintain that to ensure relevance to the actual data under study the hypothetical repetitions should be conditioned on certain features of the available data sample.

It is useful to frame our discussion as done by Cox and Mayo (2010). Suppose that for testing a specified null hypothesis $H_0 : \psi = \psi_0$ on an interest parameter ψ we calculate the observed value t_{obs} of a test statistic T and the associated p-value $p = P(T \geq t_{\text{obs}}; \psi = \psi_0)$. Then, if p is very low, e.g. 0.001, t_{obs} is argued as grounds to reject H_0 or infer discordance with H_0 in the direction of the specified alternative, at level 0.001.

This is not strictly valid, since it amounts to choosing the decision rule based on the observed data (Kuffner and Walker, 2017). A valid statistical test requires that the decision rule be specified in advance. However, there are two rationales for the interpretation of the p-value described in the preceding paragraph.

(1) To do so is consistent with following a decision rule with a (pre-specified) low Type 1 error rate, in the long run: if we treat the data as just decisive evidence against H_0, then in hypothetical repetitions, H_0 would be rejected in a proportion p of the cases when it is actually true.
(2) [What we actually want]. To do so is to follow a rule where the low value of p corresponds to the actual data sample providing inconsistency with H_0.

The evidential construal in (2) is only accomplished to the extent that it can be assured that the small observed p-value is due to the actual data-generating process being discrepant from that described by H_0. As noted by Cox and Mayo (2010), once the requirements of (2) are satisfied, the low error-rate rationale (1) follows.

The key to principled inference which provides the required interpretation is to ensure relevancy of the sampling distribution on which p-values are based. This is achieved through the Conditionality Principle, which may formally be stated as follows.

Conditionality Principle: *Suppose we may partition the minimal sufficient statistic for a model parameter θ of interest as $S = (T, A)$, where T is of the same dimension as θ and the random variable A is distribution constant: the statistic A is said to be ancillary. Then, inference should be based on the conditional distribution of T given $A = a$, the observed value in the actual data sample.*

In practice, the requirement that A be distribution constant is often relaxed. It is (Barndorff-Nielsen and Cox, 1994) well-established in statistical theory that to condition on the observed data value of a random variable whose distribution does depend on θ might, under some circumstances, be convenient and meaningful, though this would in some sense sacrifice information on θ.

This extended notion of conditioning is most explicit in problems involving nuisance parameters, where the model parameter θ is partitioned as $\theta = (\psi, \lambda)$, with ψ of interest and λ a nuisance parameter.

Suppose that the minimal sufficient statistic can again be partitioned as $S = (T, A)$, where the distribution of T given $A = a$ depends only on ψ.

We may extend the Conditionality Principle to advocate that inference on ψ should be based on this latter conditional distribution, under appropriate conditions on the distribution of A. We note that the case where the distribution of A depends on λ but not on ψ is just one rather special instance.

A simple illustration of conditioning on an exactly distribution constant statistic is given by Barndorff-Nielsen and Cox (1994, Example 2.20). Suppose Y_1, Y_2 are independent Poisson variables with means $(1-\psi)l, \psi l$, where l is a known constant. There is no reduction by sufficiency, but the random variable $A = Y_1 + Y_2$ has a known distribution, Poisson of mean l, not depending on ψ. Inference would, say, be based on the conditional distribution of Y_2, given $A = a$, which is binomial with index a and parameter ψ.

Justifications for many standard procedures of applied statistics, such as analysis of 2×2 contingency tables, derive from the Conditionality Principle, even when A has a distribution that depends on both ψ and λ, but when observation of A alone would make inference on ψ imprecise. The contingency table example concerns inference on the log-odds ratio when comparing two binomial variables: see Barndorff-Nielsen and Cox (1994, Example 2.22). Here Y_1, Y_2 are independent binomial random variables corresponding to the number of successes in (m_1, m_2) independent trials, with success probabilities (θ_1, θ_2). The interest parameter is $\psi = \log\{\theta_2/(1-\theta_2)\} - \log\{\theta_1/(1-\theta_1)\}$. Inference on ψ would, following the Conditionality Principle, be based on the conditional distribution of Y_2 given $A = a$, where $A = Y_1 + Y_2$ has a marginal distribution depending in a complicated way on *both* ψ *and* whatever nuisance parameter λ is defined to complete the parametric specification.

Central to our discussion, therefore, is recognition that conditioning an inference on the observed data value of a statistic which is, to some degree, informative about the parameter of interest is an established part of statistical theory. Conditioning is supported as a means of controlling the Type 1 error rate, while ensuring relevance to the data sample under test. Of course, generally, conditioning will run counter to the objective of maximising power (minimising Type 2 error rate), which is a fundamental principle of much of statistical theory. However, loss of power due to adoption of a conditional approach to inference may be very slight, as demonstrated by the following example.

Suppose Y is normally distributed as $N(\theta, 1)$ or $N(\theta, 4)$, depending on whether the outcome δ of tossing a fair coin is heads ($\delta = 1$) or tails

($\delta = 2$). It is desired to test the null hypothesis $H_0 : \theta = -1$ against the alternative $H_1 : \theta = 1$, controlling the Type 1 error rate at level $\alpha = 0.05$. The most powerful unconditional test, as given by Neyman–Pearson optimality theory, has rejection region given by $Y \geq 0.598$ if $\delta = 1$ and $Y \geq 2.392$ if $\delta = 2$. The Conditionality Principle advocates that instead we should condition on the outcome of the coin toss, δ. Then, given $\delta = 1$, the most powerful test of the required Type 1 error rate rejects H_0 if $Y \geq 0.645$, while, given $\delta = 2$ the rejection region is $Y \geq 2.290$. The power of the unconditional test is 0.4497, while the power of the more intuitive conditional test is 0.4488, only marginally less.

Further support for conditioning, to eliminate dependence of the inference on unknown nuisance parameters, is provided by the Neyman–Pearson theory of optimal frequentist inference; see, for example, Young and Smith (2005).

A key context where this theory applies is when the parameter of interest is a component of the canonical parameter in a multi-parameter exponential family model. Suppose Y has a density of the form

$$f(y;\theta) \propto h(y)\exp\{\psi T_1(y) + \lambda T_2(y)\}.$$

Then (T_1, T_2) is minimal sufficient and the conditional distribution of $T_1(Y)$, given $T_2(Y) = t_2$, say, depends only on ψ. The distribution of $T_2(Y)$ may, in special cases, depend only on λ, but will, in general, depend in a complicated way on both ψ and λ. The extended form of the Conditionality Principle argues that inference should be based on the distribution of $T_1(Y)$, given $T_2(Y) = t_2$. But, in Neyman–Pearson theory this same conditioning is justified by a requirement of full elimination of dependence on the nuisance parameter λ, achieved in the light of completeness of the minimal sufficient statistic only by this conditioning. The resulting conditional inference is actually optimal, in terms of furnishing a uniformly most power unbiased test on the interest parameter ψ: see Young and Smith (2005, Chapter 7).

Our central thesis is that the *same* Fisherian principles of conditioning are necessary to steer appropriate statistical inference in a data science era, when models and the associated inferential questions are arrived at after examination of data:

"Data science does not exist until there is a dataset".

Our assertion is that appropriate conditioning is needed to ensure validity of the inferential methods used. Importantly, however, the justifications used for conditioning are not new, but mirror the arguments used in established statistical theory.

3. Classical and 'Post-selection' Inference

In classical statistical inference, the analyst specifies the model, as well as the hypothesis to be tested, in advance of examination of the data. A classical α-level test for the specified hypothesis H_0 under the specified model M must control the Type 1 error rate

$$P(\text{reject } H_0 | M, H_0) \leq \alpha.$$

The appropriate paradigm for data science is, in our view, the structure for inference that is known as 'post-selection Inference', as described, for example, by Lee et al. (2016) and Fithian et al. (2014).

Now it is recognised that inference is performed after having arrived at a statistical model adaptively, through examination of the observed data.

Having selected a model $\hat{M}$ based on our data Y, we wish to test a hypothesis $\hat{H}_0$. The notation here stresses that $\hat{H}_0$ will be random, a function of the selected model and hence of the data Y. The key principle to follow in this context is expressed in terms of selective Type 1 error: we require that

$$P(\text{reject } \hat{H}_0 | \hat{M}, \hat{H}_0) \leq \alpha.$$

That is, we require that we control the Type 1 error rate of the test given that it was actually performed. The thinking leading to this principle is really just a 21st century re-expression of Fisherian thought.

A simple example, the 'File Drawer Effect', serves to illustrate the central ideas, and is a template (Fithian et al., 2014) for how statistical inference is performed in data science. Suppose data consists of a set of n independent observations Y_i distributed as $N(\mu_i, 1)$. We choose, however, to focus attention only on the apparently large effects, selecting for formal inference only those indices i for which $|Y_i| > 1$, $\hat{I} = \{i : |Y_i| > 1\}$. We wish, for each $i \in \hat{I}$, to test $H_{0,i} : \mu_i = 0$, each individual test to be performed at significance level $\alpha = 0.05$.

A test which rejects $H_{0,i}$ when $|Y_i| > 1.96$ is invalidated by the selection of the tests to be performed. Though the probability of falsely rejecting a given $H_{0,i}$ is certainly α, since most of the time that hypothesis is not actually tested, the error rate among the hypotheses that are actually selected for testing is much higher than α.

Letting n_0 be the number of true null effects and supposing that $n_0 \to \infty$ as $n \to \infty$, in the long run, the fraction of errors among the true nulls we test, the ratio of the number of false rejections to the number of true nulls selected for testing, tends to $P_{H_{0,i}}(\text{reject } H_{0,i}|i \in \hat{I}) \approx 0.16$.

The probability of a false rejection conditional on selection is the natural and controllable error criterion to consider. We see that

$$P_{H_{0,i}}(|Y_i| > 2.41 \mid |Y_i| > 1) = 0.05,$$

so that the appropriate test of $H_{0,i}$, given that it is selected for testing, is to reject if $|Y_i| > 2.41$.

In a formal framework of post-selection inference, we assume that our data Y lies in some measurable space with unknown sampling distribution $Y \sim F$. The task is to pose, on the basis of Y itself, a reasonable probability model $\hat{M}$, then carry out inference, using the same data Y.

Let $S \equiv S(Y)$ be the selection event. For instance, this might be the event that model $\hat{M}$ is chosen, or, in the context of the File Drawer Effect example, the event $S = \{|Y| > 1\}$.

The central proposal is that to be relevant to the observed data sample and yield precisely interpretable validity, the inference we perform should not be drawn from the original assumed distribution, $Y \sim F$, but by considering the conditional distribution of $Y|S$. This is just the Fisherian proposition being applied.

In terms of our discussion above, the selection event S will typically be informative about the quantity θ of interest, and conditioning will therefore discard information. But, to ignore the selection event loses control over the (Type 1) error rate, potentially badly. Principled inference requires conditioning on the selection event, and therefore drawing inferences from leftover information in Y, given S.

4. Example: File Drawer Effect

Consider the File Drawer Effect example, but now take the selection event as $\{Y > 1\}$. We compare 'nominal' confidence intervals, not accounting for selection, and selective confidence intervals, of coverage 95%.

Figure 2.1 compares the selective and nonselective confidence intervals, as a function of the observed value Y. If Y is much larger than 1, there is hardly any selection bias, so no adjustment for selection is really required. When Y is close to 1, the need to properly account for selection is stark.

Confidence intervals

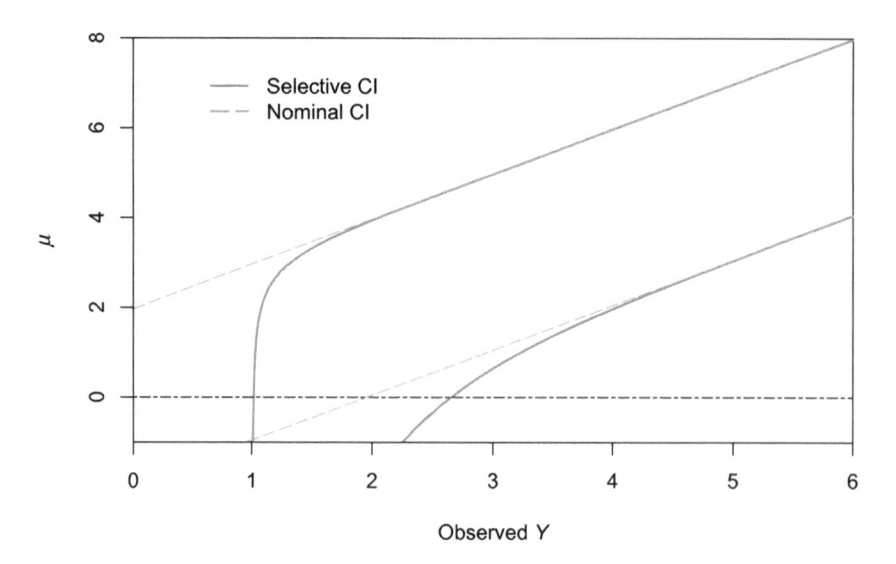

Fig. 2.1. File Drawer Effect, comparison of selective and nonselective confidence intervals.

Confidence interval length

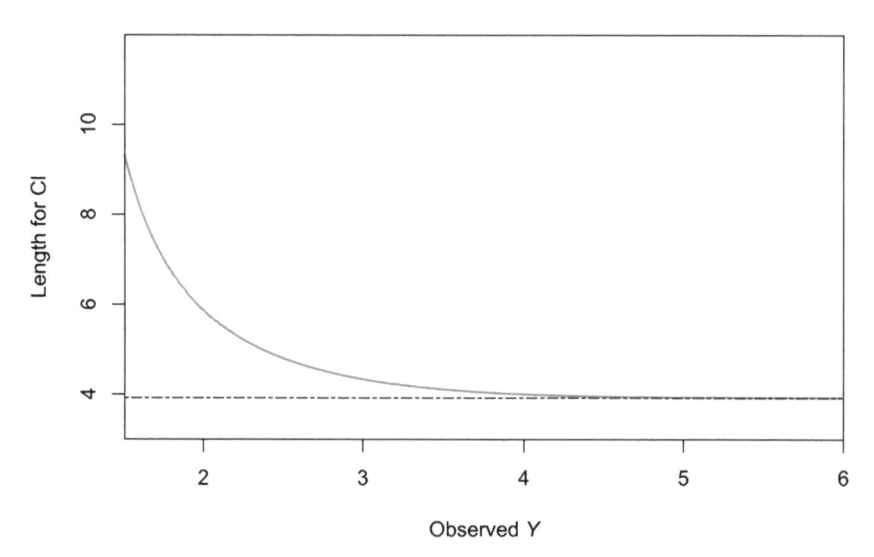

Fig. 2.2. File Drawer Effect, length of selective confidence interval compared to fixed length of nonselective interval.

Coverage of nonselective 95% confidence interval

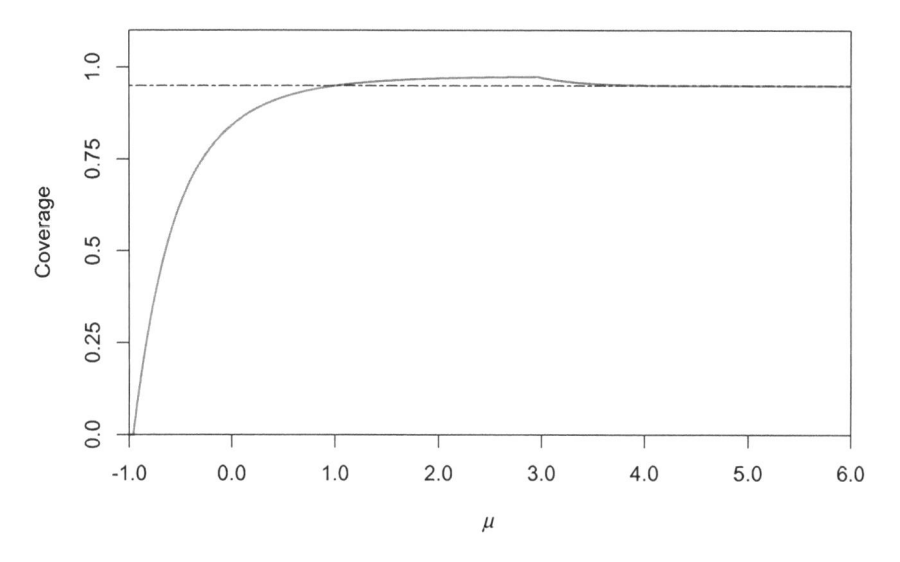

Fig. 2.3. File Drawer Effect, coverage of nonselective confidence interval.

Figure 2.2 compares the lengths of the selective and nonselective confidence intervals: the nonselective interval is $Y \pm 1.96$, and therefore has length 3.92, whatever the true mean μ or data value Y. Figure 2.3 illustrates the coverage of the invalid nonselective confidence interval: this generally exceeds 95%, but if the true mean μ is much less than 1, undercoverage is substantial. If the true mean is exactly 1, but only in this case, the nonselective interval has coverage exactly 95%.

5. Borrowing from Classical Theory

Conditioning the inference performed on the selection event is especially convenient if Y is assumed to have an exponential family distribution. Then the distribution of Y conditional on a measurable selection event $S(Y)$ is also an exponential family distribution, allowing support for the techniques of selective inference to be drawn from the established classical theory for inference in exponential families: see Fithian *et al.* (2014).

As further illustration, we consider a simple normal linear regression model. Suppose that $Y \sim N_n(\mu, \sigma^2 I_n)$, with $\mu \equiv X\beta$, β a vector of unknown parameters, and X a matrix of p predictors with columns $X_1, \ldots, X_p \in \mathbb{R}^n$. We suppose, for simplicity, that σ^2 is known.

Suppose that some variable selection procedure is utilised to select a model $M \subset \{1, \ldots, p\}$ consisting of a subset of the p predictors. Under the selected model, $\mu = X_M \beta^M$, where X_M is $n \times |M|$, with columns $(X_M)_1, \ldots, (X_M)_{|M|}$, say: we assume that X_M is of full rank, so that $\beta^M = (\beta_1^M, \ldots, \beta_{|M|}^M)$ is well-defined.

Conventional principles of inference in exponential family distributions, adapted to this selective inference context, indicate that inference on β_j^M should be based on the conditional distribution of $(X_M)_j^T Y$, given the observed values of $(X_M)_k^T Y$, $k = 1, \ldots, |M|, k \neq j$, and the selection event that model M is chosen. Use of this sampling distribution is termed (Fithian et al., 2014) inference under the 'selected model'.

If we do not take the model M seriously, there is still a well-defined linear predictor in the population for design matrix X_M. Now we define the target of inference as

$$\beta^M \equiv \arg\min_{b^M} \mathbb{E}\|Y - X_M b^M\|^2 = X_M^+ \mu,$$

$X_M^+ \equiv (X_M^T X_M)^{-1} X_M^T$ is the Moore-Penrose pseudo-inverse of X_M.

This 'saturated model' perspective is convenient as it allows meaningful inference even if, say, our variable selection procedure does a poor job.

The saturated model point of view can be advocated (Berk et al., 2013) as a way of avoiding the need, in the adaptive model determination context typical of data science, to consider multiple candidate probabilistic models.

Under the selected model, β_j^M can be expressed in the form $\beta_j^M = \eta^T \mu$, say, whereas under the saturated model there may not exist any β^M such that $\mu = X_M \beta^M$.

Compared to the selected model, the saturated model has $n - |M|$ additional nuisance parameters, which may be completely eliminated by the classical device of conditioning on the appropriate sufficient statistics: these correspond to $P_M^\perp Y \equiv (I_n - X_M(X_M^T X_M)^{-1} X_M^T) Y$.

Considering the saturated model as an exponential family, again assuming σ^2 is known, and writing the least-squares coefficient β_j^M again in the form $\eta^T \mu$, inference is based on the conditional distribution of $\eta^T Y$, the conditioning being on the observed values of $P_\eta^\perp Y \equiv (I_n - \eta^T(\eta^T \eta)^{-1} \eta^T) Y$, as well as the selection event.

The issue then arises of whether to perform inference under the selected or saturated models. Do we assume $P_M^\perp \mu = 0$, or treat it as an unknown nuisance parameter, to be eliminated by further conditioning?

Denoting by $X_{M\setminus j}$ the matrix obtained from X_M by deleting $(X_M)_j$, and letting $U = X_{M\setminus j}^T Y$ and $V = P_M^\perp Y$, the issue is whether to condition on both U and V, or only on U. Of course, conditioning on the selection event is assumed.

In the classical, nonadaptive, setting this issue does not arise, as $\eta^T Y, U$ and V are mutually independent: they are generally not independent conditional on the selection event.

If we condition on V when, in fact, $P_M^\perp \mu = 0$, we might expect to lose power, while inferential procedures may badly lose their control of (Type 1) error rate if this quantity is large, so that the selected model is actually false. We contend that such further conditioning is, however, necessary to ensure validity of the conclusions drawn from the specific dataset under analysis.

6. Example: Bivariate Regression

Suppose that Y is distributed as $N_2(\mu, I_2)$, so that $\sigma^2 = 1$ and that the design matrix is $X = I_2$.

We choose (using Least Angle Regression, lasso, or some such procedure) a 'one-sparse model', that is X_M is specified to have just one column. The selection procedure chooses $M = \{1\}$ if $|Y_1| > |Y_2|$ and $M = \{2\}$ otherwise.

Suppose the data outcome is $Y = \{2.9, 2.5\}$, so the chosen model is $M = \{1\}$.

The selected model has Y distributed as $N_2((\mu_1, 0), I_2)$. Inference on μ_1 would base a test of $H_0 : \mu_1 = 0$ against $H_1 : \mu_1 > 0$ on rejection for large values of Y_1, $Y_1 > c$, say. This test may be expressed as $H_0 : \eta^T \mu = 0$, with $\eta = (1,0)^T$. In the test of nominal Type 1 error α based on the selected model, c is fixed by requiring $P_{H_0}(Y_1 > c \mid M, |Y_1| > |Y_2|) = \alpha$, explicitly assuming that $\mu_2 = 0$. Notice that, in terms of the discussion of the previous section, there is no U in this example, since X_M has only one column. The issue is whether to condition only on the selection event, or also on $V = P_M^\perp Y \equiv P_\eta^\perp Y = Y_2$.

In the saturated model framework, we reject H_0 if $Y_1 > c'$, where c' satisfies

$$P_{H_0}(Y_1 > c' \mid Y_2 = 2.5, |Y_1| > |Y_2|) \equiv P_{H_0}(Y_1 > c' \mid |Y_1| > 2.5) = \alpha.$$

Conditioning on the observed value $Y_2 = 2.5$ as well as the selection event eliminates completely dependence of the Type 1 error rate on the value

Power, selected and saturated models

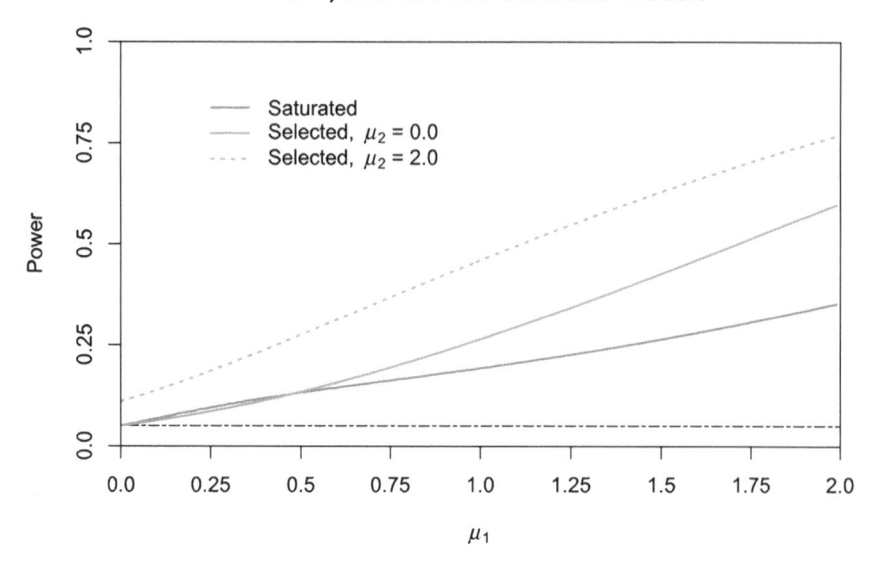

Fig. 2.4. Bivariate regression, power functions under selected and saturated models.

of μ_2. It is immediately established here that $c = 1.95, c' = 3.23$, in tests of nominal Type 1 error rate 0.05.

Figure 2.4 compares the power functions of the tests in the selected and saturated models. If the selected model is true, $\mu_2 = 0$, the test under the selected model is generally more powerful than the test derived from the saturated model, though we note the latter is actually marginally more powerful for small values of μ_1. However, if the selected model is false (the figure illustrates the case $\mu_2 = 2$), control of Type 1 error at the nominal 5% level is lost: the test of $\mu_1 = 0$ has Type 1 error rate exceeding 10% when the selected model is false and μ_2 is actually equal to 2.

Figures 2.5 and 2.6 examine the distributions of Y_2 and Y_1 respectively, conditional on the selection event $|Y_1| > |Y_2|$. Figure 2.5 demonstrates that the conditional distribution of Y_2 varies little with μ_1, the interest parameter, so that Y_2 is rather uninformative about μ_1. By contrast, the conditional distribution of Y_1, shown in Fig. 2.6, depends strongly on μ_1. Conditioning on the observed value of Y_2 is justified on the grounds that conditional on the selection event this value is, relative to Y_1, uninformative about μ_1, while this further conditioning ensures exact control of Type 1 error.

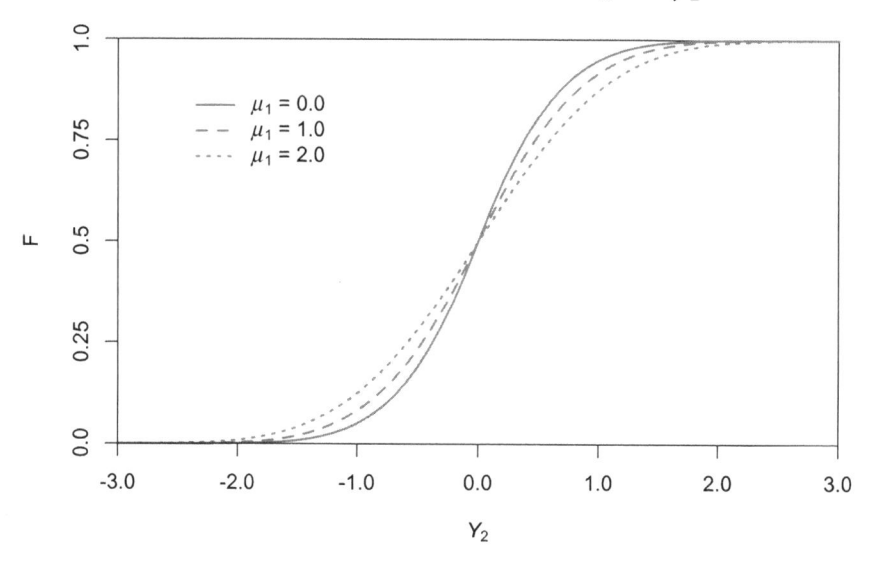

Fig. 2.5. Bivariate regression, conditional distributions of Y_2.

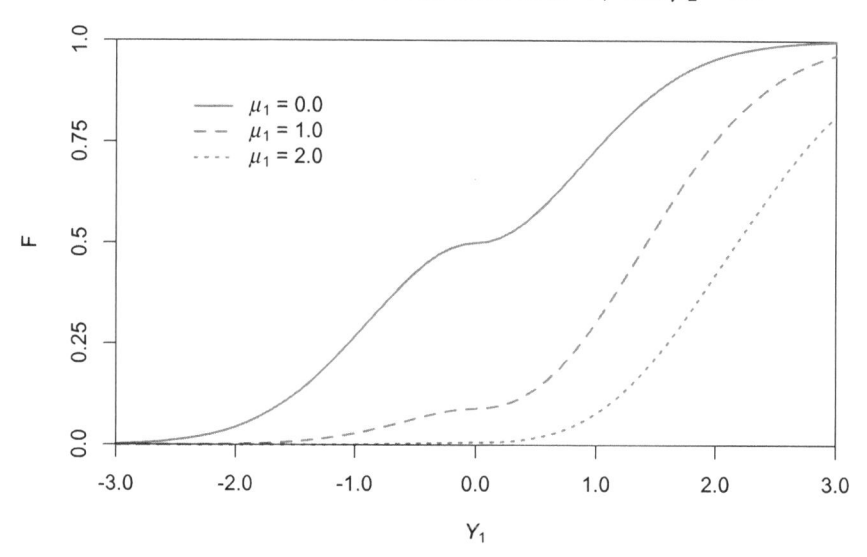

Fig. 2.6. Bivariate regression, conditional distributions of Y_1.

What do we conclude from this analysis? The operational difference between the saturated and selected model perspectives may (Fithian et al., 2014) be important in key practical contexts, such as early steps of sequential model-selection procedures. However, the case being made is that a principled approach to inference is forced to give central consideration to the saturated model in contexts such as those discussed here, where valid interpretation of significance is key. The Fisherian proposition requires conditioning on the selection event, as it is necessary (Young, 1986) to condition the inference on features of the data sample which control the propensity for extreme value of the test statistic to occur for spurious reasons. Precise control of the Type 1 error rate then demands elimination of nuisance parameter effects, achieved only by further conditioning on $P_\eta^\perp Y$: this leads to inference from the saturated model perspective.

7. Some Other Points

(i) The distribution theory necessary for inference in the saturated model perspective, under the Gaussian assumption at least, is generally easy.

In some generality, the selection event can be expressed as a polyhedron $S(Y) = \{AY \leq b\}$, for A, b not depending on Y. This is true for forward stepwise regression, the lasso with fixed penalty parameter λ, Least Angle Regression and other procedures. If inference is required for $\eta^T \mu$, then further conditioning on $P_\eta^\perp Y$ yields the conditional distribution required for the inference to be a truncated Gaussian with explicitly available endpoints, allowing a simple analytic solution.

Notice that here conditioning on $P_\eta^\perp Y$ is generally promoted (Lee et al., 2016) as a means of obtaining an analytically simple distribution for the inference. We have argued, however, that this conditioning is necessary to eliminate dependence on the nuisance parameter and provide control over Type 1 error. Marginally, that is ignoring the selection event, $\eta^T Y$ is independent of $P_\eta^\perp Y$, so the conditioning is justified by ancillarity, but this is not true conditional on the selection event: justification stronger than analytic convenience is provided by necessary elimination of the nuisance parameter.

(ii) In the non-Gaussian setting and in general under the selective model, Monte Carlo procedures, such as MCMC and acceptance/rejection methods, will be necessary to determine the necessary conditional distribution of Y, but such computational demands are unlikely to prove an obstacle to principled inference (Young and DiCiccio, 2010).

(iii) Tibshirani *et al.* (2015) offer a different perspective on selective inference, potentially relevant to data science.

Consider again the multivariate normal model. Under an alternative framework for selective inference, we recognise that for every possible selected model M, a quantity of interest, $\eta_M^T \mu$, say, is specified. When model $\hat{M}(Y)$ is selected, inference is made on the interest parameter $\eta_{\hat{M}(Y)}^T \mu$.

The notion of validity now is that, for the selected target, which is not fixed but varies according to Y, it is required that under repeated sampling of Y, a specified proportion $1-\alpha$ of the time, the inference on the selected target should be correct. Implicitly, perhaps, this is what is sought in much of data science. However, this perspective abandons the requirement that we have argued is central to principled inference, of ensuring validity and relevance to the actual data sample.

8. Conclusion

We have argued that a principled approach to inference in data science is necessary to provide the rationale by which claimed error-rate properties of inferential procedures are justified. The appropriate conceptual framework for valid inference is that discussed in the statistical literature as 'post-selection inference', which is based on ensuring relevance of sampling distributions used for inference to the particular data sample. These are classical, Fisherian ideas: no new paradigm for inference in data science is involved.

Specifically, inference after adaptive model determination ('data snooping') requires conditioning on the selection event and control of the error rate of the inference given it was actually performed. As commented by Fithian *et al.* (2014) 'the answer must be valid, given that the question was asked.'

Care is however required, as the selected model for inference may be wrong, and can lead to substantially distorted error rates. The primary cause is the assumption that nuisance parameters effects are known: elimination by the classical device of (further) conditioning ensures precise control of error rates. What we have described as the saturated model framework is the appropriate basis for inference. The potential loss of accuracy (power) through the necessary conditioning is undesirable, but may not be practically consequential: possible over-conditioning is a worthwhile price to be paid for validity.

Acknowledgement

The first author was supported by NSF DMS-1712940.

References

Barndorff-Nielsen, O. E. and Cox, D. R. (1994). *Inference and Asymptotics*, Chapman & Hall.

Berk, R., Brown, L., Buja, A., Zhang, K. and Zhao, L. (2013). Valid post-selection inference, *Ann. Statist.* **41**, 802–837.

Cox, D. R. and Mayo, D. G. (2010). Objectivity and conditionality in frequentist inference, in Mayo, D. G. and Spanos, A. (eds.) *Error and Inference: Recent Exchanges on Experimental Reasoning*, Reliability, and the Objectivity and Rationality of Science, Cambridge University Press, pp. 276–304.

Fisher, R. A. (1925). Theory of statistical estimation, *Proc. Cambridge Philos. Soc.* **22**, 700–725.

Fisher, R. A. (1934). Two new properties of mathematical likelihood, *Proc. R. Soc. Lond. A* **144**, 285–307.

Fithian, W., Sun, D. and Taylor, J. (2014). Optimal inference after model selection, preprint, arXiv:1410.2597.

Kuffner, T. A. and Walker, S. G. (2017). Why are p-values controversial? *Amer. Statist.*, DOI: https://doi.org/10.1080/00031305.2016.1277161.

Lee, J. D., Sun, D. L., Sun, Y. and Taylor, J. E. (2016). Exact post-selection inference, with application to the lasso, *Ann. Statist.* **44**, 907–927.

Speed, T. (2016). Terence's stuff: Principles, *IMS Bull.* **45**, 17.

Tibshirani, R., Rinaldo, A., Tibshirani, R. and Wasserman, L. (2015). Uniform asymptotic inference and the bootstrap after model selection, preprint, arXiv:1506.06266.

Young, G. A. (1986). Conditioned data-based simulations: Some examples from geometrical statistics, *Int. Stat. Rev.* **54**, 1–13.

Young, G. A. and DiCiccio, T. J. (2010). Computer-intensive conditional inference, in Mantovan, P. and Secchi, P. (eds.) *Complex Data Modeling and Computationally Intensive Statistical Methods*, Springer-Verlag, pp. 138–150.

Young, G. A. and Smith, R. L. (2005). *Essentials of Statistical Inference*, Cambridge University Press.

Chapter 3

Evaluating Statistical and Machine Learning Supervised Classification Methods

David J. Hand

Imperial College London and Winton Capital Management, UK
d.j.hand@imperial.ac.uk

Performance evaluation lies at the very heart of creating effective classifiers. It is needed in choosing variables, in deciding how to transform them, and in selecting an appropriate model or algorithm by which to combine them. This is true whether one is using simple logistic regression, support vector machines, deep learning, extreme gradient boosting, or whatever. A wide range of performance criteria have been created and are applied, but all too often they do not match the problem or aims. This can have serious consequences in terms of poor performance and mistaken classifications. This paper explores a number of familiar and very widely used measures, demonstrating that they have major weaknesses. These measures include misclassification rate, the F-measure, and the area under the ROC curve. Remedies are proposed, but the most important message is that it is necessary to think carefully about what one is trying to achieve when constructing and using a classification rule.

1. Introduction

In 1997 I published a book which focused on the evaluation of supervised classification methods (Hand, 1997). This book began by noting that researchers often ask what is the best type of classification method. The book concluded with the sentences: "We can now answer that question. The answer is: it depends." The aim of this paper is to expand on that statement, to illustrate some of the characteristics — of the classifier, of the problem, and of the aims of the analysis — that the answer depends on, and to describe some recent advances in supervised classifier evaluation.

The aim of supervised classification is to assign objects to one of a prespecified set of classes. For example, in medical diagnosis we will wish to decide which of several possible diseases a patient is suffering from. In speech recognition we will want to identify a spoken word as one of a set of possible words. And in selecting students or deciding whether to provide venture capital to a startup we will want to assign applicants to likely success or failure classes. And so on. The list of applications of supervised classification methods is unlimited, and it is the core technology which underlies machine learning. As a consequence of the tremendous breadth of application domains, supervised classification has been the focus of a huge amount of research. Tools date from even before Fisher's description of discriminant analysis in 1936, and range through logistic regression, classification trees, support vector machines, to deep learning neural networks, and beyond. With larger and larger datasets, in terms of both number of cases and number of descriptive features, with data arriving faster than ever (as in streaming data), and with new application domains continuing to appear, we can expect development to continue.

Formally, supervised classification begins with a set of objects, each of which has a known vector of characteristics x and for each of which the class membership is also known. This dataset is variously known as the design set (mainly in statistics) or the training set (mainly in machine learning), and it is the fact that the membership classes of objects in this design set are known which makes it *supervised* — it is as if there was a teacher or supervisor telling us the class labels.

Given the design data, the aim is to construct a rule — a formula, an algorithm, a recipe, etc. — which will allow us to assign new objects to classes purely on the basis of their vectors of characteristics. So we will construct a rule which will allow us to diagnose a new patient from their vector of signs and symptoms, to classify a spoken word on the basis of characteristics of its waveform, and so on.

In what follows, for simplicity we shall stick to the two class case, as the most important and basic case. We will label the classes as 0 or 1.

The aim, then, is to use the design set to construct a rule for mapping from $x = (x_1, \ldots, x_p)$ to the set $\{0, 1\}$. This can be done in three ways:

- directly. Systems based on strict logical rules are of this kind: if $[x_1 > 0.9]$ and $[x_2 > 0.3]$ then assign to class 1, otherwise to class 0, for example.

Evaluating Statistical and Machine Learning Supervised Classification Methods 39

- indirectly via a univariate *score*: $x \to s(x) \to \{0, 1\}$.
- indirectly via a score which is an estimate of the probability of belonging to class 1, $P(1|x) : x \to \hat{P}(1|x) \to \{0, 1\}$.

When scores or estimated probabilities are used, it is necessary also to choose a *threshold*, t, for the final stage of the mapping, so that

if $s(x) > t$ assign the object with descriptive vector x to class 1

or

if $\hat{P}(1|x) > t$ assign the object with descriptive vector x to class 1.

Note that in systems which involve logical rules, as in the example of a direct rule above, it is also often necessary to choose thresholds — but then multiple thresholds are needed (the 0.9 and 0.3 in the example). In certain classes of problems one can take advantage of this — see, for example, Kelly et al. (1998, 1999) and Kelly and Hand (1999).

Since the score is to be compared with a threshold, if measured in terms of how many class 0 and how many class 1 cases are correctly classified the performance of a classification rule will be invariant to monotonic transformations of the score function: if $s > t$ then $f(s) > f(t)$ for a monotonic increasing function f. This means that systems which use scores which are not probability estimates can easily be converted to such estimates via an extra *standardisation step*. To avoid overfitting issues, this may require classified data beyond the design set. Examples of systems which do not use probability estimates are

- credit scores: e.g. the FICO classic credit score has a range from 300 to 850, and FICO bankcard scores range between 250 and 900.
- medical scores such as the Apgar score of neonatal health, which ranges from 0 to 10, and the Beck Depression Inventory which ranges from 0 to 63.

Incidentally, it is worth noting that score scales can be used for more than mere classification. For example, a credit score can be used as the basis of a lend/not-lend decision, but it can also be used to determine an appropriate rate of interest.

In what follows, for simplicity I shall assume that the scores have been standardised: henceforth my scores are estimates of the probability of belonging to class 1. Letting $\hat{f}_i(s)$ be the probability density function for scores from class i, for $i = 0, 1$, and π_i be the class priors (that is the terminology used in supervised classification for the "sizes" of the classes — the proportion of objects in the overall population which belong to each class), this means that we have $s = \hat{P}(1|x) = \pi_1 \hat{f}_1(s)/\hat{f}(s)$ where $\hat{f}(s) = \pi_1 \hat{f}_0(s) + \pi_0 \hat{f}_1(s)$ is the overall probability density function (and where we have slightly abused the notation to take $\hat{P}(1|s) = \hat{P}(1|x)$). It also follows from the standardisation that

$$\hat{f}_0(s) = \frac{\hat{f}(s) \times (1-s)}{\pi_0}, \quad \hat{f}_1(s) = \frac{\hat{f}(s) \times s}{\pi_1}, \quad \frac{\hat{f}_0(s)}{\hat{f}_1(s)} = \frac{1-s}{s} \times \frac{\pi_1}{\pi_0}. \quad (1)$$

We shall use upper case F to represent the cumulative distribution functions. A score (and estimated probability of class 1 membership in our case) is said to be *calibrated* if $s = E(i|s) = P(1|s)$, with $i = 0, 1$, the class membership. Note, however, that calibration is not classification accuracy. For example, we could assign every object a score of π_1. This would be perfectly calibrated since $P(1|s) = \pi_1$ for all s which occurred in the data, there being only $s = \pi_1$, but it would be useless for classification purposes since it assigns every object the same score and does not discriminate at all.

Performance criteria are important for a number of reasons:

- to evaluate models. For example, to answer the question, is it good enough?
- to choose between models. For example, to answer the question, which one should we use?
- to estimate parameters. For example, to determine weights in linear combinations, split points in tree models, etc.
- to choose model components. For example, to decide which components of x to use (often it is better not to use all of them, to avoid overfitting), to determine an appropriate number of hidden nodes in a neural network, etc.

It is important to distinguish between two fundamentally different types of performance measure: problem-based measures and classification "accuracy" measures. This paper is concerned with the latter, but the former are illustrated by:

- speed of construction and updating (e.g. important in internet classification problems; spam detection);

- speed of classification (e.g. important in credit card fraud detection);
- ability to handle large datasets (sampling is not always possible);
- ability to handle problems where x has many features but relatively few cases (e.g. in genomics);
- ability to cope with incomplete data, a universal problem;
- interpretability can be important in some applications (e.g. as a result of recent legislation requiring an ability to be able to explain a decision based on an algorithm);
- extent to which the classifier permits the identification of important characteristics (e.g. in epidemiology);
- how well the classifier copes with unbalanced classes, where one is much smaller than the other (e.g. in credit card fraud detection).

Bob Duin (1996) has made some important observations about performance-based measures. He noted that "In comparing classifiers one should realise that some classifiers are valuable because they are heavily parametrized and thereby offer a trained analyst a large flexibility in integrating his (sic) problem knowledge in the classification procedure. Other classifiers on the contrary, are very valuable because they are entirely automatic and do not demand any user parameter adjustment. As a consequence they can be used by anybody." And "we are interested in the real performance for practical applications. Therefore, an application domain has to be defined. The traditional way to do this is by a diverse collection of datasets. In studying the results, however, one should keep in mind that such a collection does not represent any reality. It is an arbitrary collection, at most showing partially the diversity, but certainly not with any representative weight. It appears still possible that for classifiers showing a consistently bad behaviour in the problem collection, somewhere an application exists for which they are perfectly suited."

In general, it is important to recognise that performance is not an *intrinsic* property of a classifier. For classifier performance evaluation, what matters is the product of *method* by *user* by *problem* by *data*, and, equally important, by just what is meant by *best*.

The next section looks at the range of "accuracy" based performance measures, showing the variety of different definitions of accuracy (of what is meant by "best") which have been proposed and used (see also Hand (2012)). Subsequent sections focus down on two particular widely-used measures, showing that they are fundamentally misleading and should not be used for evaluating classification and machine learning algorithms.

Table 3.1. Classification table.

		True Class	
		0	1
Predicted Class	0	a	b
	1	c	d

2. Performance Measures

2.1. *Measures based on the classification table*

Given the score continuum and threshold t we can produce the familiar cross-classification shown in Table 3.1, where $a = n\pi_0 \hat{F}_0(t)$, $b = n\pi_1 \hat{F}_1(t)$, $c = n\pi_0(1 - \hat{F}_0(t))$, $d = n\pi_1(1 - \hat{F}_1(t))$, with n the total design set size.

Our aim is to reduce the four values a, b, c, and d to a single measure, so that it can be used to compare classification rules.

First observe that there are really only three independent degrees of freedom here since $a + b + c + d = n$. In fact, beyond this, for fixed class priors, $a + c = n\pi_0$ and $b + d = n\pi_1$, so they reduce to two independent degrees of freedom. The key question is how to reduce these two to one.

The two degrees of freedom can be described in various ways. For example, we can look at proportion of each true class which are correctly classified, or look at proportion in each predicted class which really do belong to that predicted class. Since supervised classification problems are so ubiquitous, different disciplines have devised different names for the same concept. Thus, for example (regarding class 1 as "cases"):

- the proportion of true class 1 objects which are correctly predicted, $d/(b + d)$ is variously called recall, sensitivity, and true positive rate;
- the proportion of predicted class 1 objects which are correctly predicted, $d/(c + d)$ is variously called precision, and positive predictive value. Its complement, $c/(c + d)$, is the false discovery rate.

Likewise, the two degrees of freedom have been condensed into one in a variety of ways, with different names for the same concept, and with different disciplines favouring different condensations — often with little rationale. So, for example, misclassification rate (error rate, the complement of proportion correct) is very widely used, especially in the machine learning literature, where it is by far the dominant measure (see, e.g. Jamain and Hand (2008)). This is despite the fact that it treats the two kinds of misclassification (misclassifying a class 0 point as class 1 and the converse) as equally serious while this is rarely appropriate. The impact of this is especially brought home in situations involving unbalanced classes, where typically misclassifying the rare class is more serious than misclassifying the common class. For example, in credit card fraud detection, a ball-park figure is that 1 in a 1000 transactions are fraudulent. Ignoring the relative severity of misclassifying a fraudulent transaction as legitimate compared to the converse would mean that if we classified everything as legitimate we would achieve the very low error rate of 0.001. It looks good but would be useless. (See Hand *et al.* (2008), for criteria which overcome this problem in plastic card fraud applications.)

An important variant of misclassification rate, Cohen's Kappa, adjusts for chance agreement. If the classes have equal priors, and we classify equal numbers to the two classes, then simple random assignment would give us a misclassification rate of 0.5. Kappa is defined as (*observed proportion correct − chance proportion correct*)/(*1 − chance proportion correct*). In terms of the misclassification table the observed proportion correct is $p_c = (a+d)/n$ and the chance proportion correct (i.e. the proportion expected to be correctly classified if we assigned objects to classes at random with the given class priors and the given proportions assigned to each class) is $p_e = (a+b)(a+c)/n^2 + (b+d)(c+d)/n^2$ so that Kappa is $(p_c - p_e)/(1 - p_e)$.

Misclassification rate, $(b+c)/n$ can be written as a weighted sum of the proportions misclassified in each of the two true classes, or in each of the two predicted classes. In general, since there are many different measures of classification performance but only two degrees of freedom in the misclassification table, the measures are obviously related. Some mathematical relationships and bounds are given in Sec. 3.4 of Hand (2012).

2.2. *Choosing the classification threshold*

The choice of threshold determines how $a+c$ is split into a and c, and how $b+d$ is split into b and d in Table 3.1. And clearly these splits are jointly determined. This means, for example, that a compromise has to be struck between the proportion of class 0s which are correctly classified and the proportion of class 1s which are correctly classified (in medical screening terminology, with class 1 objects as cases, this would be a compromise between specificity and sensitivity). The decision should ideally be made on the basis of understanding the problem and aims. For example, in answer to questions such as:

- what is the desired (estimated) proportion to be assigned to class 1?
- what is the desired (estimated) class 1 rate amongst those assigned to class 1?
- what is the minimum (estimated) probability of class 1 membership for which we want to assign objects to class 1?

The reader will immediately recognise that the underlying abstract problem has much in common with the logic of hypothesis testing. In that case, the conventional choice is to fix the rate of one of the types of misclassification, misclassifying class 0 objects as class 1, at, say 5%, and to minimise the rate of misclassifying class 1 objects (i.e. maximising test power) by choice of test and design of study.

2.2.1. Misclassification rate

Using the notation introduced above, the proportion correctly classified (the complement of misclassification rate) is

$$\max_t(\pi_0 \hat{F}_0(t) + \pi_1(1 - \hat{F}_1(t))).$$

Elementary calculus then yields the optimal threshold to be the t which satisfies $\pi_0 \hat{f}_0(t) = \pi_1 \hat{f}_1(t)$, and since $\hat{P}(1|t) = \pi_1 \hat{f}_1(t)/(\pi_0 \hat{f}_0(t) + \pi_1 \hat{f}_1(t))$, we obtain $\hat{P}(1|t) = 1/2$ which in turn, because of the standardisation we are assuming, yields $t = 1/2$. We see that misclassification rate classifies each object to the class from which it is (estimated to be) most likely to have arisen. This seems perfectly reasonable — but, as we remarked above, it ignores the relative severity of the two kinds of errors: the classifications are based solely on the estimated class 0 and class 1 membership probabilities.

2.2.2. Kolmogorov–Smirnov measure

A second commonly used measure is the Kolmogorov–Smirnov (KS) statistic familiar in the context of nonparametric two-sample tests (and widely used in the retail credit scoring industry). It is defined as

$$\max_t(|\hat{F}_0(t) - \hat{F}_1(t)|).$$

This leads to $\hat{f}_0(t) = \hat{f}_1(t)$, so that $t = \hat{P}(1|t) = \pi_1$. Once again, this choice ignores the relative severities of the two kinds of misclassification.

For convenience in what follows, we will assume that the class 1 distribution stochastically dominates the class 0 distribution, so that $\hat{F}_0(s) > \hat{F}_1(s)$: that is, we will assume that class 1 objects tend to score higher than class 0 objects.

2.2.3. Given misclassification costs

In many, arguably most, real classification problems, it is important to take misclassification costs into account: one would prefer a self-driving car to err on the side of caution, and stop more often than was strictly necessary, rather than going ahead regardless in possibly dangerous situations. So, let the cost of misclassifying a class 0 case be k and the cost of misclassifying a class 1 case be $1 - k$. Then the overall estimated loss at threshold t is

$$L(t) = k\pi_0(1 - \hat{F}_0(t)) + (1-k)\pi_1 \hat{F}_1(t).$$

We see immediately that if $k = 1/2$ this reduces to misclassification rate and if $k = \pi_1$ it reduces to $1-(\hat{F}_0(t) - \hat{F}_1(t))$ which, because of our stochastic dominance assumption, leads to the complement of the KS measure. The second of these observations means that another interpretation of the KS measure is that it is the overall loss if the costs are such that misclassifying *all* the class 0 cases equals the overall loss from misclassifying *all* the class 1 cases.

In general, for a given k, the threshold which minimises the overall loss is given by the value of t which satisfies $k = \pi_1 \hat{f}_1(t)/\hat{f}(t)$. Since we assumed our scores had been standardised to be probability estimates, we have the optimal t to be $t = k$. (And again we see immediately that misclassification rate is the special case when $k = 1/2$ — when the costs are equal.)

2.2.4. The F-measure

Another measure which is widely used in certain applications (e.g. especially in information retrieval, computer science, and record linkage — see for example (Hand and Christen, 2017)) is the *F-measure* (also called the *Dice coefficient* in numerical taxonomy). If class 1 objects are regarded as "cases" then the F-measure is the harmonic mean of the proportion of true class 1 objects which are correctly predicted, and the proportion of predicted class 1 objects which really do come from class 1. In computer science terminology, these are the *recall* and *precision* respectively, and in terms of the notation of Table 3.1 they are:

- Recall $= R = d/(b+d)$
- Precision $= P = d/(c+d)$

so that the F-measure is $F = 2\left[P^{-1} + R^{-1}\right]^{-1}$.

From a formal perspective this seems to be a (rather ugly) combination of noncommensurate (estimated) conditional probabilities. However, there is another way to express it which sheds useful light on a possible interpretation.

Using the notation from Table 3.1, we can rewrite F as

$$F = 2\left[P^{-1} + R^{-1}\right]^{-1}$$
$$= \frac{2d}{b+c+2d}$$
$$= \frac{c+d}{b+c+2d}\frac{d}{c+d} + \frac{b+d}{b+c+2d}\frac{d}{b+d}$$
$$= pP + (1-p)R$$

where $p = (c+d)/(b+c+2d)$. That is, F can also be viewed as a *weighted arithmetic mean*. This gives it a direct probability interpretation. As we shall see, it also opens a path to defining the F-measure in terms of the problem and the researchers' aims.

With this weighted arithmetic mean interpretation, the weights p and $1-p$ give the importance assigned to precision and recall respectively. And the reader will see that they depend on the numbers in Table 3.1. That is, the weights — the relative importance assigned to precision and recall — will depend on the classifier used. This is not sensible: precision and recall capture different aspects of classifier performance and the relative importance attached to them should be a function of the problem, the user, and the objectives, not of the classifier which happens to be chosen. We would not say that precision is more important than recall if logistic regression was used, but less important if naive Bayes was used.

To make the comparison fair, the value of p must be the same for all methods being compared (for the particular problem in question). It means that the ratio $p/(1-p)$ must be the same. This ratio is equal to $(c+d)/(b+d)$; that is, to the ratio of the number predicted to be class 1 to the number actually in class 1. Since the latter is fixed, a property of the problem and design data, this means that we must choose the thresholds for each of the classifiers being compared so that they all predict the same number to class 1, and, in particular, so that

$$\#\,(\text{Pred Class 1}) = \#\,(\text{True Class 1}) \cdot \frac{p}{1-p},$$

where the second factor is the ratio of the relative importance accorded to precision and recall. To do otherwise means that one would not be comparing the classifiers using the same instrument — it would be analogous to measuring lengths using an elastic ruler which was stretched differently for different objects being measured.

This is an important conclusion which deserves stressing: when using the F-measure to compare classifiers it is necessary, for the results to be meaningful, that the different classifiers assign the same number of test set objects to class 1.

2.3. *Distributions of misclassification costs*

2.3.1. *The H-measure*

As we have seen, the misclassification rate and KS measure are equivalent to choosing a classification threshold, and this in turn is equivalent to minimising the overall loss for particular values of the cost k. This means that if one knows the relative costs of the two kinds of misclassification, then one can choose the best threshold. However, identifying costs is difficult — and experience shows this to be the case even in financial situations where, at least in principle, different situations use money as a common numéraire, let alone in medical and other situations. This experience has led to the suggestion that, instead of point cost values, we might use a distribution of possible costs, with most weight being placed on those values thought most likely to be relevant. This section explores this idea (for more details see Hand (2009, 2010), Hand and Anagnostopoulos (2013, 2014), and Hand and Zhou (2010)).

To explore this idea we shall begin by looking at another very widely used measure of classifier performance, the area under the Receiver Operating Characteristic (ROC) curve. The ROC curve is a plot of $1 - \hat{F}_1(t)$ on the vertical axis against $1 - \hat{F}_0(t)$ on the horizontal axis (sometimes other axes are used, but they simply represent various reflections of this plot). With these axes, when $t = 1$ all objects are classified into class 0, corresponding to a point at the bottom left of the plot, and when $t = 0$ all objects are classified as class 1, corresponding to a point at the top right.

A value of t corresponding to perfect classification would have $1 - \hat{F}_1(t) = 1$ and $1 - \hat{F}_0(t) = 0$, corresponding to a point at the top left of the plot. The diagonal of the plot corresponds to chance classification, and the extent to which the curve lies above the diagonal is a measure of how much the classifier is better than chance. The area beneath the curve (ranging from 1/2 for chance to 1 for perfect classification), the AUC, is equivalent to the Mann–Whitney–Wilcoxon two sample test statistic and is widely used as a measure of classifier performance. A little calculus shows $AUC = \int \hat{F}_0(t) \hat{f}_1(t) dt$. For more detail of ROC curves see Krzanowski and Hand (2009).

With that definition in hand, let us return to using cost weighted loss based on a distribution $w(k)$ of possible cost values. If we let $L_{\min}(k)$ represent the minimum loss for a given cost (i.e. the loss which arises if one chooses the threshold to minimise the loss for costs k and $1-k$) the average minimum cost is

$$\int L_{\min}(k) w(k) dk = \int [k\pi_0(1 - \hat{F}_0(k)) + (1-k)\pi_1 \hat{F}_1(k)] w(k) dk.$$

Now, we have seen that the threshold t which minimises the loss at cost k is $t = k$, so we have $k = \pi_1 \hat{f}_1(k)/\hat{f}(k)$. This gives

$$\int L_{\min}(k) w(k) dk$$
$$= \int \left[\frac{\pi_1 \hat{f}_1(k)}{\hat{f}(k)} \pi_0 (1 - \hat{F}_0(k)) + \frac{\pi_0 \hat{f}_0(k)}{\hat{f}(k)} \pi_1 \hat{F}_1(k) \right] w(k) dk,$$

and a little algebra shows that if we choose $w(k) = \hat{f}(k)$ we obtain

$$\int L_{\min}(k) \hat{f}(k) dk = 2\pi_0 \pi_1 (1 - AUC).$$

That is, the AUC is equivalent to (i.e. it is proportional to the complement of) a cost-weighted average of misclassification rates, where the averaging function is the overall score mixture distribution $\hat{f}(k)$, *which depends on the data*.

This is nonsensical. It means one is using a different weight function for each classifier being compared — since different classifiers are almost certain to produce different population score distributions $\hat{f}(s)$. Since the score has been standardised, averaging over different score distributions is as if one said "If you use logistic regression you believe misclassifying a class 1 object as class 0 is nine times as serious as the converse, but if you use naive Bayes it is only three times as serious." The distribution of possible weights must be a function of the problem and aims, not of the classifiers being used.

Incidentally, if two classifiers produce the same overall score distribution $\hat{f}(s)$, then the results in (1) (which follow from the standardisation) would mean that the classifiers would produce identical classification results: the classifiers would be indistinguishable in terms of performance.

The implication is that the AUC is a potentially misleading measure of the performance of classification rules and should not be used to evaluate them. Given the breadth of application of supervised classification, and how widespread is the use of AUC (see Hand and Anagnostopoulos (2013)), this can have serious consequences.

The remedy is straightforward. In place of the classifier-dependent weight function $w(k) = \hat{f}(k)$, use a function which is independent of the classifier. Ideally, one would choose a function which properly reflected ones beliefs about the problem in question. Here Bayesian probability elicitation methods can be used.

Alternatively, and we recommend *in addition*, a conventional standard distribution should be used. In Hand and Anagnostopoulos (2014) we proposed that the Beta$(1 + \pi_1, 1 + \pi_0)$ distribution be used. This leads to the *H-measure* described in Hand (2009, 2010), Hand and Anagnostopoulos (2013, 2014). The H-measure takes the average loss, as described above, and then standardises and subtracts from 1, to yield a measure which takes a maximum of 1 and for which large values correspond to good performance — see the above references, and for code see http://www.hmeasure.net.

It is perhaps worth noting that, in those (rare) cases when the relative misclassification costs are known, obviously these should be used — and then misclassification rate with the optimal threshold for this cost is the appropriate measure, and in such circumstances AUC is irrelevant.

I am occasionally asked about interpretations of the H-measure. Such questions often begin with the comment that the AUC has a straightforward interpretation. But this is misleading. The most familiar interpretation of the AUC is that it is the probability that a randomly chosen class 0 object will have a score lower than a randomly chosen class 1 object. While this interpretation is fine in some situations (e.g. when comparing two probability distributions, as in applications of the Mann–Whitney–Wilcoxon test statistic) it is generally irrelevant to classification problems: objects typically do not arrive in pairs, one from each class. A second interpretation of the AUC is that it is the fraction by which the classifier reduces the expected minimum misclassification loss, compared with that of a random classifier. While correct, the expectation in this interpretation depends on the classifier being used — as explained above. Finally, a third interpretation is that the AUC is the expected proportion of class 0 objects correctly classified if the threshold is randomly chosen so that the proportion of class 1 objects correctly classified is uniform. This is based on the screening idea described in the next subsection. However, as we shall see, the expectation here is based on an unrealistic choice of a uniform distribution.

The second of the interpretations of the AUC just outlined can be mapped directly to the H-measure, where the shortcoming of the AUC is resolved. This leads to: The H-measure is

> H1: the fraction by which the classifier reduces the expected minimum misclassification loss, compared with that of a random classifier;

or

> H2: 100 times the H-measure is "the percentage reduction in expected minimum misclassification loss when the classifier is used" (compared with that of a random classifier).

In each case, the expectation is over the chosen distribution function — for example, the Beta$(1 + \pi_1, 1 + \pi_0)$ described above.

2.3.2. *Screening*

The above derivation depended on choosing the threshold which minimised the misclassification rate for each value of the cost k, over the distribution of these costs. However, there are situations where this is not an appropriate thing to do. In particular, in *screening* we seek to identify those members of a population which are most likely to belong to class 1, perhaps so that they can be investigated further, or so that they can be treated in some way (e.g. medical investigation, granted a loan, accepted for a university course, etc.).

Once again, if we know what proportion of objects we wish to select then this proportion should be used. However, if we do not know this proportion it again makes sense to average over a distribution of possible proportions.

It is now easy to see that

$$\int [\pi_0(1-\hat{F}_0(t)) + \pi_1 \hat{F}_1(t)]\hat{f}(t)\mathrm{d}t = \frac{\pi_0^2 + \pi_1^2}{2} + 2\pi_0\pi_1(1-AUC).$$

That is, if one uses the overall score population distribution $\hat{f}(t)$ as the averaging distribution for the scores, one again obtains (something equivalent to) the AUC. But using $\hat{f}(t)$ in this way is equivalent to assuming that each fraction of the population is equally likely to be chosen as the proportion to be selected. That is, it is equivalent to saying we think it equally likely that we will want to select 90% of the population or 10% or 1%.

This is unrealistic. While one might not know exactly what proportion of the population one will want to select, the range is likely to be quite small — we might, for example, regard 5% or 10% as realistic possible values in medical screening, or 80% or 90% if selecting applicants for a loan, but a distribution which regards each possible proportion over the entire range from 0 to 1 as equally likely is not realistic.

The solution, the same as that in converting the AUC to the H-measure, is to replace the uniform distribution by one which better reflects ones true beliefs about the likely proportions of the population one will wish to select.

In summary, when classifying objects based on minimising the overall loss, the AUC is equivalent to an average loss where the averaging distribution varies from classifier to classifier. This is nonsensical because it contravenes the basic principle of evaluation — that the same instrument should be used to assess each thing being measured — each classifier in this case. And when screening, if the proportion of the population to be selected is initially unknown (it might depend on what one will be able to afford in the future) the AUC is equivalent to assuming a uniform distribution of possible proportions, and this unrealistic.

3. Conclusion

This paper began by pointing out that, without further qualification, it is misleading and meaningless to ask what is the best type of classifier. The answer will depend on the aims, the problem, the data, the user of the classifier, as well as by what is meant by "best". A nice illustration of the importance of the last point was given by Benton (2001, Fig. 4.1). He showed the directions which maximised the gradient of different classifier performance measures in the ionosphere data from the UCI Data Repository. In particular, he found that the optimal direction when using misclassification rate was at almost 60° to the optimal direction when using AUC. Quite clearly, use of an inappropriate measure for any particular problem could lead to many misclassifications.

We showed that many familiar and widely used measures, such as misclassification rate, the KS statistic, the F-measure, and the AUC have implicit assumptions which may be inappropriate for any particular problem. We also showed how to overcome their shortcomings.

Although this paper has delved into the details of particular measures, the most important conclusion is the general one: when constructing and evaluating classification rules think carefully about the intended application. It is critically important that an appropriate and relevant performance measure be used. Doing otherwise is to risk poor classification performance, with consequent possible misdiagnoses, loss of money, or even catastrophic failure, depending on the application.

References

Benton, T. (2001). *Theoretical and Empirical Models*, Ph.D. thesis, Department of Mathematics, Imperial College, London.

Duin, R. (1996). A note on comparing classifiers, *Pattern Recognit. Lett.* **17**, pp. 529–536.

Hand, D. (1997). *Construction and Assessment of Classification Rules*, John Wiley & Sons, Chichester.

Hand, D. (2009). Measuring classifier performance: a coherent alternative to the area under the ROC curve, *Mach. Learn.* **77**, pp. 103–123.

Hand, D. (2010). Evaluating diagnostic tests: the area under the ROC curve and the balance of errors, *Stat. Med.* **29**, pp. 1502–1510.

Hand, D. (2012). Assessing the performance of classification methods, *Int. Stat. Rev.* **80**, pp. 400–414.

Hand, D. and Anagnostopoulos, C. (2013). When is the area under the receiver operating characteristic curve an appropriate measure of classifier performance? *Pattern Recognit. Lett.* **34**, pp. 492–496.

Hand, D. and Anagnostopoulos, C. (2014). A better beta for the H-measure of classification performance, *Pattern Recognit. Lett.* **40**, pp. 41–46.

Hand, D. and Christen, P. (2017). A note on using the F-measure for evaluating record linkage algorithms, *Statist. Comput.*, doi:10.1007/s11222-017-9746-6.

Hand, D., Whitrow, C., Adams, N., Juszczak, P. and Weston, D. (2008). Performance criteria for plastic card fraud detection tools, *J. Oper. Res. Soc.* **59**, pp. 956–962.

Hand, D. and Zhou, F. (2010). Evaluating models for classifying customers in retail banking collections, *J. Oper. Res. Soc.* **61**, pp. 1540–1547.

Jamain, A. and Hand, D. (2008). Mining supervised classification performance studies: A meta-analytic investigation, *J. Classification* **25**, pp. 87–112.

Kelly, M. and Hand, D. (1999). Credit scoring with uncertain class definitions, *IMA J. Math. Appl. Business Industry* **10**, pp. 331–345.

Kelly, M., Hand, D. and Adams, N. (1998). Defining the goals to optimise data mining performance, in Agrawal, R. Stolorz, P. and Piatetsky-Shapiro, G. (eds.) *Proc. Fourth Int. Conf. Knowledge Discovery and Data Mining*, AAAI Press, Menlo Park, pp. 234–238.

Kelly, M., Hand, D. and Adams, N. (1999). Supervised classification problems: how to be both judge and jury, in Hand, D. Kok, J. and Berthold, M. (eds.) *Advances in Intelligent Data Analysis*, Springer, Berlin, pp. 235–244.

Krzanowski, W. and Hand, D. (2009). *ROC Curves for Continuous Data*, Chapman and Hall, London.

Chapter 4

Diversity as a Response to User Preference Uncertainty

James Edwards[*] and David Leslie[†]

*Department of Mathematics and Statistics, Lancaster University,
Lancaster LA1 4YF, UK*
[*]*j.edwards4@lancaster.ac.uk*
[†]*d.leslie@lancaster.ac.uk*

This chapter considers the problem of choosing a set of website elements to present to a user. An often desirable property of such a set is that it is diverse, i.e. the elements are not all similar to one another. Often this is presented as being a separate objective from that of choosing elements that match the user in some way and which are therefore more likely to be clicked. We present a range of simple and intuitive models based on uncertainty about user preferences that show how diversity emerges naturally as a result of seeking to maximise the probability that the user will click on an element. As such we give an argument as to why diversity is desirable which avoids the need for it as a separate objective. The exact model used affects the diversity of sets chosen as well as the likelihood that the user will click on an element.

1. Introduction

A common problem faced by websites is to choose which *elements* (e.g. adverts, news stories or retail items) to display to a user. The aim is to choose elements that are useful or attractive to the user so that they choose or *click* the element. How likely an element is to be clicked depends not only on its inherent quality or general attractiveness but also on its relevance to the particular user. For example, a news story about a big football game might attract more interest than a relatively niche story about astronomy but if it is known that the user enjoys science news and has little interest in sport then they may be more likely to click on the latter story.

Usually elements will not be presented in isolation but as a part of a list or set of other elements. If elements are very similar to one another then there will be *redundancy* in the set. That is, if an element does not appeal to the user then it is unlikely that a similar element will do so either. So if our belief about the user in the previous example is wrong then a selection of mainly astronomy stories would be very inappropriate and lead to a dissatisfied customer. This illustrates the intuitive idea that element sets should be *diverse*.

How to achieve appropriate diversity is a current challenge in the field of *Recommender Systems*, which are techniques for suggesting items to a user (Ricci et al., 2011). Items that are best for the user (most *accurate*) will be the ones that most closely match the user's interests and so will usually be similar to one another. Therefore the direct approach of choosing elements that are most accurate individually will frequently lead to a lack of diversity.

The usual approach (e.g. Carbonell and Goldstein (1998); Vargas and Castells (2011); Hurley and Zhang (2011); Zhou et al. (2010)) is to explicitly trade-off accuracy against diversity by setting these as joint objectives and maximising some combination. This, however, introduces the additional question of how the two objectives should be weighted in importance. In this chapter we will demonstrate that treating diversity as a separate objective can be unnecessary. Instead diversity arises naturally as a result of maximising a single, realistic objective (click through rate) under uncertainty about user preferences.

These two alternative views of diversity are described by Radlinski et al. (2009) as intrinsic and extrinsic needs for diversity. When the need is intrinsic the diversity is regarded as desirable in itself, for example by providing variety and novelty in a recommender system. With an extrinsic need, diversity emerges as a characteristic of good solutions even though it is not in itself an objective. This chapter builds on the extrinsic viewpoint taken in Information Retrieval (El-Arini et al., 2009; Agrawal et al., 2009). We will show that these existing models often result in only moderate set diversity, then give an extended family of models in which higher diversity is induced.

Our approach is based on the idea that each user has a latent preference or *state*. This state provides information about what type of element a user is likely to click on. The state could take many forms: it could be the intended meaning of an ambiguous search term, the genre of movie the user wishes to watch, or some subgroup of the user population that the user belongs to. If the state was known then elements could be chosen that are appropriate for that state. However we will assume throughout that we are provided only with a probability distribution over the user's states. Therefore it may be desirable to choose elements appropriate for several different states to ensure that there is a good chance of a click whichever of the possible states is true. In this way we choose a diverse set simply by seeking to maximise the probability of a click.

We argue that this approach results in *appropriate* diversity. If we are sure a user wishes to watch an action movie then there is little to be gained from including sport or comedy movies in the recommended set; this would correspond to inappropriate diversity. However when we are uncertain about the user's desires, perhaps because we have little information on the user or because their preferences vary, then we need a variety of genres in the set to cover these different realities. The diversity of the element set should depend on the reliability of available information about the user's preferences — the greater our uncertainty, the greater the need for diversity.

Section 2 will formally state the problem we will investigate together with a continuum of models for user click behaviour based on our knowledge of their preferences. Algorithms for choosing element sets are given in Sec. 3 and their performance and behaviour will be investigated in a simulation study in Sec. 4. Section 5 concludes.

2. Problem Formulation

A user arrives with a *state* $x \in \{1, \ldots, n\}$ which gives potentially useful information about the user as described in Sec. 1. This state is hidden, so we consider it a random variable X with distribution which is observed and given by a topic preference vector $\mathbf{q}$ such that $Pr(X = x) = q_x$. In response to the topic preference vector we present m elements as an (ordered) set $A \subseteq \mathcal{A}$. The user will respond by selecting (or clicking) at most one element of the set.

Each element $a \in \mathcal{A}$ is characterised by a weight vector $\mathbf{w}_a$ of length n with $w_{a,x} \in [0,1]$ for $x \in \{1, \ldots, n\}$. The weight $w_{a,x}$ represents the probability a user with state x will click element a and we call this the *element click through rate*. In practice each $w_{a,x}$ would not be known exactly but in this chapter we will assume that each $\mathbf{w}_a$ is known. Let $\mathbf{w}_A$ denote the set of vectors $\{\mathbf{w}_a\}, a \in A$.

This framework is complete if $m = 1$ element is to be displayed and x is known: the click probability if a is presented is simply $w_{a,x}$. However if x is latent and $m > 1$ we need to build a model of receiving a click on the *set* of elements A, what we term simply the *click through rate (CTR)*. While the cascade model (Craswell et al., 2008) is often used to model *which* of a set of elements might be selected, we instead require a model of *whether* an element will be selected. Two intuitive models are presented, which are shown to be extreme examples of a general click model.

The consequences of the choice of model will be the main focus of this work. Each model is initially specified for known x but easily extends to latent x as given at the end of this section.

Definition 1. The *Probabilistic Click Model (PCM)* is closely related to models for document retrieval in Agrawal et al. (2009); El-Arini et al. (2009). The user considers each element in A in turn until they either click an element or have considered all the elements in A. Each element a currently considered will be clicked with probability $w_{a,x}$ which is independent of any other elements $a \setminus A$. Therefore the CTR of the set A for known x is,

$$r_{\text{PCM}}(x, A, \mathbf{w}_A) = 1 - \prod_{a \in A}(1 - w_{a,x}).$$

This model captures in a simple way the idea of diminishing returns as more elements are added. Although it will be shown later that the PCM does indeed encourage diversity in the element set, as in Agrawal et al. (2009), an obvious issue is that a set of two identical elements gives a higher CTR than a single such element, which is an unrealistic representation of user click behaviour. We present a new model which avoids this problem.

Definition 2. In the *Threshold Click Model (TCM)* each user has a threshold u drawn independently from the $U(0,1)$ distribution. They consider each element in turn, clicking the first element $a \in A$ such that $w_{a,x} > u$. The probability of a click is thus the probability that U is less than the maximal $w_{a,x}$:

$$r_{\text{TCM}}(x_t, A, \mathbf{w}_{A_t}) = \int_0^1 1 - \prod_{a \in A_t}(1 - \mathbb{1}_{w_{a,x_t} > u_t}) \, du_t.$$

$$= \int_0^{\max_{a \in A_t} w_{a,x_t}} 1 \, du_t + \int_{\max_{a \in A_t} w_{a,x_t}}^1 0 \, du_t$$

$$= \max_{a \in A_t} w_{a,x_t}.$$

The TCM thus represents a user who, with preference x, will click an advert if its relevance $w_{a,x}$ exceeds a user-specific threshold u. This user-behaviour model can be related to models of consumer purchasing behaviour in economics (Van Ryzin, 2012). The $w_{a,x}$ corresponds to the price of a good while u corresponds to the consumer's *willingness-to-pay* threshold. The good is purchased (corresponding to a click) if the price is no greater than the user's willingness-to-pay.

These two models form the extreme ends of the following parameterised continuum of models.

Definition 3. In the *General Click Model (GCM)* there is a single parameter $d \in [1, \infty)$. Let $a^* \in \operatorname{argmax}_{a \in A} w_{a,x}$ with ties broken arbitrarily. The click probability for element a^* is $w_{a^*,x}$ and for all other elements $a \in A \setminus a^*$ it is $(w_{a,x})^d$. Therefore the CTR of the set A is

$$r^d_{\text{GCM}}(x, A, \mathbf{w}_A) = 1 - (1 - w_{a^*,x}) \prod_{a \in A \setminus a^*} (1 - (w_{a,x})^d). \tag{1}$$

As d increases the user's click likelihood becomes increasingly dependent on the element they find most attractive with other elements increasingly unlikely to be clicked. Setting $d = 1$ gives PCM and $d \to \infty$ results in TCM. Thus GCM gives us a method to investigate the effect of click model choice over a continuum.

Since x is unobserved, our objective is actually to optimise expected reward over $\mathbf{q}$. Since, in any particular instance, $\mathbf{q}$ and $\mathbf{w}_A$ are fixed, we write our objective function as

$$\text{CTR}^d(A) = \mathbb{E}_{x \sim \mathbf{q}}[r^d_{\text{GCM}}(x, A, \mathbf{w}_A)], \tag{2}$$

which is easy to calculate since q is discrete. The expected reward for PCM is therefore given by $\text{CTR}^1(A)$ and for TCM we denote the expected reward by $\text{CTR}^\infty(A)$. In Sec. 4 we demonstrate how the diversity of the CTR-optimising element set changes with d.

3. Solution Method

Choosing an element set $A \subseteq \mathcal{A}$ to maximise the CTR is not straightforward as there is a combinatorial explosion in the number of possible sets as the number of available elements increase. Therefore calculating the CTR for all possible sets will be too slow for the web-based primary applications of this problem. A number of algorithms for choosing element sets will be given including a method which exploits a property of the click models, submodularity, which will be demonstrated below. In Sec. 4 the performance of these will be assessed as well as how the set diversity varies with click model and selection algorithm.

The reward functions for our models possess a property, *submodularity*, that has been well studied (for an overview see Krause and Golovin (2014)) and which gives good results for a simple heuristic algorithm. Submodularity in our context captures the intuitive idea of diminishing returns as the number of elements chosen increases — adding an element to a large set gives a smaller increase in set CTR than adding it to a smaller subset.

Definition 4. A set function f is *submodular* if for every $A \subseteq B \subseteq \mathcal{A}$, and $a \in \mathcal{A} \setminus B$ it holds that

$$f(A \cup \{a\}) - f(A) \geq f(B \cup \{a\}) - f(B).$$

A submodular function for which the $f(A \cup \{a\}) - f(A)$ are all nonnegative is said to be *monotone*.

Proposition 1. *CTR under GCM is monotone submodular.*

Proof. Let $A \subseteq B \subseteq \mathcal{A}$ and $a \in \mathcal{A} \setminus B$ and $\mathbf{q}, \mathbf{w}_\mathcal{A}$ be given. All expectations in the proof are over $x \sim \mathbf{q}$. Let $a^* \in \text{argmax}_{b \in A} w_{b,x}$ and $b^* \in \text{argmax}_{b \in B} w_{b,x}$. Since $A \subseteq B$ it follows that $b^* \geq a^*$.

We will need to show that $\Delta_{a,A}^d \geq \Delta_{a,B}^d$. This will be done by considering three cases:

Case 1. $w_{b^*,x} \geq w_{a^*,x} \geq w_{a,x}$,
Case 2. $w_{b^*,x} \geq w_{a,x} > w_{a^*,x}$,
Case 3. $w_{a,x} > w_{b^*,x} \geq w_{a^*,x}$.

To make the proof easier to read we will use the notation $C = \prod_{b \in A \setminus a^*} [1 - (w_{b,x})^d]$ and $D = \prod_{b \in B \setminus b^*} [1 - (w_{b,x})^d]$. Note that $C \geq D$ since $(A \setminus a^*) \subseteq (B \setminus b^*)$ and $w_{b,x} \in [0,1]$ for all $b \in B$.

Case 1.
$$\Delta^d_{a,A} = \mathbb{E}[1-(1-w_{a^*,x})(1-(w_{a,x})^d)C] - \mathbb{E}[1-(1-w_{a^*,x})C]$$
$$= \mathbb{E}[(1-w_{a^*,x})C - (1-w_{a^*,x})(1-(w_{a,x})^d)C]$$
$$= \mathbb{E}[(w_{a,x})^d(1-w_{a^*,x})C],$$

while similarly,
$$\Delta^d_{a,B} = \mathbb{E}[1-(1-w_{b^*,x})(1-(w_{a,x})^d)D] - \mathbb{E}[1-(1-w_{b^*,x})D]$$
$$= \mathbb{E}[(w_{a,x})^d(1-w_{b^*,x})D]$$
$$\leq \mathbb{E}[(w_{a,x})^d(1-w_{b^*,x})C]$$
$$\leq \mathbb{E}[(w_{a,x})^d(1-w_{a^*,x})C]$$
$$= \Delta^d_{a,A}.$$

Case 2.
$$\Delta^d_{a,A} = \mathbb{E}[1-(1-w_{a,x})(1-(w_{a^*,x})^d)C] - \mathbb{E}[1-(1-w_{a^*,x})C]$$
$$= \mathbb{E}[(1-w_{a^*,x})C - (1-w_{a,x})(1-(w_{a^*,x})^d)C]$$
$$= \mathbb{E}\{[(1-w_{a^*,x}) - (1-w_{a,x})(1-(w_{a^*,x})^d)]C\}$$
$$\geq \mathbb{E}\{[(1-w_{a^*,x}) - (1-w_{a,x})(1-(w_{a^*,x})^d)]D\}.$$

Here $\Delta^d_{a,B}$ is the same as in Case 1 and rewriting this gives,
$$\Delta^d_{a,B} = \mathbb{E}\left[(w_{a,x})^d(1-w_{b^*,x})D\right]$$
$$= \mathbb{E}\left\{\left[(1-(w_{b^*,x})^d) - (1-w_{b^*,x})(1-(w_{a,x})^d)\right]D\right\}.$$

So we need to show that
$$\mathbb{E}[(1-w_{a^*,x}) - (1-w_{a,x})(1-(w_{a^*,x})^d)]$$
$$\geq \mathbb{E}[(1-(w_{b^*,x})^d) - (1-w_{b^*,x})(1-(w_{a,x})^d)]$$
$$\iff \mathbb{E}[w_{a,x} + (w_{a^*,x})^d - w_{a^*,x} - (w_{a,x})^d$$
$$+ (w_{a,x})^d w_{b^*,x} - (w_{a^*,x})^d w_{a,x}] \geq 0,$$

which holds since $(w_{a,x})^d w_{b^*,x} \geq (w_{a^*,x})^d w_{a,x}$ and $w_{a,x} - w_{a^*,x} \geq (w_{a,x})^d - (w_{a^*,x})^d$. The first part is by the $w_{b^*,x} \geq w_{a,x} > w_{a^*,x}$ condition and the second since $a - b \geq a^d - b^d$ for any $1 \geq a \geq b \geq 0$ and $d \geq 1$.

Case 3. Here $\Delta_{a,A}^d$ is the same as in Case 2 so,
$$\Delta_{a,A}^d \geq \mathbb{E}\{[(1-w_{a^*,x})-(1-w_{a,x})(1-(w_{a^*,x})^d)]D\};$$
$$\begin{aligned}\Delta_{a,B}^d &= \mathbb{E}[1-(1-w_{a,x})(1-(w_{b^*,x})^d)D] - \mathbb{E}[1-(1-w_{b^*,x})D] \\ &= \mathbb{E}[(1-w_{b^*,x})D - (1-w_{a,x})(1-(w_{b^*,x})^d)D] \\ &= \mathbb{E}\{[(1-w_{b^*,x})-(1-w_{a,x})(1-(w_{b^*,x})^d)]D\}.\end{aligned}$$
Therefore $\Delta_{a,A}^d \geq \Delta_{a,B}^d$ since $w_{b^*,x} \geq w_{a^*,x}$ and the required condition is met for this and therefore all cases which completes the proof. □

We now describe a number of heuristic algorithms for choosing element sets which will be evaluated in Sec. 4. Maximising a submodular function is NP-hard but for monotone submodular functions a computationally feasible greedy heuristic algorithm is known to have good properties (Nemhauser and Wolsey, 1978). This algorithm starts with the empty set then iteratively adds the element that most increases the objective function. It will be referred to here as the **sequential algorithm (SEQ)**.

SEQ is known (Nemhauser and Wolsey, 1978) to produce a solution within $1 - 1/e \approx 0.63$ of optimal. In practical terms 0.63 of optimal represents a considerable loss so in Sec. 4 we test the method using simulation to better estimate what the true loss is, as well as measuring the robustness of the method to model misspecification, and quantifying the diversity of the sets chosen for different click models.

For comparison we present here a number of other algorithms which are natural alternatives. For the first of these, as well as SEQ, the algorithm requires that a click model be assumed since CTR calculations are made for element sets with more than one member. The remaining methods are independent of click model and depend only on $\mathbf{w}_A$ and $\mathbf{q}$.

Optimal (OPT). For small studies, we can optimise (2). Note that we retain the expectation over latent state $x \sim \mathbf{q}$.

Naive (NAI). Elements are ranked in order of independent element CTR $\mathbb{E}_{x \sim q} w_{a,x} = \mathbf{q} \cdot \mathbf{w}_a$ and the top m elements are selected in order.

Most Frequent User Preference (MFUP). We fix $\tilde{x} = \mathrm{argmax}_x q_x$ and select the m elements with highest $w_{a,\tilde{x}}$.

Ordered User Preference (OUP). For $i \in 1, \ldots, m$, $\tilde{x}_i$ are selected in order of decreasing probability of occurrence q_x.[a] Then for each i select $a_i = \mathrm{argmax}_{a \notin \{a_j : j < i\}} w_{a,\tilde{x}_i}$.

---

[a] To ensure that all $q_{\tilde{x}_i} > 0$, if $|\{x : q_x > 0\}| < m$ then fill the remaining slots by repeating the sequence $\{x : q_x > 0\}$ until $|\tilde{\mathbf{x}}| = m$.

The last two algorithms give simple deterministic ways of handling the uncertainty about x. The NAI algorithm does use the full distribution given by $\mathbf{q}$ but ignores interactions between elements in the set and therefore the problem of redundancy.

4. Simulation Study

In this section we will give the results of experiments investigating the CTR and diversity of sets chosen by each of the algorithms from Sec. 3 with clicks simulated with different click models from Sec. 2. Both SEQ and OPT depend on the click model assumed and we will test versions of both algorithms using each of PCM and TCM. These algorithms will be named OPT-PCM, OPT-TCM, SEQ-PCM and SEQ-TCM. Two sets of simulations will be run, to investigate CTR (Sec. 4.1) and set diversity (Sec. 4.2).

Results are based on 1000 instances. Each instance represents a unique user for whom we must select a set of m elements from the k available, given a $\mathbf{q}$ and $\mathbf{w}_A$. On each instance, the state distribution $\mathbf{q}$ is sampled from a Dirichlet distribution with all n parameters equal to $1/n$. Each weight $w_{a,x}$ for $a = 1, \ldots, k$, $x = 1 \ldots, n$ is drawn independently from a mixture distribution; with probability ξ the weight is *relevant* and is drawn from a Beta(α, β) distribution, otherwise the weight is 0.001. The values of the parameters ξ, α, β will be given with the results. Throughout our simulations there are $n = 20$ possible states for x, a choice of $k = 40$ elements and a set size of $m = 3$. Varying these parameters did not change the overall pattern of results. On each instance, each algorithm chooses a set of elements.

4.1. Experimental results: CTR

Table 4.1 gives the percentage *lost CTR* which is the difference between the mean CTR of the element sets chosen by the optimal and the heuristic methods as a percentage of the mean optimal CTR. The simulations were run using both PCM and TCM to determine the simulated clicks. Since OPT and SEQ assume a click model we are able to test the effect of click model misspecification (for example SEQ-PCM when TCM is used to simulate clicks). The other algorithms do not change with click model. The absolute CTRs of OPT using the correct click model with $\beta = 2$ and $\beta = 9$ respectively are 0.877 and 0.451 for PCM, and 0.773 and 0.316 for TCM.

Table 4.1. Lost CTR as a percentage of optimal CTR with $n = 20$, $k = 40$, $m = 3$, $\xi = 0.1$, $\alpha = 1$ and $\beta \in \{2, 9\}$.

| | \multicolumn{4}{c}{True Click Model and Beta Value} |
Algorithm Click Model	PCM $\beta = 2$	PCM $\beta = 9$	TCM $\beta = 2$	TCM $\beta = 9$
OPT-PCM	0.0%	0.0%	3.4%	6.6%
OPT-TCM	9.2%	19.9%	0.0%	0.0%
SEQ-PCM	0.0%	0.0%	3.4%	6.6%
SEQ-TCM	8.9%	19.8%	0.1%	0.1%
NAI	4.2%	0.6%	10.6%	9.6%
MFUP	17.0%	13.6%	25.6%	27.2%
OUP	9.8%	20.7%	1.1%	1.4%

It can be seen that SEQ algorithms perform similarly to the corresponding OPT algorithms with performance being much better than the theoretical guarantees when the assumed click model is correct. However, both methods do badly when the click model is incorrectly specified. The other methods perform poorly on at least one of the click models with OUP better on TCM and NAI better on PCM. These preferences can be explained by the set diversity for each as will be given in the next section.

The performance of NAI illustrates a possible issue with PCM as a choice for click model. Despite NAI ignoring interaction effects, for PCM with $\beta = 9$ it performs well. When $\mathbf{w}_a$ is small, $r_{\text{PCM}}(x, A, \mathbf{w}_A) = 1 - \prod_{a \in A}(1 - w_{a,x}) \approx \sum_{a \in A} w_{a,x}$, and NAI is optimal for the problem of maximising the expected value of this last quantity. So a belief that interactions between elements matter is inconsistent with a belief that PCM represents the users' click behaviour, if weights are small (which will be the case in many web applications where CTRs are low).

4.2. *Experimental results: Diversity*

To compare set diversity of different methods we first need a measure of diversity for our model. The "pairwise dissimilarity between recommended items" is commonly used (Vargas and Castells, 2011). Based on this we define the *overlap* of a set of two elements $A = \{a_1, a_2\}$ as

$$\text{overlap}(A) = \frac{\sum_{x=1}^{n} \min(w_{1,x}, w_{2,x})}{\min[\sum_{x=1}^{n}(w_{1,x}), \sum_{x=1}^{n}(w_{1,x})]}.$$

For sets of elements larger than 2 the overlap is given by

$$\frac{2}{|A|(|A|-1)} \sum_{a_i, a_j \in A, i<j} \text{overlap}(\{a_i, a_j\}).$$

The *diversity* of the set A is given by $1 - \text{overlap}(A)$. Note that these measures are independent of the click model used. For two elements, if overlap $= 1$ then the weights for one element are all larger than the corresponding weights of the other element, and the lesser of the two elements contributes nothing under TCM. However, it does contribute under other GCM. If overlap $= 0$ then the weight vectors of all elements are pairwise orthogonal and $\text{CTR}_A^d = \sum_{a \in A} \text{CTR}_a^d$ for all d (and for TCM).

For the simulation to investigate diversity we measure the mean overlap values of element sets chosen by algorithms. These are given in Fig. 4.1 over a range of GCM parameter values d assumed by the OPT and SEQ algorithms. The other methods ignore the click model and so have unchanging overlap over d. The overlap of the optimal sets decreases with d which shows how the diversity requirements change with the click model. SEQ shows a very similar pattern and chooses similar sets to OPT but with generally slightly greater overlap.

NAI and MFUP choose sets that are insufficiently diverse for any model which explains their poor performance in the CTR simulation results particularly where clicks are simulated using TCM. OUP has low overlap which is at an appropriate level for TCM and higher d but which is too low for PCM. This fits with the poor CTR on PCM. It is notable that no method is

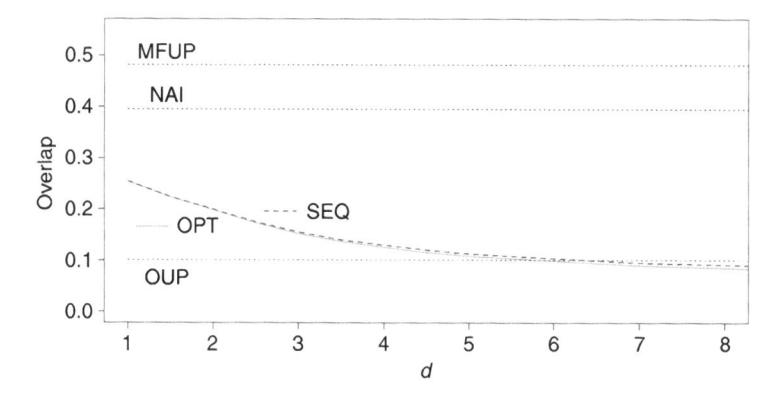

Fig. 4.1. Overlap for set choosing algorithms over $d \in [1, 8]$ with $m = 3$, $n = 20$, $\xi = 0.1$ and $k = 40$ elements each with $\alpha = 1$ and $\beta = 2$.

as diverse as OPT and SEQ with high d indicating that maximising rewards when TCM is assumed is an effective method to produce diverse sets.

5. Discussion

We considered the problem of selecting a set of website elements to display to a user. Intuitively, elements in this set should not be too similar to one another, as would be the case if we selected the elements on individual merit without considering interaction effects. However we argue that diversity in the set of elements does not need to be a separate objective from maximising click probability.

Instead, by using an appropriate click model, good quality sets will be diverse because this is needed in response to uncertainty about user preferences. As well as simplifying the objective this also provides a clearer and less arbitrary statement about why diversity is desirable compared to when it is set as a separate objective. Secondly, the diversity of chosen sets can be seen to adapt to the level of uncertainty about user preferences. If we have high certainty about user preferences then there is less need for diversity than if we have little knowledge of the user or if the user's preferences are very variable. This gives a motivation for better quantifying uncertainty about users and their preferences in recommender system applications. In addition we see two main questions that motivate future work.

First, we found that selecting the correct click model is important. However "correct" will depend on the application and can only be ascertained from examining data. Our experiments indicate that algorithms which assume PCM are more robust to a misspecified click model than those that assume TCM. This is because assuming PCM will generally result in choosing elements with larger overall weights. However assuming PCM does not promote high diversity, and so contrasts with intuition as to what makes for good recommendation. One example which fits our setup, but which lacks an explicit click model, is tweet recommendation (Pennacchiotti et al., 2012). Here, the stated objective to "span interests" is suggestive of TCM where duplicate information should be avoided. This, though, depends on how topics are defined: broad topic definitions may favour PCM as a more appropriate model, as elements with the same topic may not actually be redundant, while narrower topics would favour using TCM, as elements within the same topic will be very similar.

Second, we have assumed that the element weights $\mathbf{w}$ and user topic preference vectors $\mathbf{q}$ are known. In practice we would at best have some best estimate of both of these with which to use the algorithms given here. In a search setting, **q** will already exist, since it is the topic preference vector used to provide search results. In extensions of this work we derive bandit schemes to estimate **w**. We note that the explore-exploit challenge becomes especially interesting when both can be carried out simultaneously (since more than one element can be displayed at a time) and the information returned is more subtle (which element, if any, was clicked, alongside the presence of state uncertainty). Simultaneously learning **q** and **w** on the basis of user feedback is currently an open challenge.

Acknowledgements

This work was funded by a Google Faculty Research Award. James Edwards was supported by the EPSRC funded EP/H023151/1 STOR-i centre for doctoral training.

References

Agrawal, R., Gollapudi, S., Halverson, A. and Ieong, S. (2009). Diversifying search results, in *ACM Conf. Web Search and Data Mining (WSDM)*, pp. 5–14.

Carbonell, J. and Goldstein, J. (1998). The use of MMR, diversity-based reranking for reordering documents and producing summaries, in *Proc. ACM SIGIR*, pp. 335–336.

Craswell, N., Zoeter, O., Taylor, M. and Ramsey, B. (2008). An experimental comparison of click position-bias models, in *Proc. Int. Conf. Web Search and Web Data Mining*, pp. 87–94.

El-Arini, K., Veda, G., Shahaf, D. and Guestrin, C. (2009). Turning down the noise in the blogosphere, in *ACM Conf. Knowledge Discovery and Data Mining*, pp. 289–298.

Hurley, N. and Zhang, M. (2011). Novelty and diversity in top-N recommendation–analysis and evaluation, *ACM Trans. Internet Technol.* **10**, 4, pp. 1–29.

Krause, A. and Golovin, D. (2014). Submodular function maximization, in *Tractability: Practical Approaches to Hard Problems*, Vol. 3, Cambridge University Press.

Nemhauser, G. L. and Wolsey, L. A. (1978). Best algorithms for approximating the maximum of a submodular set function, *Math. Oper. Res.* **3**, 3, pp. 177–188.

Pennacchiotti, M., Silvestri, F., Vahabi, H. and Venturini, R. (2012). Making your interests follow you on twitter, in *Proc. 21st ACM Int. Conf. Information and Knowledge Management, CIKM'12*, pp. 165–174.

Radlinski, F., Bennett, P. N., Carterette, B. and Joachims, T. (2009). Redundancy, diversity and interdependent document relevance, *SIGIR Forum* **43**, 2, pp. 46–52.

Ricci, F., Rokach, L., Shapira, B. and Kantor, B. P. (eds.) (2011). *Recommender Systems Handbook*, Springer US, Boston, MA.

Van Ryzin, G. A. (2012). *Models of Demand*, Chapter 18, Oxford University Press, London.

Vargas, S. and Castells, P. (2011). Rank and relevance in novelty and diversity metrics for recommender systems, in *Proc. Fifth ACM Conf. Recommender Systems*, ACM, New York, NY, pp. 109–116.

Zhou, T., Kuscsik, Z., Liu, J.-G., Medo, M., Wakeling, J. R. and Zhang, Y.-C. (2010). Solving the apparent diversity-accuracy dilemma of recommender systems, *Proc. Natl. Acad. Sci. USA* **107**, 10, pp. 4511–4515.

Chapter 5

L-kernel Density Estimation for Bayesian Model Selection

Mark Briers
The Alan Turing Institute,
British Library, 96 Euston Road, London, UK
mbriers@turing.ac.uk

The chapter introduces a novel density estimation procedure that utilises and exploits the output structure of a Markov chain based simulation procedure, in order to improve density estimation performance, when compared to the traditional kernel density estimation procedure. The density estimator is demonstrated in the context of Bayesian model selection applied to a problem of clustering in Single Nucleotide Polymorphism (SNP) data.

1. Introduction

The use of Monte Carlo methods, or specifically Markov Chain Monte Carlo (MCMC) techniques, has exploded within the past twenty years. As a result, the simplistic models which were previously adopted to facilitate tractable inference can now be replaced with far more realistic models, resulting in enhances in applications that were hitherto considered impossible.

The development of density estimation techniques from the output of a Markov chain simulation has not had the same effort devoted to it. This is, in part, due to the presence of the intuitively appealing and simplistic kernel density estimator. Whilst this density estimation technique is useful in a plethora of application domains, intuitively, it can be considered to be a density estimator based on a series of independent approximations; i.e. the kernel density estimation technique does not exploit the Markovian nature of the simulation algorithm used. This can lead to poor approximations of the true density. Moreover, selection of the kernel bandwidth can also cause problems, especially for high-dimensional spaces. Should one be able to develop more sophisticated density estimation techniques that exploit known algorithmic properties, then one is able to directly employ them on a wide array of statistical problems: from the efficient visualisation of densities, to the calculation of marginal likelihood estimates for model selection.

In this chapter we provide a novel density estimator that attempts to exploit the Markovian nature of the problem; this density estimation can be considered to be a unique interpretation/extension of the method devised by Chen (1994) but which is more universally applicable.

The chapter is structured as follows: we start by providing a brief review of the MCMC literature before presenting the density estimator in Sec. 3, where we are also able to prove almost sure convergence using standard results. We then show in Sec. 4 how it is possible to determine marginal likelihood estimates from the output of *any* MCMC technique — Chib and Jeliazkov have several publications (Chib, 1995; Chib and Jeliazkov, 2001, 2005) relating to specific MCMC techniques for the calculation of marginal likelihood estimates. We apply this marginal likelihood estimation procedure to model selection for a well-studied Gaussian mixture model. Finally, conclusions are drawn in Sec. 5.

2. Markov Chain Monte Carlo

Traditional Markov chain analysis involves determining the invariant distribution of a Markov chain given a specified transition kernel and initial distribution. Markov chain Monte Carlo (MCMC) methods, on the other hand, are used to target a specific stationary distribution (taken to be the distribution of interest π) through the simulation of a Markov chain where the transition kernel is suitably defined such that it admits the desired distribution as its stationary distribution (Andrieu *et al.*, 2003; Robert and Casella, 1999; Liu, 2001). Thus, arguably, the MCMC literature is primarily concerned with the determination of transition kernels that allow one to converge (in some sense) to the stationary distribution as quickly as possible. We now review some Markov chain theory before examining the most general form of the MCMC algorithm, the Metropolis–Hastings algorithm. The reader is referred to Meyn and Tweedie (1993) for an excellent, in-depth analysis, of Markov chain theory.

2.1. Markov chains

Within this section we are concerned with a discrete time E-valued stochastic process, $X = \{X_n; n \in \mathbb{N}\}$, i.e. each random variable X_n takes values in E and are (individually) assumed to be measurable functions.

2.1.1. Transition kernel

Consider a (Markov) transition kernel $K(x, A) = P(X_n \in A | X_{n-1} = x)$ defined on the space $(E, \mathcal{E})$ as follows:

(1) For any fixed $A \in \mathcal{E}$, the function $K(\cdot, A)$ is measurable.
(2) For any fixed $x \in E$, the function $K(x, \cdot)$ is a probability measure.

A stochastic process X defined on $(E, \mathcal{E})$ is called a time-homogeneous Markov chain with initial distribution μ if the (finite-dimensional) distributions of X satisfy:

$$P_\mu(X_0 \in A_0, \ldots, X_n \in A_n) = \int_{x_0 \in A_0} \cdots \int_{x_n \in A_n} \mu(dx_0) K(x_0, dx_0) \cdots K(x_{n-1}, dx_n) \quad (1)$$

for every n. The existence of such a stochastic process is proved in Meyn and Tweedie (1993). We write the conditional distribution of X_n given X_0 as

$$P(X_n \in A | X_0 = x_0) = K^n(x_0, A) = \int_E K^{n-1}(y, A) K(x_0, dy), \quad (2)$$

where K^n denotes the nth iterate of the kernel K. The initial kernel iterate, K^0, is defined as

$$K^0(x_0, A) = \delta_{x_0}(A). \quad (3)$$

We want to construct a Markov chain which has π as its invariant distribution, i.e.

$$\pi(dy) = \int_{x \in E} \pi(dx) K(x, dy) \quad (4)$$

for $x, y \in E$. It is possible to construct a Markov chain whose stationary distribution is π by considering a reversible Markov chain (Roberts and Rosenthal, 2004).

Definition 1. A Markov chain is reversible with respect to a probability distribution π if
$$\pi(dx)K(x,dy) = \pi(dy)K(y,dx), \quad x,y \in E. \tag{5}$$

This leads us to the following proposition.

Proposition 1. *If a Markov chain is reversible with respect to π, then $\pi(\cdot)$ is stationary for the chain.*

Proof.
$$\int_{x \in E} \pi(dx)K(x,dy) = \int_{x \in E} \pi(dy)K(y,dx)$$
$$= \pi(dy) \int_{x \in E} K(y,dx) = \pi(dy). \tag{6}$$

□

A stronger condition than reversibility is that of detailed balance (e.g. Robert and Casella (1999)):

Definition 2. A Markov chain with transition kernel K (with density K) satisfies the detailed balance condition if there exists a function f satisfying
$$K(y,x)f(y) = K(x,y)f(x) \tag{7}$$
for every (x,y).

This detailed balance condition is not a necessary but sufficient condition to ensure that f is an invariant measure associated with the Markov chain. If f is a density function (e.g. $f = \pi$), then detailed balance implies that the chain is also reversible.

We now know how to define a Markov chain that has an invariant distribution that is the desired distribution π; however, there are no guarantees that such a Markov chain will ever converge to its stationary distribution. We have to impose some further conditions on the Markov chain to ensure such convergence.

2.1.2. *Convergence of Markov chains*

As discussed by Tierney (1994), the invariant distribution π is a stationary distribution of the Markov chain if for π-almost all x
$$\lim_{n \to \infty} K^n(x,A) = \pi(A) \tag{8}$$
for all measurable sets A. Such a simple statement poses several difficult questions:

(1) Can we generalise the statement in Eq. (8) for all $x \in E$? That is, can we ensure that π is a stationary distribution of the Markov chain irrespective of the initial condition?
(2) Is π the only stationary distribution of the Markov chain?
(3) Can we show that an appropriate distance metric between the measures K^n and π decreases to zero as $n \to \infty$?
(4) For such a distance metric, can we provide any rates of convergence?

To answer these questions we need to introduce some concepts relating to a chain's behaviour and its ability to traverse the space for a given initial condition.

Informally, we would like to define a chain that is able to reach all parts of the space in a finite number of steps irrespective of the starting point. Such a concept is known as *irreducibility*. We therefore want an irreducible Markov chain. Unfortunately, for a general state space, this naïve condition is impossible since the probability of returning to a single state $\{x\}$ (for a certain class of transition kernel) is zero. Instead, we need to define a weaker condition known as ψ-irreducibility (Roberts and Rosenthal, 2004).[a]

Definition 3. A chain is ψ-irreducible if there exists a nonzero σ-finite measure ψ on $(E, \mathcal{E})$ such that for all $A \in \mathcal{E}$ with $\psi(A) > 0$, and for all $x \in E$, there exists a positive integer $n = n(x, A)$ such that $K^n(x, A) > 0$.

For our purposes it is natural to take $\psi = \pi$. This definition merely states that we are able to reach any set $A \in \mathcal{E}$ which has positive (target) probability $\pi(A) > 0$ from any initial condition (not just π-almost all x). Hence, a π-irreducible Markov chain is guaranteed (with positive probability) to explore all parts of the space of interest from a practitioners perspective.

As discussed in Robert and Casella (1999), the behaviour (or stability) of a Markov chain is an important consideration to guarantee a good approximation of the simulated model. We know already that we are able to visit any (interesting) part of the space from the irreducibility property for any $x \in E$. The question is then: how often will a set $A \in \mathcal{E}$ (for $\pi(A) > 0$) be visited? We want to ensure that such a set will be visited infinitely often (i.o.). This leads to a definition of recurrence (Tierney, 1994).

---

[a] Several equivalent definitions of ψ-irreducibility can be found in Meyn and Tweedie (1993).

Definition 4. A π-irreducible Markov chain with invariant distribution π is recurrent, if for each A with $\pi(A) > 0$:

$$P(X_n \in A \text{ i.o.}|X_0 = x) > 0 \quad \text{for all } x,$$
$$P(X_n \in A \text{ i.o.}|X_0 = x) = 1 \quad \text{for } \pi\text{-almost all } x.$$

The chain is Harris recurrent if $P(X_n \in A \text{ i.o.}|X_0 = x) = 1$ for all x.

Clearly Harris recurrence is the most stringent condition and it consequently allows one to determine stronger convergence results. We will return to Harris recurrence shortly. Within this thesis we are concerned with π as a probability distribution, and so the total mass of π is finite, meaning that the chain is classed as being *positive* recurrent.

Tierney (1994) presents a contradiction argument to show that if K is π-irreducible and has π as an invariant distribution, then K *must* be recurrent. Moreover, if K is π-irreducible and positive recurrent, having π as an invariant (probability) distribution then π is its unique invariant distribution. Intuitively, the chain is able to reach any part of the space which has positive probability (π-irreducibility) from any $x \in E$ which implies that the chain is able to traverse the space freely meaning it will visit all sets A infinitely often with a nonzero probability (positive recurrence). Since all sets $A \in \mathcal{E} : \pi(A) > 0$ are visited infinitely often then the limiting distribution of the chain can only be described by its invariant distribution π, otherwise the chain would be limited in its movement (in some sense).

Although the chain is able to reach any part of the space from any other and visit each set infinitely often (under the conditions imposed), the Markov chain may still exhibit local unusual behaviour when making a transition from one set to another. We would like the Markov chain to be completely free to move around the space and have no repeated properties: we would like the chain to be aperiodic (Roberts and Rosenthal, 2004).

Definition 5. A Markov chain with stationary distribution π is aperiodic if there does not exist $d \geq 2$ and disjoint subsets $A_1, \ldots, A_d \subseteq \mathcal{E}$ with $K(x, A_{i+1}) = 1$ for all $x \in E_i$ ($1 \leq i \leq d - 1$) and $K(x, A_1) = 1$ for all $x \in E_d$, such that $\pi(A_1) > 0$ (and hence $\pi(A_i) > 0$ for all i).

In other words, a chain is periodic if there are portions of the state space, it can only visit at certain regularly spaced times; otherwise the chain is aperiodic.

Before stating the first convergence result, we define the total variation distance, a distance metric used to measure the distance between two probability measures.

Definition 6. The *total variation distance* between two probability measures ν_1 and ν_2 is

$$||\nu_1(\cdot) - \nu_2(\cdot)|| = \sup_A |\nu_1(A) - \nu_2(A)|. \qquad (9)$$

Based on this definition we can now state a convergence result for Markov chains as follows (taken from Roberts and Rosenthal (2004); see this reference for a proof).

Theorem 1. *If a Markov chain on a state space with countably generated σ-algebra is ψ-irreducible and aperiodic, and has stationary distribution π [and so is positive recurrent]; then for π-almost everywhere $x \in E$*

$$\lim_{n \to \infty} ||K^n(x, \cdot) - \pi|| = 0. \qquad (10)$$

In particular, $\lim_{n \to \infty} K^n(x, A) = \pi(A)$ *for all measurable* $A \subseteq \mathcal{E}$.

This theorem proves the statement made in the beginning of this section (8) under very minimal and verifiable assumptions. Essentially, we require that the chain is able to reach all nonnegligible measurable parts of the space from any other parts of the space infinitely often, and that the chain does not exhibit any cyclical behaviour making approximations to the simulated model stable.

The only minor concern with the above theorem is that the chain is not guaranteed to converge (in total variation distance) from all starting points $x \in E$. To guarantee convergence in this case, we need to ensure that the chain is positive Harris recurrent.

Theorem 2. *If a Markov chain on a state space with countably generated σ-algebra is ψ-irreducible, aperiodic and positive Harris recurrent, and has stationary distribution π, then for all $x \in E$:*

$$\lim_{n \to \infty} ||K^n(x, \cdot) - \pi|| = 0. \qquad (11)$$

The conditions on both of these theorems are necessary and sufficient. It is straightforward to show that a Metropolis–Hastings kernel K_{MH} (defined in Sec. 2.2) is Harris recurrent.

2.1.3. *Ergodicity*

Whilst the above theorems prove that the Markov chain will converge in total variation distance to the stationary distribution, they do not offer any clues as to how fast convergence occurs. To study such rates of convergence, we need to consider an ergodic Markov chain. An ergodic Markov chain is defined to be one that is positive Harris recurrent and aperiodic. Such a definition still does not quantify the rate of convergence. We have to consider stronger forms of ergodicity Roberts and Rosenthal (2004).

Definition 7. A Markov chain with stationary distribution $\pi(\cdot)$ is geometrically ergodic if

$$\|K^n(x,\cdot) - \pi(\cdot)\| \leq M(x) r^n, \quad n = 1, 2, 3, \ldots \quad (12)$$

for some $r < 1$ where $M(x) < \infty$ for π-almost everywhere $x \in E$.

This definition tells us that the rate of convergence is at least geometric but *is dependent* upon the initial state x. A stronger condition than geometric ergodicity is provided through the following definition (Roberts and Rosenthal, 2004).

Definition 8. A Markov chain having stationary distribution π is uniformly ergodic if

$$\|K^n(x,\cdot) - \pi(\cdot)\| \leq M r^n, \quad n = 1, 2, 3, \ldots \quad (13)$$

for some $r < 1$ and $M < \infty$.

One equivalence of uniform ergodicity is the following proposition.

Proposition 2. *A Markov chain with stationary distribution $\pi(\cdot)$ is uniformly ergodic if and only if* $\sup_{x \in \mathcal{E}} \|K^n(x,\cdot) - \pi(\cdot)\| < 1/2$ *for some* $n \in \mathbb{N}$.

The difference between uniform and geometric ergodicity is that now the constant M may not depend on the initial state x so that the convergence rate is uniform over the whole space.

Whilst such definitions do not appear to offer much to the statistical practitioner, we will return to them when trying to establish a central limit theorem for estimators based on the output of a Monte Carlo simulation of a Markov chain.

We now analyse the fundamental algorithmic component underlying most Markov Chain Monte Carlo algorithms; the Metropolis–Hastings kernel.

2.2. Metropolis–Hastings kernel

The Metropolis–Hastings kernel underpins all of the commonly known and used MCMC algorithms, for example, the Gibbs sampling algorithm and the Reversible-Jump algorithm. This review section intends to review the basic building blocks of the algorithm.

The Metropolis–Hastings kernel is written as

$$K_{\mathrm{MH}}(x, dx') = Q(x, dx')\alpha(x, x') + \delta_x(dx') \int_E (1 - \alpha(x, u))Q(x, du) \quad (14)$$

and can be interpreted as follows: a sample is drawn from the proposal distribution Q and is accepted with probability α (first term on the right-hand side); the new sample is rejected with probability $(1 - \alpha)$ (second term on the right-hand side). We need to ensure that the detailed balance condition holds to ensure that K is reversible. Thus, it is necessary and sufficient to show that:

$$\pi(dx)Q(x, dx')\alpha(x, x') = \pi(dx')Q(x', dx)\alpha(x', x) \quad (15)$$

holds. We now recall a proposition from Tierney (1998) which provides an important result with respect to symmetric measures.

Proposition 3 (Tierney, 1998). *Let $\mu(dx, dx') \triangleq \pi(dx)Q(x, dx')$, which is a σ-finite measure defined on the product space $(E \times E, \mathcal{E} \times \mathcal{E})$. Also let $\mu^T(dx, dx') = \mu(dx', dx) \triangleq \pi(dx')Q(x', dx)$. Then there exists a symmetric set $R \in \mathcal{E} \times \mathcal{E}$ such that μ and μ^T are mutually absolutely continuous on R (i.e. the measures are equivalent) and mutually singular on the complement of R, R^c. The set R is unique up to sets that are null for both μ and μ^T. Let μ_R and μ_R^T be the restrictions of μ and μ^T to R (i.e. such that the measures are, by construction, mutually absolutely continuous). Then there exists a version of the density*

$$r(x, x') = \frac{\mu_R(dx, dx')}{\mu_R^T(dx, dx')} \quad (16)$$

such that $0 < r(x, x') < \infty$ and $r(x, x') = 1/r(x', x)$ for all $x, x' \in E$.

Based on this proposition, analysis of Eq. (14) suggests that we have to impose certain conditions on α such that detailed balance can be attained. Such conditions are presented in Tierney (1998) through the following theorem.

Theorem 3 (Tierney, 1998). *A Metropolis–Hastings kernel satisfies the detailed balance condition if and only if the following two conditions hold:*

(1) *The function α is μ-almost everywhere zero on R^c.*
(2) *The function α satisfies $\alpha(x, x')r(x, x') = \alpha(x', x)$ μ-almost everywhere on R.*

- Draw a candidate from Q.
- Accept the candidate with probability α given in Eq. (17) with the density r given in Eq. (19).

Fig. 5.1. Metropolis–Hastings algorithm.

With these two conditions in mind, it is straightforward to show that the standard Metropolis–Hastings acceptance probability can be written as

$$\alpha(x, x') = \begin{cases} \min(1, r(x', x)) & \text{if } (x, x') \in R, \\ 0 & \text{if } (x, x') \notin R, \end{cases} \quad (17)$$

since $r(x, x') = 1/r(x', x)$ on R.

2.2.1. Metropolis–Hastings algorithm

Consider the case where both π and Q are dominated by a common measure, ν, i.e. $\pi(dx) = \pi(x)\nu(dx)$ and $Q(x, dx) = q(x, x')\nu(dx')$. The set R is then taken to be the set of state pairs for which the densities are of the transitions from x to x' and from x' to x are strictly positive. That is

$$R = \{(x, x') : \pi(x)q(x, x') > 0 \text{ and } \pi(x')q(x', x) > 0\}. \quad (18)$$

The density $r(x, x')$ appearing in Eq. (17) can be written as

$$r(x, x') = \frac{\pi(x)q(x, x')}{\pi(x')q(x', x)}, \quad (19)$$

which is α's usual more familiar form. The algorithm is now summarised in Fig. 5.1.

2.2.2. Gibbs sampling algorithm

It is possible to define a transition kernel as a cycle of Metropolis–Hastings moves; informally, the state-space is broken into disjoint subsets such that blocks of variables are moved conditioned on all other blocks of variables. A complete cycle of moves, i.e. one which cycles through all blocks that make up the state-space, is completed. This allows one to explore the space of highly correlated variables more effectively (Andrieu et al., 2003; Chib and Greenberg, 1995).

The Gibbs sampling algorithm is one such blocking scheme. The transition kernel is defined as the product of full-conditional distributions:

$$K(x, dy) = \prod_{i=1}^{d} K_i(x, S_{x,i,dy}), \quad (20)$$

where $S_{x,i,dy} = \{y \in E: y_j = x_j \text{ for } j \neq i, \text{ and } y_i \in dy\}$ with $x = (x_1, \ldots, x_d)$ (Roberts and Rosenthal, 2004). It is straightforward to show that the acceptance probability when one uses the exact full-conditional distributions is equal to one.

2.3. LLN and the CLT for MCMC

It is possible to approximate posterior distributions of interest using an ergodic Markov chain through the following sample average:

$$\hat{\pi}(g) = \frac{1}{n} \sum_{i=1}^{n} g(X_i). \quad (21)$$

Based on this approximation an LLN can then be stated.

Theorem 4. *Consider an ergodic Markov chain X with stationary distribution π. For any real-valued function g where $\pi(|g|) < \infty$, the following holds almost surely: $\hat{\pi}(g) \to \pi(g)$.*

Proof. See Meyn and Tweedie (1993, Theorem 17.0.1) for example. □

A natural progression is then to determine rates of convergence of such estimators. Asymptotic variance expressions are possible through the CLT. Verifying the mixing conditions within these theorems is difficult to do in practice, as we will discuss.

Theorem 5. *Consider a geometrically ergodic Markov chain X with stationary distribution π. For any real-valued function g such that $\pi(|g|^{2+\delta}) < \infty$ for some $\delta > 0$, the distribution of*

$$\sqrt{n}(\hat{\pi}(g) - \pi(g)) \quad (22)$$

converges weakly to a normal distribution with mean 0 and (finite) variance σ_g^2, for any initial distribution.

Proof. See Roberts and Rosenthal (2004). □

If it is possible to show that the chain is uniformly ergodic (a stronger condition than geometric ergodicity) then we can write the following CLT.

Theorem 6. *Consider a uniformly ergodic Markov chain X with stationary distribution π. For any real-valued function g such that $\pi(|g|^2) < \infty$, the distribution of*

$$\sqrt{n}(\hat{\pi}(g) - \pi(g)) \tag{23}$$

converges weakly to a normal distribution with mean 0 and (finite) variance σ_{g*}^2, for any initial distribution.

Proof. See Jasra and Yang (2006). □

Such ergodicity conditions within the above two theorems are difficult to show in practice. For instance, to show that a chain is geometrically ergodic requires one to establish a drift condition and associated minorisation condition for the underlying Markov chain (Roberts and Rosenthal, 2004). An excellent overview of such concepts, directed towards the statistical practitioner, can be found in Jones and Hobert (2001).

Finally, note that the proofs to the above CLTs can be derived using regeneration theory from operational research; such an exposition relies upon definitions of small sets and regeneration theory from operational research. Proofs derived in such a fashion become intuitively appealing (almost) on first reading (Jasra and Yang, 2006; Roberts and Rosenthal, 2004; Jones, 2004).

2.4. Sequential Monte Carlo samplers

Sequential Monte Carlo is typically used when one is interested in distributions defined on an increasing dimensional space $E_t = E^t$. This is not always the case. For example, one may be interested in defining a sequence of distributions $\{\pi_t\}_{t \geq 1}$ defined on a common measurable space ($E_t = E$ for all t), such that one can transition from an easy-to-sample distribution to a highly complex target distribution through a sequence of intermediate distributions (Neal, 2001). Alternatively, in Bayesian inference applications, one may be interested in the estimation of a static parameter based on a large dataset and so to avoid computing expensive likelihoods it may be desirable to impute the data points sequentially until one arrives at the desired target distribution (Chopin, 2004; Ridgeway and Madigan, 2003).

Both cases are possible through the sequential Monte Carlo samplers (SMCS) framework (Moral et al., 2004, 2006; Peters, 2005), which forms a complete generalisation of the work in Neal (2001); Chopin (2004); Ridgeway and Madigan (2003), and can also be considered to be a population Monte Carlo approach (Jasra et al., 2006), whereby one exploits the use of interacting chains to better explore the space of interest. Note also that the SMCS approach is complementary to MCMC since one can employ MCMC kernels within the SMCS framework (Moral et al., 2006). The basic idea behind SMCS is to define an extended target distribution $\tilde{\pi}$ (on the joint space $E_t = E^t$) which admits the desired distribution π_t (defined on the space E) as a marginal distribution. Thus, consider an artificial joint distribution:

$$\tilde{\pi}_t(x_{1:t}) = \frac{\tilde{\gamma}_t(x_{1:t})}{Z_t}, \qquad (24)$$

where $\tilde{\gamma}_t(x_{1:t})$ is defined as

$$\tilde{\gamma}_t(x_{1:t}) = \gamma_t(x_t)\tilde{\gamma}_t(x_{1:t-1}|x_t)$$
$$= \gamma_t(x_t) \prod_{n=1}^{t-1} L_n(x_{n+1}, x_n). \qquad (25)$$

By definition this joint distribution (defined on E^t) admits the desired target distribution $\pi(x_t)$ (defined on E) as a marginal distribution and so one can use the SISR (sequential importance sampling with resampling) framework to provide an estimate of this distribution (and its normalising constant).

Since we follow the standard SISR framework, we need to define the incremental importance weight with (24) as the target distribution. This is constructed as follows:

$$w(x_{1:t}) = \frac{\tilde{\pi}_t(x_{1:t})}{\tilde{\pi}_{t-1}(x_{1:t-1}K_t(x_{t-1}, x_t))}$$
$$= \frac{\tilde{\pi}_t(x_t)L_{t-1}(x_t, x_{t-1})}{\tilde{\pi}_{t-1}(x_{t-1})K_t(x_{t-1}, x_t)}. \qquad (26)$$

One is now left with the problem of specifying how one should choose the so-called auxiliary kernels L_{t-1}. Moral et al. (2004, 2006) and Peters (2005) provide a theoretical justification for the optimal choice of the auxiliary kernels, with respect to minimising the variance of the incremental importance weights (26), using justification from the asymptotic variance expressions. The exact details of this is outside the scope of this thesis and so we merely state the case where one considers using an MCMC kernel K_t of invariant distribution π_t. An approximation to the optimal auxiliary kernel in this case is given by

$$L_{t-1}(x_t, x_{t-1}) = \frac{\pi_t(x_{t-1}) K_t(x_{t-1}, x_t)}{\pi_t(x_t)}, \qquad (27)$$

which leads to an incremental importance weight:

$$w_t(x_{t-1}, x_t) = \frac{\pi_t(x_{t-1})}{\pi_{t-1}(x_{t-1})}. \qquad (28)$$

Note that one is able to determine the importance weights prior to sampling (i.e. prior to employing the mutation kernel) since the incremental weights at time t do not depend upon the sampled variate $X_t^{(i)}$, and so one should perform resampling (if necessary) to help boost particles before mutation in the correct region of space prior. Analysis of (28) shows that one will have near uniform weights if $\pi_t \approx \pi_{t-1}$, i.e. π_t and π_{t-1} are close to one another in some sense. If one is employing an annealing schedule to move from an easy-to-sample distribution to the highly complex target distribution (Neal, 2001) then care should be taken when defining the annealing schedule since increasing the temperature too quickly will result in poor algorithmic performance; see Jasra et al. (2006). As discussed in Moral et al. (2006) and Peters (2005), one can also consider a mixture of transition kernels K_t (resulting in a mixture of auxiliary kernels L_t) which leads to a transdimensional SMCS algorithm.

3. Density Estimation for Markov Chain Simulation

Density estimation from the output of a Markov chain simulation is useful in a plethora of statistical applications; from the calculation of marginal likelihood estimates (Chib, 1995) useful in model selection, to visualisation of the density of an underlying random variable, readily allowing statistical conclusions to be drawn (Silverman, 1986). Perhaps the most common method of density estimation (from the output of an MCMC algorithm) is that of kernel density estimation, where it has been shown that for any point x, the estimator is asymptotically normal with a rate of convergence (i.e. asymptotic variance) dependent on the dimensionality d and strictly slower than $1/\sqrt{N}$ (where N is the number of simulated samples) (Rosenblatt, 1970; Yakowitz, 1969).

3.1. *Invariance of the Markov chain*

As previously discussed, constructing an MCMC algorithm simply requires one to define a reversible Markov chain whose stationary distribution is the target distribution of interest, $\pi(\cdot)$ (we acknowledge that there has been recent interest in nonreversible Markov chains, see Neal (2004) for example). That is

$$\pi(dy) = \int_{x \in E} \pi(dx) K(x, dy). \tag{29}$$

Ritter and Tanner (1992) were amongst the researchers to spot that one can use such stationarity of the Markov chain, Eq. (29), to estimate the density of interest (also denoted π). Specifically, Ritter and Tanner (1992) discussed density estimation through the use of a (deterministic-scan) Gibbs sampling algorithm. Let

$$K(x, dy) = K_i(x, S_{x,i,dy}), \tag{30}$$

where $S_{x,i,dy} = \{y \in E : y_j = x_j \text{ for } j \neq i, \text{ and } y_i \in dy\}$ with $x = (x_1, \ldots, x_d)$, that is, let the transition probabilities be the product of full conditional distributions (Roberts and Rosenthal, 2004). Through the use of such a (deterministic-scan) Gibbs sampling algorithm, performed for N iterations (the sampler is assumed to be started from the invariant distribution), the density of the target distribution can be estimated as follows:

$$\hat{\pi}(y) = \frac{1}{N} \sum_{i=1}^{N} K(X^{(i)}, y), \tag{31}$$

where $X^{(i)}$, $i = 1, \ldots, N$, are samples from the target distribution and the transition probabilities are defined through (30). It is straightforward to show, under mild ergodicity conditions, that

$$\lim_{N \to \infty} \hat{\pi}(y) = \pi(y) \tag{32}$$

holds almost surely.

A recent generalisation of this density estimation approach has appeared in the literature and is referred to as the "look-ahead" density estimator (Henderson and Glynn, 2001). By assuming that the transition kernel and the stationary distribution are dominated by a common measure, one is able to use (31) for a more general class of Markov kernels K. Henderson and Glynn (2001) provide rates of convergence for their look-ahead density estimator, showing that the errors decrease at a rate of $1/\sqrt{N}$, which is independent of the dimensionality of the space d. This result is attractive from a density estimation point-of-view since the asymptotic variance expression for the widely used kernel density estimator *is* dependent upon the dimensionality, and is thus slower than the stated $1/\sqrt{N}$. Moreover, the use of the look-ahead density estimator removes the selection problem of a bandwidth parameter h, a problematic issue that still receives attention today (Zhang et al., 2006). A significant problem with the generality of the look-ahead density estimation approach is the assumption that the transition kernel and stationary distribution are dominated by a common measure; this is not the case for the Metropolis–Hastings algorithm (for example) and so one is not able to readily apply this density estimation technique in some useful cases of interest.

To circumvent this problem, in this chapter we introduce a density estimation technique that allows one to use any Markov kernel, and importantly, one that may be unrelated to the Markov kernel used in the MCMC simulation stage. Based on this derivation, it is possible to use an "approximate look-ahead" density estimation procedure that is more widely applicable than that presented in Henderson and Glynn (2001). We also discuss how this density estimator relates to that of Chen (1994).

3.2. *L-kernel density estimation*

We begin by introducing a Markov transition kernel, L, (which is possibly unrelated to the Markov transition kernel K used in our MCMC algorithm). Assume that L admits a density (also denoted $L \ \forall \ x \in E$) with respect to the same dominating measure as that which dominates the target distribution (no such assumption has been made on the kernel K). Also assume that we can evaluate the target density pointwise up to an (unknown) normalising constant:

$$\pi(x) = \frac{\gamma(x)}{Z}. \tag{33}$$

Then

$$\pi(x) = \pi(x) \int L(x, dy)$$

$$= \frac{\gamma(x)}{Z} \int L(x, y) dy$$

$$= \frac{\gamma(x)}{Z} \int \frac{L(x,y)}{\frac{\gamma(y)}{Z}} \pi(dy)$$

$$= \gamma(x) \mathbb{E}_\pi \left[\frac{L(x,y)}{\gamma(y)} \right]. \qquad (34)$$

One is therefore able to specify an approximation to the target density as follows:

$$\hat{\pi}(x) = \frac{\gamma(x)}{N} \sum_{i=1}^{N} \frac{L(x, X^{(i)})}{\gamma(X^{(i)})}. \qquad (35)$$

Crucially, the samples $\{X^{(i)}\}_{i=1}^{N}$ have been generated by an MCMC kernel K of invariant distribution π which may be unrelated to the selection of L. In the following proposition, we show that the LLN for the density estimator holds.

Proposition 4. *Suppose that* $X = \{X^{(1)}, X^{(2)}, \ldots\}$ *is a positive Harris recurrent chain with invariant distribution π (for transition kernel K). Then*

$$\lim_{n \to \infty} \hat{\pi} = \pi \qquad (36)$$

holds almost surely.

Proof. We have to show that:

$$\lim_{N \to \infty} \frac{1}{N} \sum_{i=1}^{N} \frac{L(x, X^{(i)})}{\gamma(X^{(i)})} \to \mathbb{E}_\pi \left[\frac{L(x,y)}{\gamma(y)} \right] \qquad (37)$$

almost surely. This is true since:

$$\int \frac{L(x,y)}{\gamma(y)} \frac{\gamma(y)}{Z} dy = \frac{1}{Z} \qquad (38)$$

and so the result follows from Meyn and Tweedie (1993, Theorem 17.0.1). □

3.2.1. Choice of L-kernel

It is possible to show that the look-ahead density estimation technique (Henderson and Glynn, 2001) is a special case of the L-kernel technique presented here. Consider the case where L is taken to be the reversal kernel associated with the MCMC kernel of invariant distribution π, i.e.

$$L(x,y) = \frac{\gamma(y)K(y,x)}{\gamma(x)}. \tag{39}$$

Substituting (39) into (35) yields the following:

$$\hat{\pi}(x) = \frac{\gamma(x)}{N} \sum_{i=1}^{N} \frac{1}{\gamma(X^{(i)})} \frac{\gamma(X^{(i)})K(X^{(i)},x)}{\gamma(x)}$$

$$= \frac{1}{N} \sum_{i=1}^{N} K(X^{(i)}, x). \tag{40}$$

Clearly this is equivalent to (31) and, by construction, the MCMC kernel K needed to be chosen such that it admits a density with respect to the same dominating measure as the target distribution for this choice of L kernel to be valid.

When this choice of L-kernel is not available, for example, when one has used a Metropolis–Hastings kernel for the MCMC simulation (i.e. K is a Metropolis–Hastings kernel) then we recommend using an approximation of (39), where K in this instance is chosen to be an approximate Gibbs kernel.

Example 1. Consider a simple M/M/1 queuing example given in Henderson and Glynn (2001). Specifically, consider a first-in first out (FIFO) queue defining a sequence of customer waiting times $W = (W(t) : t \geq 0)$ such that

$$W(t+1) = [W(t) + Y(t+1)]^+, \tag{41}$$

where $[x]^+ \triangleq \max(x,0)$, and defining $V(t)$ as the service time of the tth customer, and $U(t+1)$ as the inter-arrival time between the tth and $(t+1)$th customer such that $Y(t+1) = V(t) - U(t+1)$. In Fig. 5.2 we compare the look-ahead density estimator, an approximate look-ahead density estimator (where we perturb the traffic intensity such that it forms an approximation of K) and a kernel density estimator for the approximation to the waiting time density. All density estimates were based upon (the same) 10,000 samples with the initial state simulated from the (known) stationary distribution. The arrival time and waiting time rate were taken to be the same as in Henderson and Glynn (2001). One can see that the approximate look-ahead density estimate yields extremely good performance for visualisation of the stationary density.

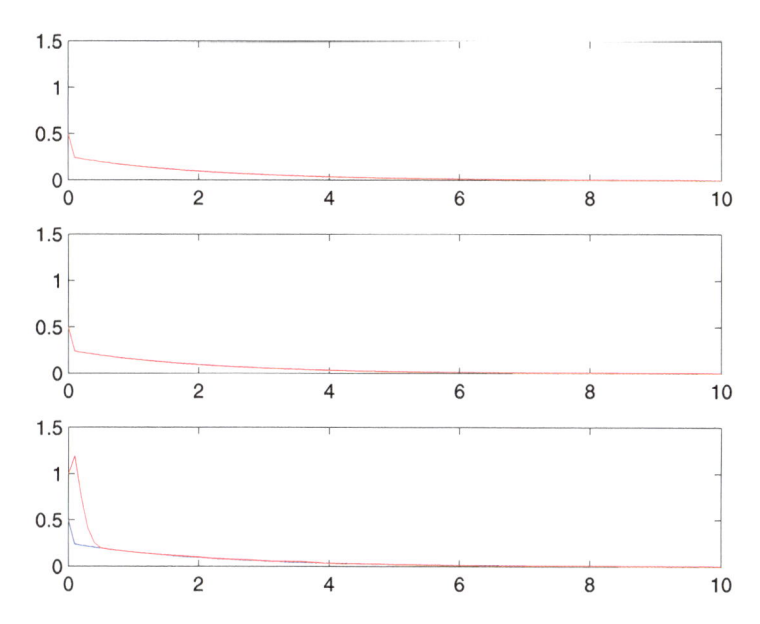

Fig. 5.2. Density estimates for: look-ahead density estimator (top); L-kernel density estimator (middle); kernel density estimator (bottom) for the waiting time density; (blue line = true density; red line = density approximation).

3.2.2. *Relationship to the existing literature*

Chen's early work (Chen, 1994) was primarily concerned with marginal density estimation. This research was adopted from importance sampling to generalise the work in Gelfand *et al.* (1992) that used the full conditional densities from a Gibbs sampler to estimate marginal densities of interest. Thus, instead of being able to evaluate the joint density of interest as is performed within this chapter, Chen's approach concentrates on an estimate of the marginal density, through marginalisation of the joint density as follows. Following the notation in Chen (1994), let $\theta = (\theta_1, \theta_2)$ be a parameter vector (generalisation to a k-dimensional vector is straightforward). One is able to determine estimates of the *marginal* density at a particular point θ_1^* as follows:

$$\begin{aligned} \pi_1(\theta_1^*) &= \int \pi(\theta_1^*, \theta_2) d\theta_2 \\ &= \int \pi(\theta_1^*, \theta_2) d\theta_2 \int w(\theta_1|\theta_2) d\theta_1 \\ &= \int \pi(\theta_1^*, \theta_2) w(\theta_1|\theta_2) d\theta, \end{aligned} \quad (42)$$

where $w(\theta_1|\theta_2)$ is *any* conditional density and we have applied Fubini's theorem. One can further manipulate this as follows:

$$\pi_1(\theta_1^*) = \int \pi(\theta_1^*, \theta_2) \frac{\pi(\theta)}{\pi(\theta)} w(\theta_1|\theta_2) d\theta$$

$$= \mathbb{E}_\pi \left[\frac{\pi(\theta_1^*, \theta_2)}{\pi(\theta)} w(\theta_1|\theta_2) \right]. \tag{43}$$

It is possible to approximate (43) by drawing M samples from the (joint) target distribution π to give

$$\hat{\pi}_1(\theta_1^*) = \frac{1}{M} \sum_{j=1}^{M} \frac{\pi(\theta_1^*, \theta_2^{(j)})}{\pi(\theta_1^{(j)}, \theta_2^{(j)})} w(\theta_1^{(j)}|\theta_2^{(j)}). \tag{44}$$

It is easy to see the L-kernel density estimation technique presented here is related to that of Chen's marginal density estimation technique, for the cases where one is interested in the joint density, rather than specific marginal densities as is required in Chen (1994).

4. Marginal Likelihood Estimation

Model selection is an important element of a statistical analysis, for example, the determination of the number of components in a mixture model or variable selection within regression. Typically, model selection is performed through the calculation of Bayes factors, which necessitates the calculation of a marginal likelihood $p(y|M)$ for a finite set of models $M = 1, \ldots, M_{\max}$. Calculation of the marginal likelihood, under model M, is typically analytically intractable. This is more so the case when one is required to use techniques such as MCMC to explore the posterior distribution.

In this section we show how it is possible to use the L-kernel density estimation technique to determine estimates of the marginal likelihood. We will discuss this in the context of the existing literature, and show how our technique is invariant to the MCMC methodology adopted.

4.1. *L-kernel estimation of marginal likelihood*

In Chib (1995), the marginal likelihood was determined through the use of a simple rearrangement of Bayes' rule which was referred to as the *basic marginal likelihood identity* (BMI):

$$p(y) = \frac{p(y|\theta)p(\theta)}{p(\theta|y)}. \tag{45}$$

For a given point, θ^*, it is possible to determine an estimate of the marginal likelihood as follows:

$$\log \hat{p}(y) = \log p(y|\theta^*) + \log p(\theta^*) - \log \hat{p}(\theta^*|y). \quad (46)$$

Evaluation of the first and second terms on the right-hand side of (46) are simply the evaluation of the (log) likelihood function and (log) prior density at the point θ^*, respectively. In its simplest interpretation, one can consider the seminal work of Chib (Chib, 1995) and its recent extensions (Chib and Jeliazkov, 2001, 2005) as novel density estimation techniques for the evaluation of $\hat{p}(\theta^*|y)$ tailored for specific MCMC-based algorithms. Whilst these approaches exploit idiosyncratic properties of the MCMC algorithm, and can thus be argued to be more "accurate than" straightforward density estimation approaches (Chib and Jeliazkov, 2001), general MCMC (or more general Monte Carlo) techniques cannot be used without significant methodological work.

It is possible to use the BMI with an L-kernel density estimate, as stated in (35), leading to an estimate of the marginal likelihood as

$$\log \hat{p}(y) = \log \sum_{i=1}^{N} \frac{L(\theta^*, \theta^{(i)})}{p(y|\theta^{(i)})p(\theta^{(i)})} - \log N. \quad (47)$$

The use of the L-kernel density estimator in this context allows one to devise (or reuse) sophisticated and possibly tailored Monte Carlo based algorithms for the exploration of the (model conditional) posterior distribution, without the need to execute further Monte Carlo simulations as would be required with Chib's approaches.

Chen (2005) utilises his density estimation technique (Chen, 1994) (see above) by considering a latent variable model, such as those appearing in normal random effects models, regression models with latent variables, etc.

Consider the estimation of the marginal posterior density, $p(\theta|y) = \int p(\theta, u|y) du$ where θ is a hidden variable and u is a latent variable introduced into the model. One can estimate the marginal posterior density, $p(\theta|y)$ as follows:

$$\hat{p}(\theta^*|y) = \frac{1}{M} \sum_{j=1}^{M} \frac{p(\theta^*, u^{(j)}|y)}{p(\theta^{(j)}, u^{(j)}|y)} w(\theta^{(j)}|u^{(j)}). \quad (48)$$

Using similar notation to that in Chen (2005), one can write the following:

$$p(\theta^*|y) = p(\theta^*) \int \frac{p(y|\theta^*, u)f(u|\theta^*)}{p(y|\theta, u)f(u|\theta)p(\theta)} w(\theta|u)p(\theta, u|y) d\theta du. \quad (49)$$

Substitution of (49) into the BMI (45) gives

$$p(y) = \frac{p(\theta^*|y)}{\mathbb{E}\left[\frac{p(y|\theta^*,u)f(u|\theta^*)}{p(y|\theta,u)f(u|\theta)p(\theta)}w(\theta|u)\right]}. \quad (50)$$

The remainder of Chen's paper discusses the choice of w. Specifically, it is proved (through a simple application of the Cauchy–Schwarz inequality) that the optimal choice of w, the conditional density, is $w = p(\theta|u, y)$. This expression can be attained since (49) can be written as

$$p(\theta^*|y) = \int p(\theta^*|u, y)p(u|y)du, \quad (51)$$

where samples of $p(u|y)$ are readily obtained when one performs MCMC on the joint distribution $p(\theta, u|y)$.

The fundamental difference between the L-kernel density estimation approach presented here and Chen's approach (Chen, 1994) is the determination of the complete joint density estimate without the need for any marginalisation of latent variables. This allows for the determination of marginal likelihood estimates for a larger class of problems than those involving latent variables. For example, in the galaxy data example, we demonstrate that it is possible to employ a Metropolis–Hastings algorithm for a finite mixture model, without the need to include the latent mixture component labels, and still be able to accurately calculate the marginal likelihood.

4.2. *Mixture modelling*

For the remainder of this chapter we are concerned with the estimation of the marginal likelihood for data modelled by finite mixture distributions; the marginal likelihood will allow us to determine the number of components within the mixture distribution. We now introduce some notation relating to mixture modelling and briefly discuss the symmetric nature of the posterior distribution. We will use standard notation as in Jasra (2005); Jasra et al. (2005); Stephens (1997); the reader is referred to these sources for more detailed information.

4.2.1. *Likelihood*

Consider data $y = \{y_1, \ldots, y_M\}$ such that the likelihood can be written as follows:

$$p(y|\theta, k) = \prod_{i=1}^{M} \left\{ \sum_{j=1}^{k} \pi_j f_j(y_i|\phi_j) \right\}, \quad (52)$$

where $f_j(y_i|\phi_j)$ are component specific densities (taken to be the normal distribution in the examples to be considered here) parameterised by ϕ_j and π_j are the component weights such that $\sum \pi_j = 1$. $\theta = (\pi_1, \ldots, \pi_k, \phi_1, \ldots, \phi_k)$ is the vector of parameters.

It is possible to permute the labelling of the parameter vector θ such that we attain an equivalent likelihood to that specified in Eq. (52):

$$p(y|\nu(\theta), k) = \prod_{i=1}^{M} \left\{ \sum_{j=1}^{k} \pi_{\nu(j)} f_{\nu(j)}(y_i|\phi_{\nu(j)}) \right\}, \quad (53)$$

for any permutation $\nu(\theta) = (\pi_{\nu(1)}, \ldots, \pi_{\nu(k)}, \phi_{\nu(1)}, \ldots, \phi_{\nu(k)})$.

4.2.2. Prior distribution

For the examples considered within this chapter (univariate and multivariate mixtures of normal distributions) we use the prior distribution specified in Richardson and Green (1997) for one dimension and its generalisation in Stephens (1997) to $d > 1$ dimensions in the multivariate case.

Specifically, for one dimension, we take:

$$\mu_j \sim \mathcal{N}(\eta, \kappa^{-1}), \quad (54)$$

$$\sigma_j^{-2}|\beta \sim \Gamma(\alpha, \beta), \quad (55)$$

$$\beta \sim \Gamma(g, h), \quad (56)$$

$$\pi \sim \mathcal{D}(\delta, \ldots, \delta). \quad (57)$$

This is commonly referred to as the "random beta model" since the hierarchical nature of the model induced by treating β as a random variable helps to ensure that one does not encounter problems with degenerate variance expressions.

For the d-dimensional case, the generalisation is given as follows (Stephens, 1997):

$$\mu_j \sim \mathcal{N}_d(\eta, \kappa^{-1}), \quad (58)$$

$$\Sigma_j^{-2}|\beta \sim \mathcal{W}_d(2\alpha, (2\beta)^{-1}), \quad (59)$$

$$\beta \sim \mathcal{W}_d(2g, (2h)^{-1}), \quad (60)$$

$$\pi \sim \mathcal{D}(\delta, \ldots, \delta). \quad (61)$$

The calculation of the parameters of the prior distributions (in both instances) is based upon the data i.e. we use a reference prior, with the intention of being as uninformative as we can without leading to an improper posterior distribution.

4.2.3. Label switching

One can see that the symmetric nature of the likelihood (i.e. the invariance to the labelling of the mixture components) combined with the prior specification above, which is also invariant to a permutation of the labelling, yields a posterior distribution that is symmetric under the $k!$ possible label permutations. Thus, the posterior distribution is highly multimodal when k is large. Such lack of identifiability means that calculation of component specific estimators will yield exactly the same results for all k components; the marginal posterior is identical for each component since they will be averaged over all permutations of the label, and will thus be unidentifiable. To counter this problem, several approaches have been proposed in the literature; see Jasra (2005) for an excellent review. When using Monte Carlo methods to perform inference, we believe that it is necessary to explore the complete posterior distribution (i.e. all $k!$ mixture permutations) and then perform some post-processing if one would like to compute component specific estimators. Such exploration of the whole space provides an excellent (MCMC, for example) convergence diagnostic allowing one to be more confident, when the sampler is switching between permutations of the labels, that the posterior distribution has been completely explored [A. Jasra, personal communication]. This is in contrast to the advice in reference Geweke (2007), which states that it is only important to ensure that one has samples from the posterior distribution under just one of the $k!$ label permutations. Such exploration allows one to use a "simple" Monte Carlo algorithm for inference. Whilst this does result in an easier coding task, the additional reassurance that convergence of the Monte Carlo algorithm has (almost certainly) been attained with an advanced Monte Carlo algorithm is believed to offset any benefits from using a more primitive Monte Carlo technique under which it is harder to diagnose convergence. It is worth noting, however, for a large number of components k the complete target distribution is going to be extremely large due to the $k!$ label permutations and so exploration, with even the most advanced technique, is going to be extremely difficult.

4.3. Inference

Within the examples presented in this chapter, we employ the sequential Monte Carlo samplers (SMCS) approach of Moral *et al.* (2006) (as an advanced Monte Carlo approach known to work well for the problems considered). Specifically, we use a sequence of tempered densities, where the target density at "time" t is

$$\pi_t(x) \propto (p(y|x))^{\psi_t} p(x), \qquad (62)$$

where $0 \leq \psi_t \leq 1$ is a temperature parameter. This formulation is equivalent to that in Jasra *et al.* (2006); however, we employ a piecewise linear tempering scheme over 100 time instances.

For all experiments, we take the transition kernel K in the SMC sampler to be a Gibbs kernel with the introduction of latent class membership variables (see Nobile (1994); Stephens (2000) for the specification of the full conditional distributions) and iterate this kernel 50 times per time instance (per particle). We also employ the approach of Frühwirth-Schnatter (2001) of randomly permuting the labels at the end of each Gibbs sampling iteration. This has the effect of ensuring that we explore the $k!$ symmetric modes, which in combination with the (sophisticated) SMC sampler, allows us to be confident that we are indeed targeting the correct distribution. We resample when the number of effective samples falls below $N/2$. By employing such an MCMC kernel within the SMC sampler, the weight update equation at time t becomes independent of the particle at time t, and we therefore perform resampling (if necessary) before iterating the Gibbs kernel. This ensures that we have a diverse population of samples at the final time instance. In this case, the weight update is given by

$$w_t \propto (p(y|x))^{\psi_t - \psi_{t-1}}. \qquad (63)$$

Intuitively, one can see that we are progressively increasing the influence of the likelihood on the distribution that we are targeting. At the beginning stages of the SMCS execution, we need to ensure that the samples are able to freely traverse the support of the distribution and hence the reason for the low-gradient temperature update (the successive target distributions for the first 33% of the data are very close to one another).

4.4. *Example: Galaxy data*

The Galaxy dataset is a commonly analysed dataset within finite mixture modelling. The data are measurements of the velocities of galaxies diverging from our own and a histogram of the data can be found in Fig. 5.3. We executed the SMCS algorithm using $N = 1000$ particles. We calculate the marginal likelihood estimate using the reversal of the Gibbs kernel K as the L-kernel within the posterior density estimate (see Eq. (40)). This differs from the approach of Chib (1995) since we also impute the latent variables into the density estimate. The marginal likelihood estimates for differing

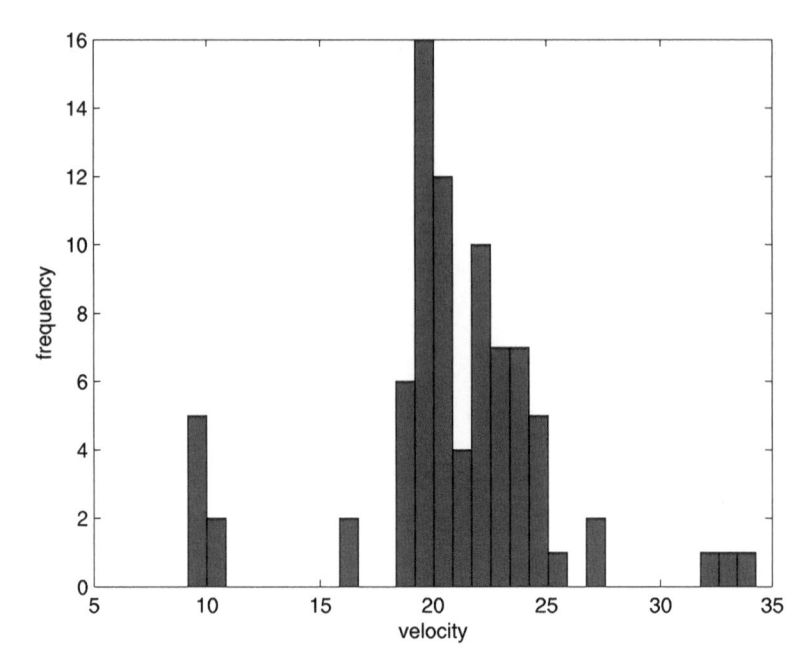

Fig. 5.3. Histogram of the galaxy dataset. It is possible (by eye) to determine at least 3 components within the data.

choices of L-kernel (which is not necessarily related to the kernel K used in the SMCS algorithm) are presented in the table below. We verified the marginal likelihood estimates using a naïve Monte Carlo approximation of the marginal likelihood; i.e. we sampled 1 million samples from the prior and approximated the resulting integral.

Components	$L =$ Gibbs	$L =$ MH	Prior
2	-235.48	-235.12	-235.08
3	-226.54	-226.22	-226.60
4	-228.27	-229.01	-228.56

One can see that the SMCS approximation of the marginal likelihood using the L-kernel density approximation agrees with the naïve Monte Carlo approach. Moreover, the selection of three components for this dataset (under the stated prior) agrees with the results produced by a reversible jump MCMC algorithm in Stephens (2000). It is clear that choosing a

Metropolis–Hastings (MH) kernel still results in accurate estimates of the marginal likelihood, which supports the proposition that the L-kernel density estimation technique can yield good density estimation performance. Based on such results, it would seem possible therefore that the L-kernel density estimate can be practically useful for a larger class of problems than the existing approaches discussed previously.

5. Discussion

In this chapter we have introduced a density estimation technique based upon the introduction of a Markov transition kernel that can be completely independent of any Monte Carlo technique used to perform inference. We have related this to the literature, and shown how the look-ahead density estimator is a special case of the L-kernel density estimator introduced here. The research is also discussed in the context of similar approaches appearing in the literature that marginalise parts of the space, or latent variables within the model, to produce density estimates. Finally, we apply the density estimation technique to the calculation of marginal likelihood estimates for finite mixture models.

Acknowledgements

The author would like to acknowledge the sponsors of the Defence and Security Programme at The Alan Turing Institute.

References

Andrieu, C., de Freitas, J. F. G., Doucet, A. and Jordan, M. I. (2003). An introduction to MCMC for machine learning, *Mach. Learn.* **50**, pp. 5–43.
Chen, M.-H. (1994). Importance-weighted marginal Bayesian posterior density estimation, *J. Amer. Statist. Assoc.* **89**, 427, pp. 818–824.
Chen, M.-H. (2005). Computing marginal likelihoods from a single MCMC output, *Statist. Neerlandica* **59**, 1, pp. 16–29.
Chib, A. and Greenberg, E. (1995). Understanding the Metropolis–Hastings algorithm, *Amer. Statist.* **49**, 4, pp. 327–335.
Chib, S. (1995). Marginal likelihood from the Gibbs output, *J. Amer. Statist. Assoc.* **90**, 432, pp. 1313–1321.
Chib, S. and Jeliazkov, I. (2001). Marginal likelihood from the Metropolis–Hastings output, *J. Amer. Statist. Assoc.* **96**, 453, pp. 270–281.
Chib, S. and Jeliazkov, I. (2005). Accept–Reject Metropolis–Hastings sampling and marginal likelihood estimation, *Statist. Neerlandica* **59**, pp. 30–44.

Chopin, N. (2004). Central limit theorem for sequential Monte Carlo methods and its application to Bayesian inference, *Ann. Statist.* **32**, 6, pp. 2385–2411.

Frühwirth-Schnatter, S. (2001). Markov chain Monte Carlo estimation of classical and dynamic switching and mixture models, *J. Amer. Statist. Assoc.* **96**, pp. 194–209.

Gelfand, A. E., Smith, A. F. M. and Lee, T. M. (1992). Bayesian analysis of constrained parameter and truncated data problems using Gibbs sampling, *J. Amer. Statist. Assoc.* **87**, pp. 523–532.

Geweke, J. (2007). Interpretation and inference in mixture models: Simple MCMC works, *Comput. Statist. Data Anal.* **51**, 7, pp. 3529–3550.

Henderson, S. G. and Glynn, P. W. (2001). Computing densities for Markov chains via simulation, *Math. Oper. Res.* **26**, 2, pp. 375–400.

Jasra, A. (2005). *Bayesian Inference for Mixture Models via Monte Carlo Computation*, Ph.D. thesis, University of London.

Jasra, A., Holmes, C. C. and Stephens, D. A. (2005). Markov chain Monte Carlo methods and the label switching problem in Bayesian mixture modeling, *Statist. Sci.* **20**, pp. 50–67.

Jasra, A., Stephens, D. A. and Holmes, C. C. (2006). On population-based simulation for static inference, Tech. Rep., University College London.

Jasra, A. and Yang, C. (2006). A regeneration proof of the central limit theorem for uniformly ergodic Markov chains, Tech. Rep., University of Toronto.

Jones, G. L. (2004). On the Markov chain central limit theorem, *Probab. Surveys* **1**, pp. 299–320.

Jones, G. L. and Hobert, J. P. (2001). Honest exploration of intractable probability distributions via Markov chain Monte Carlo, *Statist. Sci.* **16**, pp. 213–334.

Liu, J. (2001). *Monte Carlo Strategies in Scientific Computing*, Springer.

Meyn, S. P. and Tweedie, R. L. (1993). *Markov Chains and Stochastic Stability*, Springer-Verlag: London.

Moral, P. D., Doucet, A. and Jasra, A. (2004). Sequential Monte Carlo Samplers, Tech. Rep. CUED/F-INFENG/TR 443, Department of Engineering, Cambridge University.

Moral, P. D., Doucet, A. and Jasra, A. (2006). Sequential Monte Carlo Samplers, *J. Roy. Statist. Soc. Ser. B* **68**, 3, pp. 1–26.

Neal, R. M. (2001). Annealed importance sampling, *Statist. Comput.* **11**, pp. 125–139.

Neal, R. M. (2004). Improving asymptotic variance of MCMC estimators: Non-reversible chains are better, Tech. Rep. 0406, University of Toronto.

Nobile, A. (1994). *Bayesian Analysis of Finite Mixture Distributions*, Ph.D. thesis, Carnegie Mellon University.

Peters, G. W. (2005). *Topics in Sequential Monte Carlo Samplers*, Master's thesis, University of Cambridge.

Richardson, S. and Green, P. J. (1997). On Bayesian analysis of mixture models with an unknown number of components, *J. Roy. Statist. Soc. Ser. B* **59**, pp. 731–792.

Ridgeway, G. and Madigan, D. (2003). A sequential Monte Carlo method for Bayesian analysis of massive datasets, *J. Knowl. Discovery Data Mining* **7**, pp. 301–319.

Ritter, C. and Tanner, M. A. (1992). Facilitating the Gibbs sampler: The Gibbs stopper and the Griddy–Gibbs sampler, *J. Amer. Statist. Assoc.* **87**, pp. 861–868.

Robert, C. P. and Casella, G. (1999). *Monte Carlo Statistical Methods*, Springer-Verlag, New York.

Roberts, G. O. and Rosenthal, J. S. (2004). General state space Markov chains and MCMC algorithms, *Probab. Surveys* **1**, pp. 20–71.

Rosenblatt, M. (1970). Density estimates and Markov sequences, in Puri, M. (ed.) *Nonparametric Techniques in Statistical Inference*, pp. 199–213.

Silverman, B. W. (1986). *Density Estimation*, Chapman and Hall, London.

Stephens, M. (1997). *Bayesian Methods for Mixtures of Normal Distributions*, Ph.D. thesis, University of Oxford.

Stephens, M. (2000). Bayesian analysis of mixture models with an unknown number of components — An alternative to reversible jump methods, *Ann. Statist.* **28**, pp. 40–74.

Tierney, L. (1994). Markov Chains for exploring posterior distributions, *Ann. Statist.* **22**, pp. 1701–1762.

Tierney, L. (1998). A note on Metropolis–Hastings kernels for general state spaces, *Ann. Appl. Probab.* **8**, pp. 1–9.

Yakowitz, S. (1969). Nonparametric density and regression estimation for Markov sequences without mixing assumptions, *J. Multivariate Anal.* **30**, pp. 124–136.

Zhang, X., King, M. L. and Hyndman, R. J. (2006). Bandwidth selection for multivariate kernel density estimation using MCMC, *Comput. Statist. Data Anal.* **50**, 11, pp. 3009–3031.

Chapter 6

Bayesian Numerical Methods as a Case Study for Statistical Data Science

François-Xavier Briol[*,†,§] and Mark Girolami[†,‡,¶]

Department of Statistics, University of Warwick, Coventry CV4 7AL, UK

†*Department of Mathematics, Imperial College London, London SW7 2AZ, UK*

‡*The Alan Turing Institute, London NW1 2DB, UK*

§*f-x.briol@warwick.ac.uk*

¶*m.girolami@imperial.ac.uk*

Probabilistic numeric is an emerging field which considers numerical methods from the point of view of statistics and probability. This position paper discusses the relevance of probabilistic numerics to the advent of data science. In particular, we argue that statisticians have an important role to play in data science, especially in the context of uncertainty quantification. Furthermore, probabilistic numeric is an important example of where controlling uncertainty really matters. The present paper is also a concise first introduction to Bayesian probabilistic numerics and presents some of the related issues and important questions in the field with minimal technical details.

1. The Rise of Data Science

1.1. *Data science: Does it matter, or is it all hype?*

In 2012, the Harvard Business Review published an article claiming that the role of data scientist was the "sexiest job of the 21st century" (Davenport and Patil, 2012). Since then, the interest in data science has kept increasing and a multitude of new positions have opened across all industrial, commercial, and government sectors. This has of course been driven by recent successes in data science and the related fields of Machine Learning, where impressive results with e.g. self-driving cars, image recognition and recommender systems (National Research Council, 2013; Jordan and Mitchell, 2015) have awakened an interest from many leaders in their respective fields. Although this is obviously hard to predict in general, several studies have claimed that the entire job market will be radically reshaped by advances in data science (Frey and Osborne, 2017), with many existing jobs being automated. This has encouraged many governmental institutions to prepare for this shift, with the EU, UK and US each publishing reports on how to address the issues that come with this technological revolution (Cath *et al.*, 2017).

Academia has also taken notice of these changes and many universities have created new degrees to keep up with the demand in employees being able to deal with problems of data analysis. In the UK alone Warwick, UCL, Edinburgh, Bath, Glasgow, LSE and Southampton now propose (amongst many others) new bachelor or masters degrees in data science. Moreover, several national research institutes have been opened in order to increase collaboration between industry and academia; see for example the UK's Alan Turing Institute and Canada's Vector Institute.

But what exactly is this mysterious "new" science, and why does it matter so much? Furthermore, how is Statistical Science relevant to it?

The definition of data science itself can be unclear and subject to debate. What is certain is that it relates to the fact that a lot more data is being collected about pretty much everything in our lives, thanks to the increasing digitalisation which came with the rise of the internet and rapid improvements in computing hardware. One definition could therefore be that data science corresponds to a set of scientific tools and methodologies used to store, handle and analyse this heterogeneous data. As such, data science is nothing new and consists mostly of a mix of tools from the more traditional fields of statistic science and computer science, which need to be adapted to deal with the new types of complex datasets. Many pertinent issues in data science therefore relate to computing and storing facilities required to handle the data and to the efficient ways of handling and cleaning it. The popularity of data science has also encouraged more of a quantitative focus in disciplines which might have previously been more qualitative. Examples include the social sciences, urban planning and the fields of defence and security.

In his presidential address to the Royal Statistical Society, Prof. Peter J. Diggle claimed that "any numerate scholar can operate as an amateur statistician within their own substantive discipline" (Diggle, 2015), and this is often the case in the applications above. All of this leads to the important question of how statisticians can actually have an impact on this technological shift.

1.2. *Nightmares and opportunities for statisticians*

Many statisticians have long decried the poor use of statistics across the sciences. Examples include misunderstandings associated with p-values or issues related to multiple hypothesis testing. There is also often confusion related to which methodologies are appropriate for pre-processing data, which can lead to significant bias in the results. To address this issue, the American Statistical Association (ASA) recently released a statement on how to improve the use of p-values (Wasserstein and Lazar, 2016), whilst Lawrence (2017) proposed a language to formalise the quality and readiness of a dataset. There are however still claims by eminent statisticians that there is a real statistical crisis in science (Gelman and Loken, 2014), with some even arguing from a more provocative stance that "most research findings are false" (Ioannidis, 2005).

One thing is certain: it is often the case that large scale means poor statistical practice, and these issues will hence only be reinforced by the increased complexity of datasets. This potentially means that our increasing reliance on data for decision making could have catastrophic implications if we do not properly educate users of statistical methodology.

Furthermore, the increasing use of machine learning such as deep learning could also be risky due to their lack of interpretability (there has so far been very limited attempts at resolving this problem; see for example Mallat (2016)). A model might have far superior predictive abilities, but can we actually trust it with important decisions if we use it as a black box and cannot clearly understand what is happening under the hood? The answer might be yes for some applications. Take the example of a recommender system for an online company. Here, the worst-case scenario is that the wrong item is recommended to a customer, and although this might have some economic consequence, the implications are limited. On the other hand, any error in a machine learning algorithm which drives a car could have life or death consequences. It is therefore essential to repeatedly highlight the drawbacks of such approaches.

The two issues above are examples of where statisticians will need to have a pedagogical impact on data science. However, there are also several other ways in which statisticians can, and should, have an impact, especially in terms of research and development.

The first obvious area is uncertainty quantification (Sullivan, 2016), which is essential to statistics. This mostly consists of using stochastic models to account for error from the fact that we only observe a finite number of data samples. The reporting of not only a single value but of error bounds is essential for inference in the presence of randomness or incomplete information. Bayesian statistics proposes to go even further and provide an entire probability distribution on the quantities of interest. Such ideas from uncertainty quantification have already had some impact on other sciences, leading for example to an increasing interest in the Bayesian approach to inverse problems (Stuart, 2010). In the case of data science, it will be extremely important to communicate these ideas to end users since the complexity of the data will most certainly mean an exponential complexity of the underlying uncertainties.

Then there is also the idea of design of experiments which will need to be extended to deal with new challenges. The design of experiments problem consists of designing a task which could best test some hypothesis of interest, under a set of constraints. Historically, the field was mainly concerned with experimentation for designing new drugs or creating new types of crops. Nowadays, a more pressing problem with the increasing computerisation of our world is that "too much" data could potentially be collected, but we do not have enough storage capabilities to collect everything. The question therefore becomes what and how should data be collected in order to best test a given hypothesis. These new methods will need to be individually adapted to a large range of datasets including text, video, images, sound and many others.

Finally, statisticians will need to put significant effort in developing methods and software which are scalable (Diggle, 2015). Examples of developments which are already available include STAN (Carpenter *et al.*, 2016), a probabilistic programming language which provides automatic inference using Hamiltonian Monte Carlo given a model specified by the user. This type of partial automation will be essential for the wider adoption of advanced statistical methodologies, since it greatly simplifies the end user's work.

2. Probabilistic Numerical Methods

We have briefly discussed some of the objectives for the future of statistical data science, and there are many application areas in which such developments could be relevant. For the remainder of this paper, we will illustrate some of the ideas in the context of probabilistic numerics (the interested reader is referred to Briol *et al.* (2015); Cockayne *et al.* (2017) for a more complete review).

2.1. *What is probabilistic numerics?*

Numerical analysis is often described as "the study of algorithms for the problems of continuous mathematics" (Trefethen, 1992), that is, the study of how to best project continuous problems into discrete scales. Some also use the less glamorous definition of numerical analysis as the study of numerical errors. Examples include the numerical solutions of integrals, differential equations or even problems in interpolation, optimisation and linear algebra.

All of these operations are essential to mathematical modelling in many applied settings, as well as within statistics and data science themselves (National Research Council, 2013). In fact, our reliance on numerical methods has kept increasing following the increasing complexity of our models. This has also meant a growing need for computational power and the hardware that comes with it.

The numerical analysts' approach usually consists of first analysing whether the problem at hand is well-posed and the algorithm numerically stable (i.e. can we show the algorithm does not magnify approximation errors), then of studying the convergence of the algorithm and the associated order of this convergence. This is done by defining some notion of error and studying how this error decreases as the number of iterations increases, or as the discretisation is refined. These types of errors are usually chosen to be worst-case errors over some set of assumptions on the problem, and therefore provide some (very) conservative error bounds on the solution.

Such an approach might sound very familiar to statisticians reading this, as it is in fact very much related to statistical inference, where we are interested in inferring some unknown quantity (or functional thereof) by observing a finite number of values and in studying asymptotic properties of associated estimators.

As a Bayesian, a natural procedure would therefore be to think of the unknown quantity as a random variable and specify a prior on it, then updating our belief using the observations available. This is exactly the approach proposed by Bayesian probabilistic numerical methods, which was independently proposed by a number of eminent mathematicians and statisticians (Diaconis, 1988; O'Hagan, 1992; Kadane and Wasilkowski, 1985; Skilling, 1991), and most recently reviewed in Hennig et al. (2015) and Cockayne et al. (2017). Since then, a whole range of methods were invented for solving problems of numerical integration (O'Hagan, 1991; Rasmussen and Ghahramani, 2002; Briol et al., 2015; Oates et al., 2016; Karvonen and Särkkä, 2017), differential equations (Schober et al., 2014; Owhadi, 2015; Chkrebtii et al., 2016; Kersting and Hennig, 2016; Cockayne et al., 2016; Teymur et al., 2016; Raissi et al., 2017; Owhadi and Scovel, 2017), optimisation (Mahsereci and Hennig, 2015; Wills and Schön, 2017) and numerical linear algebra (Hennig, 2015; Fitzsimons et al., 2017).

For the sake of concreteness, we now illustrate Bayesian probabilistic numerical methods in the case of numerical integration of some function $f : \mathbb{R}^d \to \mathbb{R}$ for some $d \in \mathbb{N}_0$; that is, we are interested in approximating the functional $I = \int_{\mathbb{R}^d} f(x) \mathrm{d}x$ with a finite number of evaluations $\{f(x_i)\}_{i=1}^n$. A Bayesian approach to this problem, called Bayesian Quadrature (BQ) (O'Hagan, 1991; Diaconis, 1988), is to specify a functional prior on the function f, then observe some data (in this case the evaluations $\{f(x_i)\}_{i=1}^n$), and obtain a posterior on f. This can then be projected through the integral operator to obtain a posterior distribution on I. In practice, this will require choosing a prior model from a class of functions for which posteriors can be integrated in closed form, such as certain classes of Gaussian processes (see Table in Briol et al. (2015) for a range of examples). An interesting point was made by Diaconis (1988), when he noticed that certain choices of covariance kernels can given standard quadrature rules (for specific choices of points $\{x_i\}_{i=1}^n$), such as the trapezoid rule.

So what is actually the point of viewing problems from this Bayesian viewpoint? Are we just reformulating existing methods in a new way?

In a sense, the answer is yes, however there is also much more to it. First of all, an advantage of specifying a prior distribution is that we are making all of our assumptions explicit (whilst these would have previously been more implicit). The prior also allows the user to add additional information which does not fit into any of the existing methods. In the case of Bayesian

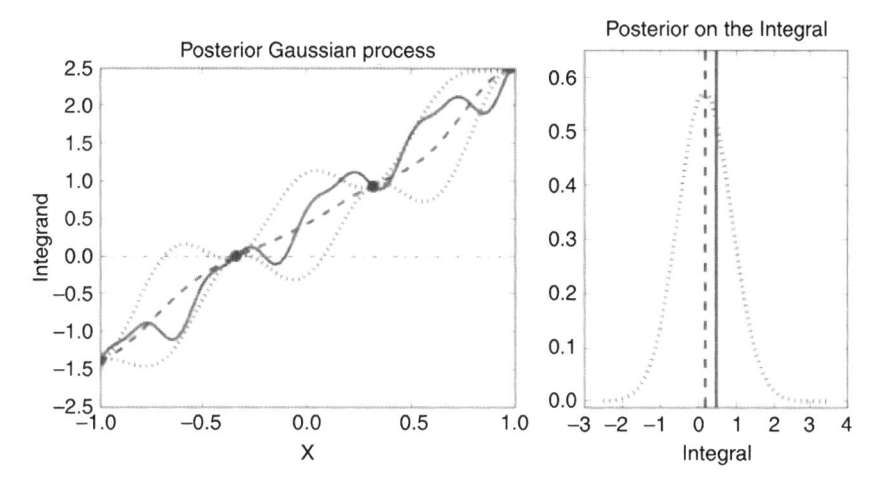

Fig. 6.1. Bayesian Quadrature with Gaussian Process prior. The left-hand side plot gives the true integrand (full line), the Gaussian Process posterior mean (dashed line) and regions of high probability (dotted lines). Finally the dashed and dotted line gives the prior mean. The right-hand side plot gives the BQ posterior distribution on the solution of the integral (dotted), the true value of the integral (full line) and the posterior mean (dashed line). The covariance kernel used is of the form $k(x,y) = a^2 + b^2(x-c)(y-c) + d^2 \exp(-\|x-y\|_2^2/e^2)$ for some $a, b, d, e > 0$ and $c \in \mathbb{R}$. This kernel is additive with a linear term and an infinitely smooth term, which were included to reflect prior knowledge of f as having a linear trend with smooth fluctuations. All of the formulae to compute the posterior on f and I can be found in Briol et al. (2015).

Quadrature, the method is very flexible and can incorporate a wide range of prior knowledge through the choice of covariance function of the Gaussian process. For example, we might know that the function is periodic or has a linear trend, perhaps through inspection of the functional form of f or via domain-specific knowledge, can directly be encoded in the numerical method, as detailed in Fig. 6.1.

Second of all, we can have Bayesian uncertainty estimates for both the function f and its integral I. This therefore clearly relates to the important role of statistics in data science which is of conveying ideas related to uncertainty quantification. Cockayne et al. (2017) also later described how many Bayesian probabilistic numerical methods can be framed as a Bayesian inverse problem. We now not only have point estimates for the quantities of interest, but can in fact provide entire Bayesian posteriors on these quantities. These should hence provide much more faithful representations of our uncertainty than the classic worst-case error bounds.

We conclude this section by discussing a recurrent question to do with the uncertainty being modelled by probabilistic numerical methods. The quantities we are modelling with random processes are usually fixed (think of the integrand f in Bayesian Quadrature), and so it is unclear how to think of the Bayesian uncertainty estimates. These actually represent epistemic uncertainty, i.e. uncertainty due to the numerical method's discrete knowledge of the continuous quantities of interest, rather than inherent uncertainty due to some sort of randomness (called aleatoric uncertainty).

2.2. The future of probabilistic numerics

It is quite clear that Bayesian probabilistic numeric is still in its infancy. Even though the general principle provides some obvious advantages in terms of uncertainty quantification, a lot of algorithmic developments are necessary to make Bayesian methods competitive with more standard numerical analysis approaches. We therefore conclude this short note with a discussion of what we believe to be some of the most important advances for the near future.

First of all, computation within Bayesian probabilistic numerical method can be complicated since we often require sampling or numerical integration in high, or even infinite, dimensions (Cockayne et al., 2017). As such, it will require many of the advances needed in Bayesian computation; see Green et al. (2015) for a general discussion and Barp et al. (2018) for a discussion relating to geometry. The current state of the art focuses on using simple models for which posterior inference can be done in closed form, or require the use of advanced Monte Carlo method. However, a shift in computation might be required and it might be of interest to consider nonexact methods such as variational inference.

There is also a need for a better understanding of how to pick priors for numerical methods. Specifically, eliciting infinite-dimensional prior information from domain experts is a challenging task which will warrant a lot of future work. An attempt for differential equations was proposed by Owhadi (2015) and further discussion was provided by Briol et al. (2016). In these cases, it would be of interest to efficiently include all information available into the method, including boundary conditions or knowledge of the smoothness satisfied by solutions of the equation. This will most likely require extending some of the existing links with the literature on Bayesian inverse problems (Cockayne et al., 2017).

There are however also further developments which are more closely related to some of the research directions for data science which were discussed in Section 1.2. For example, producing advanced and scalable software for probabilistic numerics algorithms will be essential to the widespread adoption of the methods. This will perhaps require probabilistic programming languages (equivalent to STAN) which specifically focus on numerical methods, and with implementations for all of the popular programming languages (including MATLAB, R, Python amongst others).

Finally, ideas from the field of experimental design will also be essential to improve Bayesian probabilistic numerics methodologies. As previously mentioned, Bayesian methods will be most relevant when models are complex and expensive to evaluate, in which cases the numerical error is usually the most consequent. Design of experiments can for example be used to best design how to select points at which to obtain information, or how to best allocate computational resources. Take the example of Bayesian Quadrature in the previous section, here the selection of point could be directly guided by ideas from Bayesian experimental design, as was proposed by Paul *et al.* (2016) for use in the simulation of helicopter trajectories.

3. Conclusion

This concludes our brief nontechnical introduction to Bayesian probabilistic numerical methods. We hope to have highlighted some important developments for these methods and demonstrated how these illustrate the potential impact statisticians can have on other sciences thanks to the platform given to them by data science.

Acknowledgements

FXB was supported by the EPSRC grant [EP/L016710/1]. MG was supported by the EPSRC grants [EP/J016934/3, EP/K034154/1, EP/P020720/1], an EPSRC Established Career Fellowship, the EU grant [EU/259348], a Royal Society Wolfson Research Merit Award and the Lloyds Register Foundation Programme on Data-Centric Engineering.

References

Barp, A., Briol, F.-X., Kennedy, A. D. and Girolami, M. (2018). Geometry and dynamics for Markov chain Monte Carlo, *Ann. Rev. Statist. Appl.* **5**, pp. 451–471.

Briol, F.-X., Cockayne, J. and Teymur, O. (2016). Comments on "Bayesian solution uncertainty quantification for differential equations" by Chkrebtii, Campbell, Calderhead & Girolami, *Bayesian Anal.* **11**, 4, pp. 1285–1293.

Briol, F.-X., Oates, C. J., Girolami, M., Osborne, M. A. and Sejdinovic, D. (2015). Probabilistic integration: A role for statisticians in numerical analysis? preprint, arXiv:1512.00933.

Carpenter, B., Gelman, A., Hoffman, M., Lee, D., Goodrich, B., Betancourt, M., Brubaker, M. A., Li, P. and Riddell, A. (2016). Stan: A probabilistic programming language, *J. Statist. Softw.* **76**, 1, pp. 1–32.

Cath, C., Wachter, S., Mittelstadt, B., Taddeo, M. and Floridi, L. (2017). Artificial intelligence and the "Good Society": The US, EU and UK approach, *Sci. Eng. Ethics*, pp. 1–24. Available at SSRN: https://ssrn.com/abstract=2906249 or http://dx.doi.org/10.2139/ssrn.2906249.

Chkrebtii, O. A., Campbell, D. A., Calderhead, B. and Girolami, M. (2016). Bayesian solution uncertainty quantification for differential equations, *Bayesian Anal.* **11**, 4, pp. 1239–1267.

Cockayne, J., Oates, C. J., Sullivan, T. and Girolami, M. (2016). Probabilistic meshless methods for partial differential equations and Bayesian inverse problems, preprint, arXiv:1605.07811.

Cockayne, J., Oates, C., Sullivan, T. and Girolami, M. (2017). Bayesian probabilistic numerical methods, preprint, arXiv:1701.04006.

Davenport, T. H. and Patil, D. J. (2012). Data scientist: The sexiest job of the 21st century, *Harvard Business Rev.* **October**, pp. 70–77.

Diaconis, P. (1988). Bayesian numerical analysis, in *Statistical Decision Theory and Related Topics IV*, J. Berger, S. Gupta (eds.), **1**, pp. 163–175, Springer-Verlag, New York.

Diggle, P. J. (2015). Statistics: A data science for the 21st century, *J. Roy. Statist. Soc. A* **178**, 4, pp. 793–813.

Fitzsimons, J., Cutajar, K., Osborne, M., Roberts, S. and Filippone, M. (2017). Bayesian inference of log determinants, preprint, arXiv:1704.01445.

Frey, C. B. and Osborne, M. A. (2017). The future of employment: How susceptible are jobs to computerisation? *Technol. Forecast. Soc. Change* **114**, pp. 254–280.

Gelman, A. and Loken, E. (2014). The statistical crisis in science, *Amer. Scientist* **102**, pp. 460–465.

Green, P., Latuszyski, K., Pereyra, M. and Robert, C. (2015). Bayesian computation: A summary of the current state, and samples backwards and forwards, *Statis. Comput.* **25**, pp. 835–862.

Hennig, P. (2015). Probabilistic interpretation of linear solvers, *SIAM J. Optim.* **25**, 1, pp. 234–260.

Hennig, P., Osborne, M. A. and Girolami, M. (2015). Probabilistic numerics and uncertainty in computations, *J. Roy. Soc. A* **471**, 2179.

Ioannidis, J. P. A. (2005). Why most published research findings are false, *PLoS Med.* **2**, 8. DOI: 10.1371/journal.pmed.0020124.

Jordan, M. I. and Mitchell, T. M. (2015). Machine learning: Trends, perspectives, and prospects, *Science* **349**, 6245.

Kadane, J. B. and Wasilkowski, G. W. (1985). Average case epsilon-complexity in computer science: A Bayesian view (with discussion), *Bayesian Statistics 2: Proc. Second Valencia International Meeting*, J. M. Bernardo, Morris H. Degroot, D. V. Lindley, A. F. M. Smith (eds.), pp. 361–374.

Karvonen, T. and Särkkä, S. (2017). Fully symmetric kernel quadrature, preprint, arXiv:1703.06359.

Kersting, H. and Hennig, P. (2016). Active uncertainty calibration in Bayesian ODE solvers, in *Uncertainty in Artificial Intelligence*, AUAI Press.

Lawrence, N. D. (2017). Data readiness levels, preprint, arXiv:1705.02245.

Mahsereci, M. and Hennig, P. (2015). Probabilistic line searches for stochastic optimization, in *Advances in Neural Information Processing Systems*, MIT Press, pp. 181–189.

Mallat, S. (2016). Understanding deep convolutional networks, *Philos. Trans. Roy. Soc. A: Math. Phys. Eng. Sci.* **374**, 2065.

National Research Council (2013). Frontiers in massive data analysis, Tech. Rep., The National Academies Press, Washington, D.C.

Oates, C. J., Niederer, S., Lee, A., Briol, F.-X. and Girolami, M. (2016). Probabilistic models for integration error in the assessment of functional cardiac models, preprint, arXiv:1606.06841.

O'Hagan, A. (1991). Bayes–Hermite quadrature, *J. Stat. Plan. Inference* **29**, pp. 245–260.

O'Hagan, A. (1992). Some Bayesian numerical analysis, *Bayesian Statist.* **4**, pp. 345–363.

Owhadi, H. (2015). Bayesian numerical homogenization, *SIAM Multiscale Model. Simul.* **13**, 3, pp. 818–828.

Owhadi, H. and Scovel, C. (2017). Universal scalable robust solvers from computational information games and fast eigenspace adapted multiresolution analysis, preprint, arXiv:1703.10761.

Paul, S., Ciosek, K., Osborne, M. A. and Whiteson, S. (2016). Alternating optimisation and quadrature for robust reinforcement learning, preprint, arXiv:1605.07496.

Raissi, M., Perdikaris, P. and Karniadakis, G. E. (2017). Inferring solutions of differential equations using noisy multi-fidelity data, *J. Comput. Phys.* **335**, pp. 736–746.

Rasmussen, C. and Ghahramani, Z. (2002). Bayesian Monte Carlo, in *Advances in Neural Information Processing Systems*, Curran Associates, pp. 489–496.

Schober, M., Duvenaud, D. and Hennig, P. (2014). Probabilistic ODE solvers with Runge–Kutta means, in *Advances in Neural Information Processing Systems*, Curran Associates, pp. 739–747.

Skilling, J. (1991). Bayesian solution of ordinary differential equations, in *Maximum Entropy and Bayesian Methods*, Vol. 50, Springer, pp. 23–37.

Stuart, A. M. (2010). Inverse problems: A Bayesian perspective, *Acta Numerica* **19**, pp. 451–559.

Sullivan, T. J. (2016). *Introduction to Uncertainty Quantification*, Springer.

Teymur, O., Zygalakis, K. and Calderhead, B. (2016). Probabilistic linear multistep methods. In *Neural Information Processing Systems* (pp. 4314–4321). Curran Associates, Inc.

Trefethen, L. N. (1992). The definition of numerical analysis, *SIAM News* **25**, 6. https://people.maths.ox.ac.uk/trefethen/publication/PDF/1992_55.pdf.

Wasserstein, R. L. and Lazar, N. A. (2016). The ASA's statement on p-values: context, process, and purpose, *Amer. Statistician* **70**, 2, pp. 129–133.

Wills, A. G. and Schön, T. B. (2017). On the construction of probabilistic Newton-type algorithms, preprint, arXiv:1704.01382.

Chapter 7

Phylogenetic Gaussian Processes for Bat Echolocation

J. P. Meagher[*,¶], T. Damoulas[*,†], K. E. Jones[‡] and M. Girolami[*,†,§]

[*]*Department of Statistics, University of Warwick, Coventry CV4 7AL, UK*

[†]*The Alan Turing Institute, British Library, 96 Euston Road, London, UK*

[‡]*Centre for Biodiversity and Environment Research, University College London, London WC1E 6BT, UK*

[§]*Imperial College London, London SW7 2AZ, UK*

[¶]*j.meagher@warwick.ac.uk*

The reconstruction of ancestral echolocation calls is an important part of understanding the evolutionary history of bats. General techniques for the ancestral reconstruction of function-valued traits have recently been proposed. A full implementation of phylogenetic Gaussian processes for the ancestral reconstruction of function-valued traits representing bat echolocation calls is presented here. A phylogenetic signal was found in the data and ancestral reconstruction performed. This promising preliminary analysis paves the way for more realistic models for the evolution of echolocation in bats.

1. Introduction

The emerging field of Data Science is driven by research which lies at the nexus of Statistics and Computer Science. Bioacoustics is one such area generating vast quantities of data, often through citizen science initiatives (Pettorelli et al., 2013). Bioacoustic techniques for biodiversity monitoring

(Stathopoulos et al., 2017; Damoulas et al., 2010) have the potential to make real policy impacts, particularly with regard to sustainable economic development and nature conservation.

Bats (order *Chiroptera*) have been identified as ideal bioindicators for monitoring climate change and habitat quality (Jones et al., 2009), and are of particular interest for monitoring biodiversity acoustically. Typically, a bat broadcasts information about itself in an ultrasonic echolocation call (Griffin, 1944). The development of automatic acoustic monitoring algorithms (Stathopoulos et al., 2017; Walters et al., 2012) means that large scale, noninvasive monitoring of bats is becoming possible.

Monitoring bat populations provides useful information, but an understanding of the evolutionary history is required to identify the cause and effect of any changes observed. The echolocation call structure, which reflects a bats diet and habitat (Aldridge and Rautenbach, 1987), is a key aspect of this evolutionary history. Reconstructing ancestral traits (Joy et al., 2016) relies on a statistical comparative analysis incorporating extant species and fossil records (Felsenstein and Felenstein, 2004). However, the fossil record is of limited use in inferring ancestral echolocation calls in bats. Therefore, statistical data science techniques may shed some light on this topic.

Previous studies of bat echolocation calls for both classification (Walters et al., 2012) and ancestral reconstruction (Collen, 2012) analysed features extracted from the call spectrogram. These call features relied upon domain knowledge to ensure they were sensibly selected and applied. More recently, general techniques for the classification of acoustic signals have been developed (Stathopoulos et al., 2014; Damoulas et al., 2010). General techniques for the ancestral reconstruction of function-valued traits have also been proposed (Group, 2012). Jones and Moriarty (2013) extend Gaussian Process Regression (Rasmussen, 2006) to model the evolution of function-valued traits (Meyer and Kirkpatrick, 2005) over a phylogeny, a method which was demonstrated for synthetic data by Hadjipantelis et al. (2013). This current research investigates these techniques in the context of the bat echolocation calls.

The structure of this paper is as follows. Section 2 presents details on representing echolocation call recordings as function-valued traits. Section 3 develops the model for evolution given by a phylogenetic Gaussian Process. The results of the analysis of bat echolocation calls are then presented and discussed in Sections 4 and 5.

2. Echolocation Calls as Function-Valued Traits

A functional data object is generated when repeated measurements of some process are taken along a continuous scale, such as time (Ramsay, 2006). These measurements can be thought of as representing points on a curve that varies gradually and continuously. In the context of phylogenetics, these functional data objects are function-valued traits (Meyer and Kirkpatrick, 2005).

Given a phylogenetic tree $\mathbf{T}$, representing the evolutionary relationships between the recorded bat species, we denote the (mth) call recording of the (lth) individual bat of the species observed at point $\mathbf{t} \in \mathbf{T}$ by $\{\hat{x}_{lm}^{\mathbf{t}}(n)\}_{n=0}^{N_{lm}^{\mathbf{t}}-1}$. Thus, $\{\hat{x}_{lm}^{\mathbf{t}}(n)\}$ is a series of discrete measurements of the function $x_{lm}^{\mathbf{t}}(\cdot)$, observed at the time points given by $\frac{n}{f_S}$, where f_S is the sampling rate, in samples per second (Hz), of the recording. Assume then that $x_{lm}^{\mathbf{t}}(\cdot) = x_l^{\mathbf{t}}(\cdot) + z_{lm}^{\mathbf{t}}(\cdot)$, where $x_l^{\mathbf{t}}(\cdot)$ is the representative call function for the lth individual and $z_{lm}^{\mathbf{t}}(\cdot)$ is the noise process for the mth call. Further, assume that $x_l^{\mathbf{t}}(\cdot) = x^{\mathbf{t}}(\cdot) + z_l^{\mathbf{t}}(\cdot)$ where $x^{\mathbf{t}}(\cdot)$ is the representative call function for the bat species at $\mathbf{t}$ and $z_l^{\mathbf{t}}(\cdot)$ is the noise process for the lth individual. It is the phylogenetic relationship between the species level echolocation call functions that we are interested in modelling.

The call recordings themselves are functional data objects, however modelling the phylogenetic relationships between $\{x_{lm}^{\mathbf{t}}(t)\}$ and $\{x_{l'm'}^{\mathbf{t}'}(t)\}$ directly implies that the processes are comparable at time t. This is not the case for acoustic signals, a phenomenon which is often addressed by dynamic time warping (Berndt and Clifford, 1994). Another approach to this issue is to consider an alternative functional representation of the signal.

The Fourier transform of $x_{lm}^{\mathbf{t}}(\cdot)$ is given by

$$X_{lm}^{\mathbf{t}}(f) = \int_{-\infty}^{\infty} x_{lm}^{\mathbf{t}}(t) e^{-i2\pi f t} dt.$$

The energy spectral density of $x_{lm}^{\mathbf{t}}(\cdot)$ is the squared magnitude of the Fourier transform and the log energy spectral density is given by

$$\mathcal{E}_{lm}^{\mathbf{t}}(\cdot) = 10 \log_{10} \left(|X_{lm}^{\mathbf{t}}(\cdot)|^2 \right).$$

Similarly to the call functions, $\mathcal{E}_{lm}^{\mathbf{t}}(\cdot)$ is the log energy spectral density of the mth call of the lth individual from the species at $\mathbf{t}$ where $\mathcal{E}_{lm}^{\mathbf{t}}(\cdot) = \mathcal{E}_l^{\mathbf{t}}(\cdot) + \mathcal{Z}_{lm}^{\mathbf{t}}(\cdot)$ and $\mathcal{E}_l^{\mathbf{t}}(\cdot) = \mathcal{E}^{\mathbf{t}}(\cdot) + \mathcal{Z}_l^{\mathbf{t}}(\cdot)$ where $\mathcal{Z}_{lm}^{\mathbf{t}}(\cdot)$ and $\mathcal{Z}_l^{\mathbf{t}}(\cdot)$

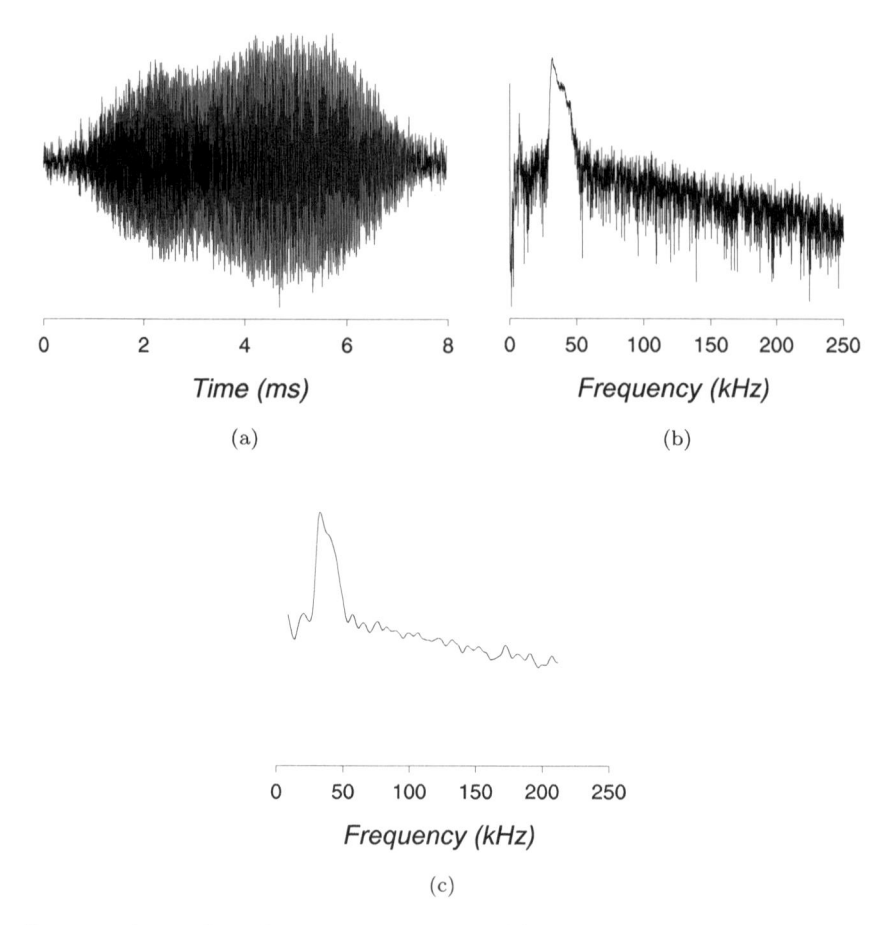

Fig. 7.1. A recording of a bat echolocation call (a) along with the log energy spectral density of the call (b) and the smooth functional representation of that spectral density restricted to the range ([9–212]) kHz (c).

are noise processes, each with an expected value of zero. The log energy spectral density is a periodic function of frequency which describes the energy of a signal at each frequency on the interval $F = [0, \frac{f_S}{2}]$ (Antoniou, 2006).

The discrete Fourier Transform (Antoniou, 2006) of $\{\hat{x}_{lm}^{\mathbf{t}}(n)\}$ provides an estimate for the log energy spectral density, the positive frequencies of which are denoted $\{\mathcal{E}_{lm}^{\mathbf{t}}(k) : k = 0, \ldots, \frac{N_{lm}^{\mathbf{t}}}{2} + 1\}$. Smoothing splines (Friedman et al., 2001) are applied to this series to obtain $\hat{\mathcal{E}}_{lm}^{\mathbf{t}}(\cdot)$, a smooth function estimating $\mathcal{E}_{lm}^{\mathbf{t}}(\cdot)$.

We now have a functional representation of each bats echolocation call where the pairs of observations $\{f, \hat{\mathcal{E}}^{\mathbf{t}}_{lm}(f)\}$ and $\{f, \hat{\mathcal{E}}^{\mathbf{t}'}_{l'm'}(f)\}$ are directly comparable. These function-valued traits can now be modelled for evolutionary inference.

3. Phylogenetic Gaussian Processes

A Gaussian process places a prior distribution over functions, $f(x) \sim \mathcal{GP}(m(x), k(x, x'))$, where $x \in \mathbf{R}^P$ is some input variable, the mean function $m(x) = \mathbf{E}[f(x)]$, and the covariance function $k(x, x') = \mathrm{cov}(f(x), f(x'))$. Given observations $\mathbf{y}$ at locations $\{x_n\}_{n=1}^N$, Gaussian noise, and kernel hyperparameters θ, a posterior predictive distribution over functions can be inferred analytically. See Rasmussen (2006) for an in depth treatment.

Jones and Moriarty (2013) extend GPs for the inference of function-valued traits over a phylogeny. Consider $\mathcal{E}^{\mathbf{t}}(\cdot)$, a functional representation of the echolocation call of the species observed at the point $\mathbf{t}$ on the phylogenetic tree $\mathbf{T}$ with respect to frequency. Modelling this as GP function, where $\mathcal{E}^{\mathbf{t}}(f)$ corresponds to a point $(f, \mathbf{t})$ on the frequency-phylogeny $F \times \mathbf{T}$, requires that a suitable phylogenetic covariance function, $\Sigma_{\mathbf{T}}((f, \mathbf{t}), (f', \mathbf{t}'))$, is defined.

Deriving a tractable form of the phylogenetic covariance function requires some simplifying assumptions. Firstly, it is assumed that conditional on their common ancestors in the phylogenetic tree $\mathbf{T}$, any two traits are statistically independent.

The second assumption is that the statistical relationship between a trait and any of its descendants in $\mathbf{T}$ is independent of the topology of $\mathbf{T}$. That is to say that the underlying process driving evolutionary changes is identical along all individual branches of the tree. We call this underlying process along each branch the marginal process. The marginal process depends on the date of $\mathbf{t}$, the distance between $\mathbf{t}$ and the root of $\mathbf{T}$, denoted t.

Finally, it is assumed that the covariance function of the marginal process is separable over evolutionary time and the function-valued trait space. Thus, by defining the frequency only covariance function $K(f, f')$ and the time only covariance function $k(t, t')$ the covariance function of the marginal process is $\Sigma((f, t), (f', t')) = K(f, f')k(t, t')$.

Under these conditions the phylogenetic covariance function is also separable and so

$$\Sigma_{\mathbf{T}}((f, \mathbf{t}), (f', \mathbf{t}')) = K(f, f')k_{\mathbf{T}}(\mathbf{t}, \mathbf{t}'). \tag{1}$$

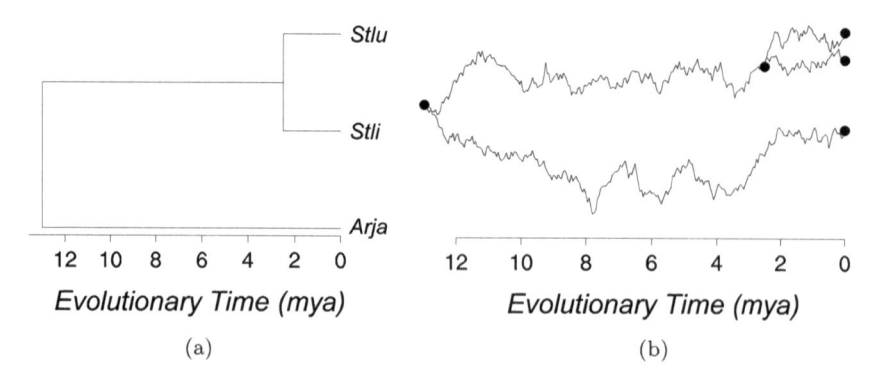

Fig. 7.2. A subtree from the full phylogeny **T** (a) and a simulated univariate phylogenetic OU GP over that subtree (b).

For a phylogenetic Gaussian Process Y with covariance function given by (1), when K is a degenerate Mercer kernel, there exists a set of n deterministic basis functions $\phi_i : F \to \mathbf{R}$ and univariate GPs X_i for $i = 1, \ldots, n$ such that

$$g(f, \mathbf{t}) = \sum_{i=1}^{n} \phi_i(f) X_i(\mathbf{t})$$

has the same distribution as Y. The full phylogenetic covariance function of this phylogenetic GP is

$$\Sigma_{\mathbf{T}}((f, \mathbf{t}), (f', \mathbf{t}')) = \sum_{i=1}^{n} k_{\mathbf{T}}^{i}(\mathbf{t}, \mathbf{t}') \phi_i(f) \phi_i(f'),$$

where $\int \phi_i(f) \phi_j(f) df = \delta_{ij}$, δ being the Kronecker delta, and so the phylogenetic covariance function depends only on $\mathbf{t}, \mathbf{t}' \in \mathbf{T}$.

Thus, given function-valued traits observed at $\mathbf{f} \times \sqcup$ on the frequency-phylogeny, where $\mathbf{f} = [f_1, \ldots, f_q]^\mathsf{T}$ and $\sqcup = [\mathbf{t}_1, \ldots, \mathbf{t}_Q]^\mathsf{T}$, an appropriate set of basis functions $\phi_F = [\phi_1^F(\mathbf{f}), \ldots, \phi_n^F(\mathbf{f})]$ for the traits $\mathcal{E} = [\mathcal{E}^{\mathbf{t}}(\mathbf{f}), \ldots, \mathcal{E}^{\mathbf{t}'}(\mathbf{f})]$, and Gaussian processes, $X_{\mathbf{T}} = [X_1^{\mathbf{T}}(\sqcup), \ldots X_n^{\mathbf{T}}(\sqcup)]$, the set of observations of the echolocation function-valued trait are then

$$\mathcal{E} = X_{\mathbf{T}} \phi_F^\mathsf{T}. \tag{2}$$

The problem of obtaining estimators $\hat{\phi}_F$ and $\hat{X}_{\mathbf{T}}$ is dealt with by Hadjipantelis et al. (2013). $\hat{\phi}_F$ is obtained by Independent Components

Analysis, as described by Blaschke and Wiskott (2004) after using a resampling procedure to obtain stable principal components for the observed traits. Given $\hat{\phi}_F$, the estimated matrix of mixing coefficients is $\hat{X}_\mathbf{T} = \mathcal{E}(\hat{\phi}_F^\mathsf{T})^{-1}$.

Each column of $X_\mathbf{T}$ is an independent, univariate, phylogenetic GP, $X_i^\mathbf{T}(\sqcup)$, modelled here with phylogenetic Ornstein–Uhlenbeck (OU) process kernel.

The phylogenetic OU process is defined by the kernel

$$k_\mathbf{T}^i(\mathbf{t}, \mathbf{t}') = (\sigma_p^i)^2 \exp\left(\frac{-d_\mathbf{T}(\mathbf{t}, \mathbf{t}')}{\ell^i}\right) + (\sigma_n^i)^2 \delta_{\mathbf{t},\mathbf{t}'}, \tag{3}$$

where δ is the Kronecker delta, $d_\mathbf{T}(\mathbf{t}, \mathbf{t}')$ is the distance along $\mathbf{T}$ between $\mathbf{t}$ and $\mathbf{t}' \in \mathbf{T}$, and $\theta^i = [\sigma_p^i, \ell^i, \sigma_n^i]^\mathsf{T}$ is the vector of hyperparameters for $X_i^\mathbf{T}(\cdot)$. The phylogenetic covariance matrix for $X_i^\mathbf{T}(\sqcup)$ is denoted $\Sigma_\mathbf{T}^i(\sqcup, \sqcup)$ and the marginal likelihood of the observed data given θ is

$$\log(p(\mathcal{E}|\theta)) \propto -\frac{1}{2}\sum_{i=1}^{n}\left(X_i(\sqcup)^\mathsf{T}\Sigma_\mathbf{T}^i(\sqcup,\sqcup)^{-1}X_i(\sqcup) + \log|\Sigma_\mathbf{T}^i(\sqcup,\sqcup)|\right) \tag{4}$$

and so θ can be estimated by type II maximum likelihood estimation.

Ancestral reconstruction of the function-valued trait for the species at $\mathbf{t}^*$ then amounts to inferring the posterior predictive distribution $p(\mathcal{E}^{\mathbf{t}^*}(\cdot)|\mathcal{E}) \sim \mathcal{N}(A, B)$ where

$$A = \sum_{i=1}^{n} (\Sigma_\mathbf{T}^i(\mathbf{t}^*, \sqcup))\left(\Sigma_\mathbf{T}^i(\sqcup,\sqcup)\right)^{-1} X_i^\mathcal{E}(\sqcup)\phi_i(\cdot)), \tag{5}$$

$$B = \sum_{i=1}^{n} (\Sigma_\mathbf{T}^i(\mathbf{t}^*, \mathbf{t}^*) - \Sigma_\mathbf{T}^i(\mathbf{t}^*, \sqcup)(\Sigma_\mathbf{T}^i(\sqcup,\sqcup))^{-1}\Sigma_\mathbf{T}^i(\mathbf{t}^*, \sqcup)^\mathsf{T})\phi_i(\cdot). \tag{6}$$

We note that the elements of θ each have intuitive interpretations. The total variation of observed points is $\sigma_p + \sigma_n$, where σ_p is the phylogenetic noise, and σ_n is the nonphylogenetic noise. σ_p is the variation depending on the evolutionary time between any $\mathbf{t}, \mathbf{t}' \in \mathbf{T}$, while σ_n accounts for variation that does not depend on the phylogeny. The length-scale parameter, ℓ, indicates the strength of the correlation between points on $\mathbf{T}$, where large values of ℓ indicate a correlation that decays slowly as $d_\mathbf{T}(\mathbf{t}, \mathbf{t}')$ increases.

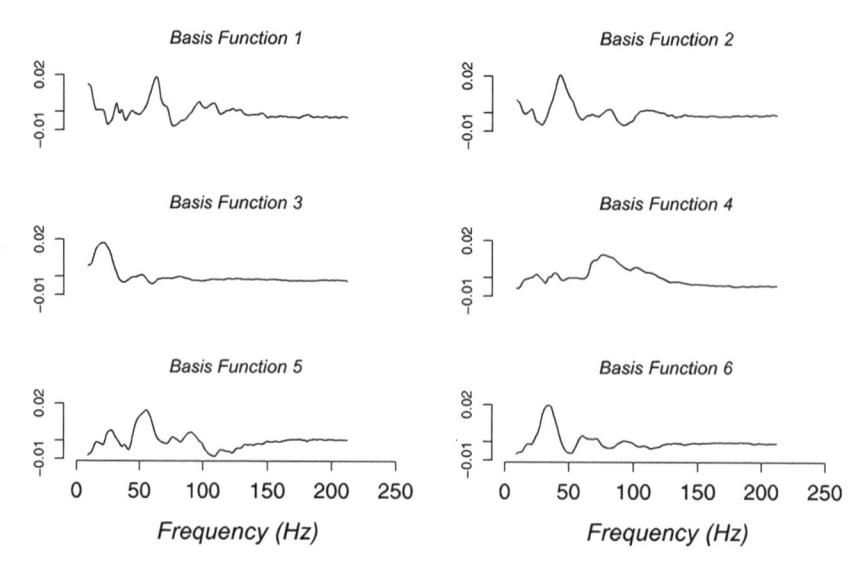

Fig. 7.3. Set of independently evolving basis functions identified for bat echolocation calls.

4. Results

4.1. Data description

Post processed echolocation call data accompanying Stathopoulos et al. (2017) was used in this analysis. Live bats were caught, identified, and recorded at a sampling frequency of 500 kHz. In total the dataset consists of 22 species from five families, 449 individual bats and 1816 individual echolocation call recordings. The distribution of these call recordings across species is summarised in Table 7.1.

Collen's (Collen, 2012) bat super-tree provided the phylogenetic tree of the recorded bat species, **T**.

4.2. Hyperparameter estimation and ancestral trait reconstruction with phylogenetic Gaussian processes

We are interested in modelling the evolution of $\mathcal{E}^t(\cdot)$, the function-valued trait representing $x_{lm}^t(\cdot)$, with a phylogenetic GP. However, only 22 species of bat are represented in **T**. The relatively small size of this dataset presents challenges for the estimation of the kernel hyperparameters in (3). A short

Table 7.1. Echolocation call dataset.

Species	Key	Individuals	Calls
Family: Emballonuridae			
1 *Balantiopteryx plicata*	Bapl	16	100
Family: Molossidae			
2 *Nyctinomops femorosaccus*	Nyfe	16	100
3 *Tadarida brasiliensis*	Tabr	49	100
Family: Vespertilionidae			
4 *Antrozous pallidus*	Anpa	58	100
5 *Eptesicus fuscus*	Epfu	74	100
6 *Idionycteris phyllotis*	Idph	6	100
7 *Lasiurus blossevillii*	Labl	10	90
8 *Lasiurus cinereus*	Laci	5	42
9 *Lasiurus xanthinus*	Laxa	8	100
10 *Myotis volans*	Myvo	8	100
11 *Myotis yumanensis*	Myyu	5	89
12 *Pipistrellus hesperus*	Pihe	85	100
Family: Mormoopidae			
13 *Mormoops megalophylla*	Mome	10	100
14 *Pteronotus davyi*	Ptda	8	100
15 *Pteronotus parnellii*	Ptpa	23	100
16 *Pteronotus personatus*	Ptpe	7	51
Family: Phyllostomidae			
17 *Artibeus jamaicensis*	Arja	11	82
18 *Desmodus rotundus*	Dero	6	38
19 *Leptonycteris yerbabuenae*	Leye	26	100
20 *Macrotus californicus*	Maca	6	53
21 *Sturnira ludovici*	Stlu	8	51
22 *Sturnira lilium*	Stli	4	20

simulation study was performed to investigate the accuracy of estimated hyperparameters for a phylogenetic GP over **T**.

We are not limited to a single observation at any given **t**. By repeatedly sampling at each observed **t**, larger samples can be obtained, improving the quality of the estimators $\hat{\theta}$. With this in mind, 1000 independent, univariate phylogenetic GPs were simulated for each of $n = \{1, 2, 4, 8\}$ according to the kernel (3) with $\theta = [1, 50, 1]^\mathsf{T}$, where n is the number of samples generated at each leaf node. The likelihood of each of these samples (4) is then maximised to give a type II maximum likelihood estimator $\hat{\theta}$ and the results summarised in Table 7.2. This simulation study indicates that at least $n = 4$ observations are needed at each leaf node to provide stable estimators $\hat{\theta}$.

Table 7.2. Summary of $\hat{\theta}$ for 1000 simulations of independent OU processes with $\theta = [1, 50, 1]^\top$ reporting: sample mean (standard error).

n	$\hat{\sigma}_p$	$\hat{\ell}$	$\hat{\sigma}_n$
1	1.09 (0.47)	10^{14} (10^{15})	0.57 (0.54)
2	0.97 (0.29)	10^{13} (10^{14})	0.99 (0.15)
4	0.97 (0.25)	63.66 (136.96)	1.00 (0.09)
8	0.99 (0.24)	56.21 (48.24)	1.00 (0.06)

Given the modelling assumptions made in Section 2 an unbiased estimator for $\mathcal{E}^\mathbf{t}(\cdot)$ is the sample mean given by

$$\hat{\mathcal{E}}^\mathbf{t}(\cdot) = \frac{1}{l_\mathbf{t}} \sum_{l=1}^{l_\mathbf{t}} \frac{1}{m_l} \sum_{m=1}^{m_l} \hat{\mathcal{E}}^\mathbf{t}_{lm}(\cdot), \qquad (7)$$

where m_l is the total number of recordings for the lth individual and $l_\mathbf{t}$ is the number of individuals recorded from the species at $\mathbf{t} \in \mathbf{T}$. However, Table 7.2 indicates that 22 samples is not enough to obtain a stable $\hat{\theta}$ by type II maximum likelihood estimation. We implement a resampling procedure to leverage multiple estimates for each $\mathcal{E}^\mathbf{t}(\cdot)$ from the dataset. This will produce a stable estimator, $\hat{\theta}$.

A resampled estimator $\hat{\mathcal{E}}^\mathbf{t}_r(\cdot)$ is obtained by sampling at random one call from n_r individuals of the species at $\mathbf{t}$ and calculating the arithmetic mean of the sample, similarly to (7). This can be repeated to create an arbitrary number of estimates for $\mathcal{E}^\mathbf{t}$. Resampling across all the species in the dataset we create a resampled dataset $\hat{\mathcal{E}}_r = [\hat{\mathcal{E}}^{\mathbf{t}_1}_{r,1}(\mathbf{f}), \hat{\mathcal{E}}^{\mathbf{t}_1}_{r,2}(\mathbf{f}), \ldots, \hat{\mathcal{E}}^{\mathbf{t}_2}_{r,1}(\mathbf{f}), \ldots]$, where $\mathbf{f}$ is the vector of frequencies over which $\hat{\mathcal{E}}^{\mathbf{t}_2}_r(\cdot)$ is sampled. The methods outlined in Section 3 can then be applied to each resampled $\hat{\mathcal{E}}_r$.

Our analysis set $n_r = 4$ and included four samples of $\hat{\mathcal{E}}^\mathbf{t}_r(\mathbf{f})$ in each $\hat{\mathcal{E}}_r$ for $r = 1, \ldots, 1000$. This reflected the structure of the dataset, for which the minimum number of individuals per species was 4, and the results of the simulations study which showed that four observations per species provided reasonably stable estimates for θ. Note also that $\mathbf{f} = [9, 10, \ldots, 212]^\top$, which reflects the spectrum of frequencies over which bats emit echolocation calls. $\hat{\phi}_F$ was obtained by identifying the first six principal components, which accounted for approximately 85% of the variation, in each $\hat{\mathcal{E}}_r$. By averaging over each sample, a single set of six stable, approximately orthogonal, basis functions were identified. These basis functions were then passed through Blaschke and Wiskott's (2004) algorithm to produce a set

Table 7.3. Summary of $\hat{\theta}_r$ over 1000 $\hat{\mathcal{E}}_r$ samples reporting: sample mean (standard error).

Basis	$\hat{\sigma}_p$	$\hat{\ell}$	$\hat{\sigma}_n$
1	2.30 (0.11)	12.27 (4.18)	1.18 (0.11)
2	3.17 (0.11)	27.63 (3.70)	1.26 (0.13)
3	4.05 (0.32)	70.50 (20.31)	1.19 (0.12)
4	3.32 (0.17)	22.86 (8.95)	1.96 (0.19)
5	3.00 (0.13)	26.93 (2.85)	1.21 (0.11)
6	3.70 (0.14)	12.82 (4.52)	1.28 (0.15)

of six independent basis functions for $\mathcal{E}^{\mathbf{t}}(\cdot)$. Thus $\hat{X}_r$, the matrix of mixing coefficients described by (2), the columns of which are modelled a phylogenetic OU processes, is obtained for each $\hat{\mathcal{E}}_r$. $\hat{\theta}_r$ is then the type II maximum likelihood estimator of (4) given $\hat{\mathcal{E}}_r$. Table 7.3 presents the results of the hyperparameter estimation procedure.

Ancestral reconstruction by a phylogenetic GP involves obtaining the posterior predictive distribution of the trait at the ancestral node $\mathbf{t}^* \in \mathbf{T}$ given by (5) and (6).

To perform ancestral trait reconstruction for $\mathcal{E}^{\mathbf{t}^*}(\cdot)$ the species level traits are estimated by (7) and the model hyperparameters are set to be the mean values of θ_r reported in Table 7.3.

5. Conclusions and Further Work

This preliminary analysis has developed a model for the evolution of echolocation in bats and identified a phylogenetic signal which allows the construction of a posterior predictive distribution for ancestral traits. The log energy spectral density has been identified as a trait representative of the echolocation call in bats. This trait, representing the energy intensity of the call across the frequency spectrum, is modelled as a series of independent components, combinations of energy intensities across the spectrum, each of which evolves according to a phylogenetic Ornstein–Uhlenbeck process. Estimating the hyperparameters governing these Ornstein–Uhlenbeck processes from observed traits provides an insight into the evolution of these traits. Each of the hyperparameters has an intuitive interpretation where $\frac{\sigma_p}{\sigma_p+\sigma_n}$ indicates the proportion of variation in the sample accounted for by the phylogenetic distance between species, while ℓ provides a measure of how quickly correlation along the phylogeny decays. We are working

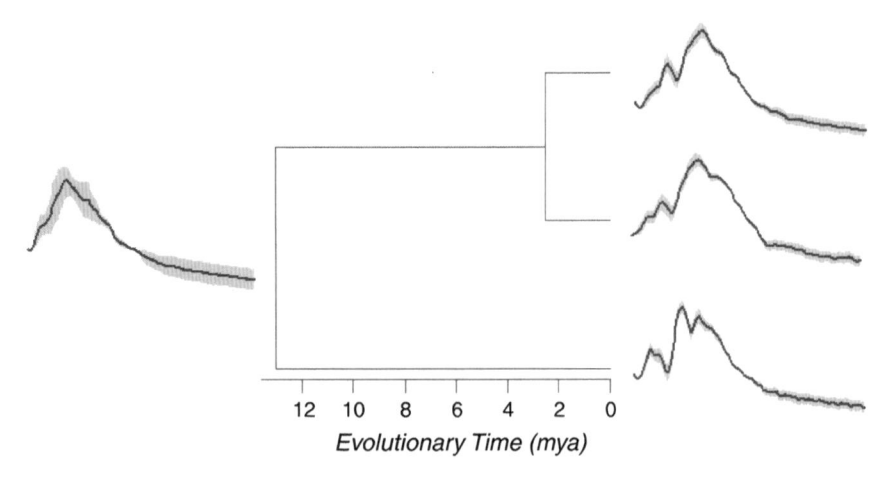

Fig. 7.4. Ancestral reconstruction of the function-valued trait representing the echolocation calls of the bat species included in the subtree shown in Fig. 7.2(a). Grey-shaded region represents one standard deviation of variation around $\hat{\mathcal{E}}^{\mathbf{t}}(\cdot)$.

towards understanding what the results of this analysis could mean with respect to the evolution of echolocation in bats.

One particular limitation of the model is the representation of the echolocation call by a log energy spectral density. Echolocation calls have complex spectral and temporal structures, much of which is lost in the log energy spectral density representation. An alternative time-frequency representation, which preserves more of this structure, is the spectrogram. Modelling the evolution of bat echolocation calls with spectrograms, and implementing this model for a larger dataset of bat echolocation calls, is to be the subject of future research.

The interested reader can access the datasets and code used to produce these results through the R package 'sdsBAT' which is still under development and can be found at https://github.com/jpmeagher/sdsBAT.

Acknowledgement

J. P. Meagher would like to thank the EPSRC for funding this work, and also acknowledge the support of the Alan Turing Institute and Gaelic Players Association.

References

Aldridge, H. D. J. N. and Rautenbach, I. L. (1987). Morphology, echolocation and resource partitioning in insectivorous bats, *J. Animal Ecol.* **56**, 3, pp. 763–778.

Antoniou, A. (2006). *Digital Signal Processing*, McGraw-Hill, Toronto, Canada.

Berndt, D. J. and Clifford, J. (1994). Using dynamic time warping to find patterns in time series, in *KDD Workshop*, Vol. 10, pp. 359–370.

Blaschke, T. and Wiskott, L. (2004). Cubica: Independent component analysis by simultaneous third-and fourth-order cumulant diagonalization, *IEEE Trans. Signal Process.* **52**, 5, pp. 1250–1256.

Collen, A. (2012). *The Evolution of Echolocation in Bats: A Comparative Approach*, Ph.D. thesis, UCL (University College London).

Damoulas, T., Henry, S., Farnsworth, A., Lanzone, M. and Gomes, C. (2010). Bayesian classification of flight calls with a novel dynamic time warping kernel, in *Ninth Int. Conf. Machine Learning and Applications (ICMLA 2010)*, pp. 424–429.

Felsenstein, J. and Felenstein, J. (2004). *Inferring Phylogenies*, Vol. 2, Sinauer Associates Sunderland.

Friedman, J., Hastie, T. and Tibshirani, R. (2001). *The Elements of Statistical Learning*, Vol. 1, Springer Series in Statistics, Springer, Berlin.

Griffin, D. R. (1944). Echolocation by blind men, bats and radar, *Science* **100**, 2609, pp. 589–590.

Group, T. F. P. (2012). Phylogenetic inference for function-valued traits: Speech sound evolution, *Trends Ecol. Evol.* **27**, 3, pp. 160–166.

Hadjipantelis, P. Z., Jones, N. S., Moriarty, J., Springate, D. A. and Knight, C. G. (2013). Function-valued traits in evolution, *J. Roy. Soc. Interface* **10**, 82, p. 20121032.

Jones, G., Jacobs, D. S., Kunz, T. H., Willig, M. R. and Racey, P. A. (2009). Carpe noctem: The importance of bats as bioindicators, *Endangered Species Res.* **8**, 1–2, pp. 93–115.

Jones, N. S. and Moriarty, J. (2013). Evolutionary inference for function-valued traits: Gaussian process regression on phylogenies, *J. Roy. Soc. Interface* **10**, 78, p. 20120616.

Joy, J. B., Liang, R. H., McCloskey, R. M., Nguyen, T. and Poon, A. F. (2016). Ancestral reconstruction, *PLoS Comput. Biol.* **12**, 7, p. e1004763.

Meyer, K. and Kirkpatrick, M. (2005). Up hill, down dale: Quantitative genetics of curvaceous traits, *Philos. Trans. Roy. Soc. London B: Biol. Sci.* **360**, 1459, pp. 1443–1455.

Pettorelli, N. *et al.* (2013). Indicator bats program: A system for the global acoustic monitoring of bats, in *Biodiversity Monitoring and Conservation: Bridging the Gap between Global Commitment and Local Action*, Wiley, pp. 211–247.

Ramsay, J. O. (2006). *Functional Data Analysis*, Wiley Online Library.

Rasmussen, C. E. and Williams, C. K. I. (2006). *Gaussian Processes for Machine Learning*, MIT Press.

Stathopoulos, V., Zamora-Gutierrez, V., Jones, K. and Girolami, M. (2014). Bat call identification with Gaussian process multinomial probit regression and a dynamic time warping kernel, *J. Mach. Learn. Res.* **33**, pp. 913–921.

Stathopoulos, V., Zamora-Gutierrez, V., Jones, K. E. and Girolami, M. (2017). Bat echolocation call identification for biodiversity monitoring: A probabilistic approach, *J. Roy. Statist. Soc. Ser. C. Appl. Statis.* DOI: 10.1111/rssc.12217.

Walters, C. L. *et al.* (2012). A continental-scale tool for acoustic identification of european bats, *J. Appl. Ecol.* **49**, 5, pp. 1064–1074.

Chapter 8

Reconstruction of Three-Dimensional Porous Media: Statistical or Deep Learning Approach?

Lukas Mosser[*,‡], Thomas Le Blévec[*,§] and Olivier Dubrule[*,†,¶]

[*]*Department of Earth Science and Engineering, Imperial College London, London SW7 2AZ, UK*

[†]*Total Laboratory, Imperial College London, London SW7 2AZ, UK*

[‡]*lukas.mosser15@imperial.ac.uk*

[§]*t.le-blevec15@imperial.ac.uk*

[¶]*o.dubrule@imperial.ac.uk*

Using X-ray computer tomography images of porous media, two approaches are compared for generating representations of porous media in three dimensions. Covariance-based simulations (CBS) of the pore space are constrained by the first- and second-order moments of the acquired images, and truncated Gaussian simulation are used to obtain realisations of the porous domain. Generative adversarial networks (GANs) have been recently developed in the context of deep learning. GANs use deep neural networks applied to a set of latent random variables to represent a distribution of training images implicitly. Sampling from this probability distribution corresponds to the generation of new stochastic image realisations. CBS and GANs are presented and compared in the context of three-dimensional image reconstruction. While GANs are a data-driven approach that aims at approximating the full probability distribution of the image datasets, CBS focuses on matching the two first moments. We show that GANs produce much more realistic representations than CBS. It is argued however, that ideas used with statistical approaches such as CBS are complementary to modern machine learning approaches. For example, in the case of image reconstruction, experimentally derived covariances can be used to quality-control images generated by GANs.

1. Introduction

The stochastic reconstruction — or simulation — of three-dimensional images is a topic that has raised much interest in the last 40 years (Torquato, 2002; Lantuejoul, 2002). Modern CT imaging now produces three-dimensional images of the distribution of pores and grains at micron resolution within millimetric samples of porous media. However, micro-CT data acquisition is expensive, time-consuming and limited to very small samples. It is important to be able to reconstruct the distribution of pores and grains over larger volumes than that of the micro-CT data, in order to run numerical experiments at larger scale. It is also useful to represent the spatial variability of the porous media over a larger domain, as a single image only provides one example of such variability. Several approaches are available to generate images sharing the same statistical properties as that of the scanned samples.

The classical reconstruction method, known as simulation in geostatistics (Quiblier, 1984; Chiles and Delfiner, 2011), consists of generating three-dimensional realisations sharing the same first- and second-order moment as the scanned image. We therefore refer to this method as covariance-based simulation (CBS). Another technique was recently developed (Mosser et al., 2017) which applies Generative adversarial networks (GANs) (Goodfellow et al., 2014) in three-dimensions. Both techniques nicely illustrate the difference between machine learning and classical statistical techniques. Volumetric CT images of three different porous media are used for the comparison. These three images, presented in Section 2, have respectively been acquired from an artificial stacking of ceramic beads, one carbonate rock sample and one sandstone rock sample. The classical CBS simulation approach is described in Section 3 and the results obtained on the three datasets are presented. Section 4 presents the GAN approach where a deep neural network is used to generate images using latent random variables as input. The results obtained by GANs on the three datasets are presented. Section 5 discusses the pros and cons of each approach. Rather than opposing them, it is stressed that the two methods can be used in a complementary manner. However the validity of both techniques for uncertainty quantification appears hard to evaluate.

2. Presentation of the Dataset and Statistical Quantification

Three previously acquired datasets are used to test the methods presented in this paper. All images have been segmented into a three-dimensional binary voxel representation of the pore space (white) and grain structure (black) as shown in Fig. 8.1. Table 8.1 describes the characteristics of the three-dimensional images. The datasets are described in more details in Mosser *et al.* (2017). With CBS, the volumetric images are assumed to be the realisation of a stationary indicator random function $I(\mathbf{x})$ of order 2, defined in three dimensions and often referred to as the characteristic

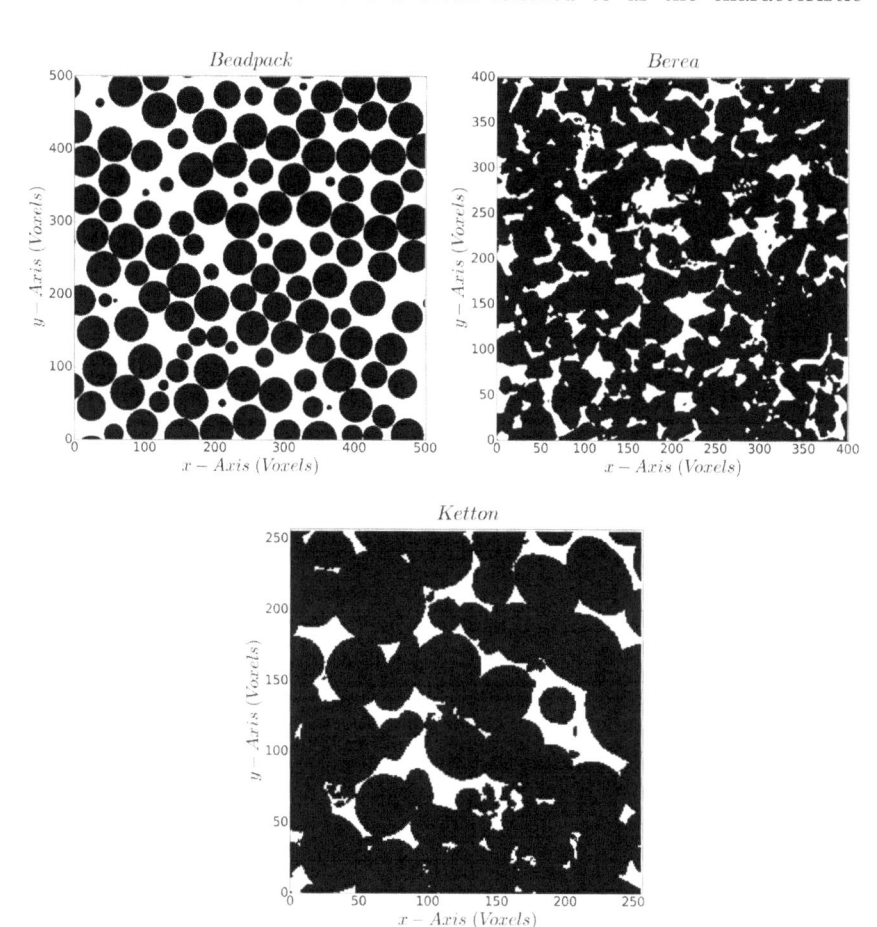

Fig. 8.1. Two-dimensional cross-sections of the volumetric CT datasets used in this study.

Table 8.1. Description of the three samples.

Sample	Composition	Image size (Voxels)	Resolution (μm)	Training image size/spacing (Voxels)
Beadpack	Ceramic grains	500^3	3	$128^3/32$
Berea	Sandstone	400^3	3	$64^3/16$
Ketton	Limestone	256^3	15.2	$64^3/8$

function (Torquato, 2002). It is assumed that $I(\mathbf{x}) = 1$ if a pore is present at location $\mathbf{x}$, $I(\mathbf{x}) = 0$ if a grain is present. The first statistical moment — or porosity Φ — and the two-point probability function $S_2(\mathbf{h})$ — with $\mathbf{h}$ a vector of R^3 — of the indicator random function are:

$$\Phi = E[I(\mathbf{x})], \quad S_2(\mathbf{h}) = E[I(\mathbf{x})I(\mathbf{x}+\mathbf{h})]. \qquad (1)$$

Since $S_2(\mathbf{h})$ is also the noncentred covariance, we will interchangeably use the term covariance or two-point probability function. As a by-product, knowledge of $S_2(\mathbf{h})$ provides quantification of some parameters of interest. For example, in three dimensions, the specific surface area S_v of the medium can be derived from the slope of the covariance at the origin: $S_V = -4S_2'(0)$. And the average chord length (Torquato, 2002) within pores is equal to:

$$l_c^{\text{pores}} = -\frac{\Phi}{S_2'(0)}. \qquad (2)$$

The experimental covariances are assumed to be isotropic and are computed as a function of the distance h only (Mosser et al., 2017). Figure 8.2 shows the experimental covariances of the three samples over a distance of 100 voxels. The $S_2(h)$ functions of the Ketton and beadpack show oscillations, also referred to as a hole-effect (Chiles and Delfiner, 2011), indicating a pseudo-periodicity in the pore–grain distribution.

3. Covariance-Based Simulation (CBS)

3.1. Modelling approach

Various algorithms are available to simulate three-dimensional realisations sharing the two first moments of $I(\mathbf{x})$. Truncated Gaussian functions (TGS) are a common approach (Armstrong et al., 2011; Chiles and Delfiner, 2011) where the indicator function $I(\mathbf{x})$ is derived from a latent standardised Gaussian random function $Z(\mathbf{x})$ (strictly speaking, $Z(\mathbf{x})$ is bi-Gaussian,

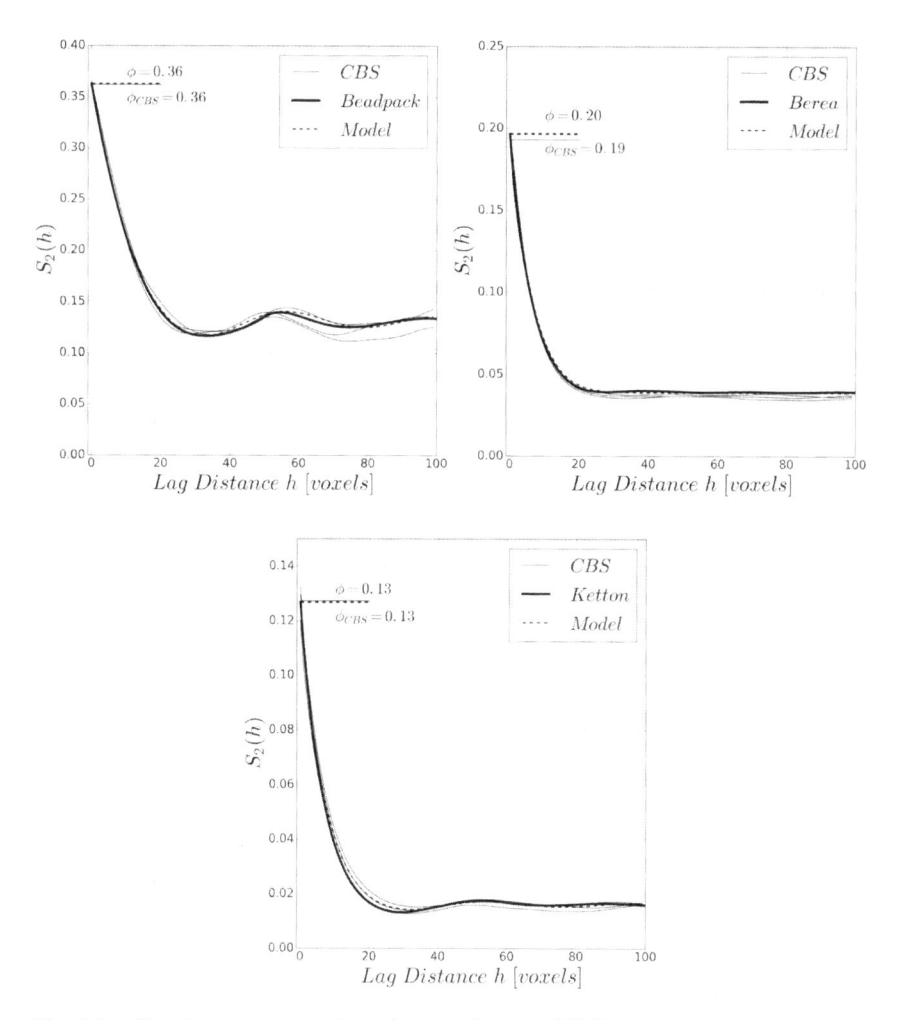

Fig. 8.2. Covariances computed on three realisations (CBS) compared with covariance model (model) and data covariance for the Berea, Ketton and beadpack samples.

meaning that any pair $(Z(\mathbf{x}), Z(\mathbf{x}+h)$ is bivariate Gaussian) by thresholding $Z(\mathbf{x})$ at truncation value t:

$$I(\mathbf{x}) = \begin{cases} 1 & \text{if } Z(\mathbf{x}) < t, \\ 0 & \text{if } Z(\mathbf{x}) > t. \end{cases} \qquad (3)$$

By using a positive definite function for the covariance of the Gaussian function $Z(\mathbf{x})$, it is guaranteed that the covariance of the resulting indicator function $I(\mathbf{x})$ is valid. This is a crucial point as it may be quite challenging to directly find indicator covariances which are valid (Dubrule, 2017).

For the first and second moments (see Eq. (1)) to be matched by the simulations the following conditions have to be satisfied:

$$\Phi = \int_{-\infty}^{t} g(u)du, \quad S_2(h) = \int_{-\infty}^{t}\int_{-\infty}^{t} g_{\Sigma_{\rho(h)}}(u,v)du\;dv, \quad (4)$$

where g is the Gaussian probability density function and $g_{\Sigma_{\rho(h)}}$ is the bi-Gaussian density with correlation $\rho(h)$.

3.2. Modelling the covariances

An isotropic covariance model of the latent Gaussian random function $Z(\mathbf{x})$ must be defined such that, after thresholding, the indicator covariance closely approximates the experimental indicator covariance. This is usually done by trial and error using Eq. (4) which is solved numerically using the R package *mvtnorm* (Genz et al., 2017). For the beadpack and the Ketton samples the hole-effect suggests the use of models such as the cardinal sine model (Chiles and Delfiner, 2011) for the latent Gaussian variable. A combination of a stable (Chiles and Delfiner, 2011) and cardinal sine covariances appears to provide the best fit:

$$\rho(h) = \beta \, \exp\left(-\left(\frac{h}{a}\right)^{\alpha}\right) + (1-\beta)\frac{b}{h}\sin\left(\frac{h}{b}\right). \quad (5)$$

For the Ketton limestone $a = 10$, $\alpha = 1.5$, $\beta = 0.8$, $b = 7$ and for the beadpack, $a = 10$, $\alpha = 2$ (Gaussian covariance), $\beta = 0.5$, $b = 7.25$ (Fig. 8.2). For the Berea sandstone, no hole-effect is observed therefore a single stable covariance model ($\beta = 1$ in Eq. (5)) is chosen for the latent Gaussian function with exponent parameter $\alpha = 1.5$, and scale factor $a = 10$. Figure 8.2 displays the results, which show a very good match between experimental and model $S_2(h)$ functions.

3.3. Results of simulation

Once the covariances have been obtained for both the latent Gaussian variable $Z(\mathbf{x})$ (and for the indicator variable $I(\mathbf{x})$), different methods exist for generating realisations of $Z(\mathbf{x})$ satisfying this covariance. The choice mainly depends on the covariance model chosen for $Z(\mathbf{x})$. If the behaviour at the origin is smooth as for a Gaussian covariance model, the turning bands simulation (Chiles and Delfiner, 2011) is a good choice. If the covariance is less regular such as a stable covariance with a lower exponent parameter, Fast Fourier Transform (FFT) (Chiles and Delfiner, 2011) may be a better choice. The R package RGeostats (Renard *et al.*, 2015) provides these methods and is used here. An FFT is performed for the Berea sample and a combination of FFT and turning bands is used for the Ketton and beadpack samples. Cross-sections of three realisations of the indicator $I(\mathbf{x})$ obtained after truncation of $Z(\mathbf{x})$ are shown in Fig. 8.3 for each of the examples on a grid of size 300^3 voxels. Figure 8.2 confirms that the experimental $S_2(h)$ functions are honoured. Comparison between Figs. 8.2 and 8.3 shows that, if the average lengths of pores and grains are honoured by each simulated image of beadpack and Ketton, on the other hand the detailed geometry

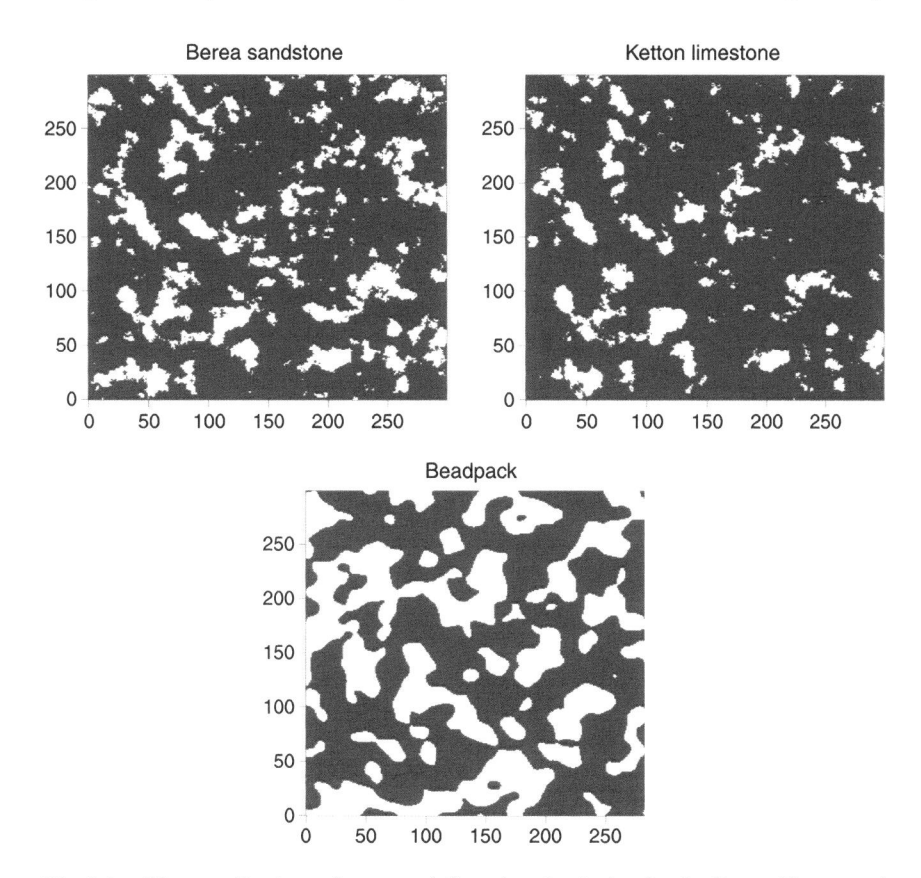

Fig. 8.3. Three realisations of truncated Gaussian simulation for the Berea, Ketton and beadpack samples.

is not properly represented. The individual spherical shapes of the bead-pack and the ovoid shape of the Ketton grains are not recovered. Moreover, it is clear that the pores of the beadpack simulation are more connected to each other than in the original image, which has important impact for permeability.

Yeong and Torquato (1998) also demonstrate that lower order correlation functions generally cannot be expected to yield perfect reconstructions, and recommend to incorporate other constraints such as chord length statistical distributions.

4. Generative Adversarial Networks (GANs)

Generative adversarial networks are presented here in the context of three-dimensional image reconstruction. GANs represent a recent technique in deep learning which has been developed (Goodfellow *et al.*, 2014) to learn a representation of a high-dimensional probability distribution from a given dataset. In the case of image reconstruction, this dataset corresponds to a set of training images that are representative samples of the probability distribution underlying the image space. GANs learn an implicit representation of the probability distribution.

GANs consist of two differentiable parametric functions: a discriminator D and a generator G. The generator maps random variables $\mathbf{z}$ drawn from a latent space to an image $x = G(\mathbf{z})$. The role of the discriminator D is to distinguish between the "fake" images sampled from the implicit probability function $p_{\text{gen}}(\mathbf{x})$ obtained from the generator and real samples that come from the data distribution $p_{\text{data}}(\mathbf{x})$. The goal is to find an approximation $p_{\text{gen}}(\mathbf{x})$ that is close to the real data distribution $p_{\text{data}}(\mathbf{x})$.

To do so, we define two cost functions, one for each of the GAN components G and D. The discriminator's goal is to maximise its ability to distinguish between samples of the real data distribution p_{data} and "fake" samples obtained from p_{gen}. For the discriminator we maximise

$$J^{(D)} = \mathbb{E}_{\mathbf{x} \sim p_{\text{data}}(\mathbf{x})}[\log\{D(\mathbf{x})\}] + \mathbb{E}_{\mathbf{x} \sim p_{\text{gen}}(\mathbf{x})}(\log[1 - D\{G(\mathbf{z})\}]). \quad (6)$$

At the same time, the generator's goal is to maximise its ability to "fool" the discriminator into believing that its samples $G(\mathbf{z})$ of $p_{\text{gen}}(\mathbf{x})$ have been obtained from the actual training data. Therefore the generator G minimises

$$J^{(G)} = \mathbb{E}_{\mathbf{x} \sim p_{\text{gen}}}(\log[1 - D\{G(\mathbf{z})\}]). \quad (7)$$

Both cost functions of the generator and the discriminator oppose each other in terms of their own optimality criterion. Therefore, both networks act as adversaries, hence the name adversarial networks.

We use convolutional neural networks to represent D and G, combined with a gradient descent-based optimisation method to optimise $J^{(G)}$ and $J^{(D)}$.

In theory, convergence is reached when the discriminator is unable to distinguish between the real data distribution $p_{\text{data}}(\mathbf{x})$ and its implicit representation $p_{\text{gen}}(\mathbf{x})$. Given this equilibrium state the value of $D(\mathbf{x})$ converges towards $\frac{1}{2}$. Once convergence is reached larger images than the set of training images can be obtained by providing larger latent vectors $\mathbf{z}$ to the generator. Due to the fully convolutional neural network used to represent G, this results in very large coherent images that do not suffer common texture synthesis artefacts such as seams or stitches.

4.1. Selecting training images within the CT images

To obtain a sufficient number of training images for the GAN approach, we subdivide the large CT datasets into smaller subdomains. Individual training images have been extracted at an overlap to maximise the number of samples. While this allows us to obtain a database of representative image samples, this also requires an assumption of stationarity within the images. The training images are also not strictly independent. The spacing of training image domains for each dataset is presented in Table 8.1.

4.2. Results

Figure 8.4 shows three samples obtained from models obtained on the previously presented image datasets. For the Berea and Ketton datasets the generated images are difficult to distinguish from the real images. The image quality of the beadpack GAN model is lower than for the other two datasets. The perfect spherical nature of the grains in the beadpack image makes it a challenging dataset; nevertheless, given the fact that all geometric features must be learned from the input image data alone, we believe that these results are impressive. In the presented beadpack model, many grains show spherical to ellipsoidal shapes and capture the juxtaposition of the spherical beadpack where grains may only touch at single points.

The challenge represented by the beadpack dataset is also reflected in the two-point probability function $S_2(h)$ measured on the three presented realisations (see Fig. 8.5). For the beadpack we observe an error in the

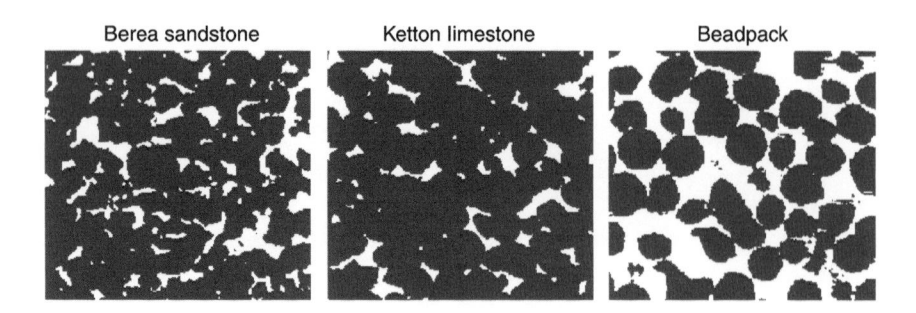

Fig. 8.4. Three realisations of GANs for the Berea, Ketton and beadpack samples.

porosity of the synthetic models by 3%. Nevertheless we observe that the hole-effect is clearly captured by the GAN representations. For the Berea and Ketton reconstructions, the behaviour of the covariances calculated on the samples matches the image data closely and deviations in the porosity in these samples is much lower than for the beadpack.

5. Discussion

The two approaches discussed here are at opposite sides of the modelling spectrum. The CBS approach honours some of the simplest statistics that can be extracted from a black-and-white image. The GAN approach is based on the latest approach available in deep learning and aims at matching the full probability distribution of the images.

5.1. *Visual and statistical quality of image reconstructions*

It is clear that for beadpack and Ketton images, GANs provide much more realistic representations than those obtained with CBS, while the results do not differ as much for the Berea image. The reason can be found in the criterion used by the two techniques. The CBS model generates images that simply have to honour the order one and two statistical moments of the Micro-CT image. From the comparison of the resulting simulations shown in Fig. 8.6 it is clear that first- and second-order moments are not sufficient to capture the morphological characteristics of the pore space. Additional morphological quantities, such as the Minkowski functionals, including porosity, specific surface area, integral of mean curvature and Euler characteristic have been shown to be closely related to effective physical properties of porous media (Scholz et al., 2015). CBS models constrain

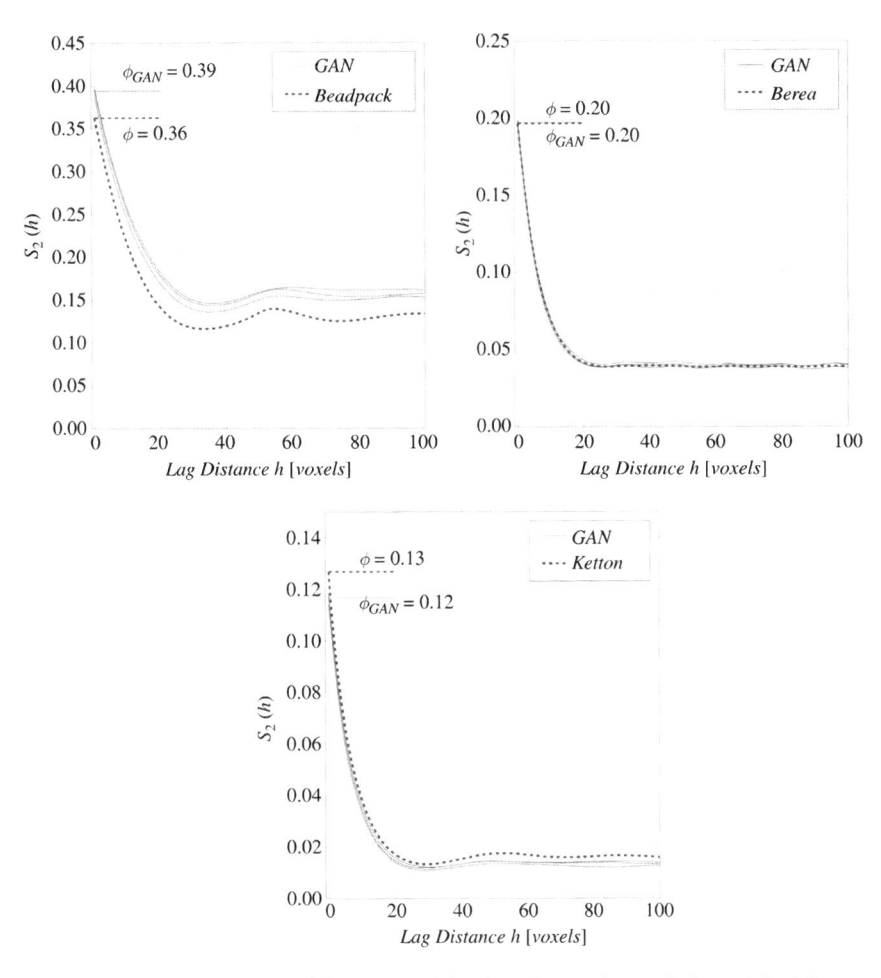

Fig. 8.5. Comparison of $S_2(h)$ for the GAN-based samples and the original image datasets.

simulations on the first- and second-order moments only, therefore capturing two of the four Minkowski functionals necessary to fully describe the pore topology. GANs do not explicitly constrain the morphological parameters, but Mosser et al. (2017) have shown evidence that at least three of the four Minkowski functionals can be captured by the GAN model. The GAN model aims to reconstruct the whole probability density function of the random set while CBS only aims to reconstruct the two first moments. The Ketton and beadpack are much more geometrically complex than the Berea, and the covariance cannot in itself represent this complexity.

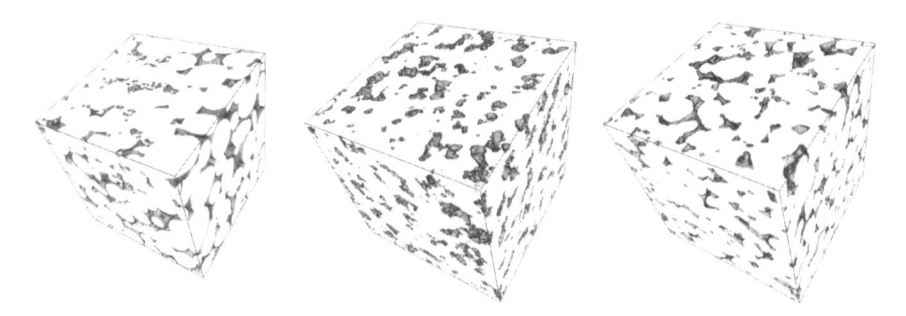

Fig. 8.6. Three-dimensional view of the Ketton dataset (left), CBS (middle) and GAN-based models.

5.2. Uncertainties

The realism of the CBS simulations and of the GANs reconstructions has just been discussed, and it was seen that GANs produce better results. Another important question in simulation is whether the images generated by a given method describe the full range of uncertainty. In other words, given a number of starting statistical assumptions and parameter values, are we spanning the space of all possible realisations satisfying these assumptions and theses parameter values? Thus the question is: for CBS, do the generated realisations cover the whole spectrum of possible indicator images that can be derived from the space of Gaussian random functions satisfying the order one and two moments? For GANs, do the realisations cover the whole range of possible images of the implicit probability density function?

The answer to the first question with regards to CBS-based methods is yes, as the simulation of Gaussian random variables is now a well-understood process. But the use of a latent Gaussian variable implicitly controls all the other moments of the generated images. And the real objective is to generate all possible indicator images, whatever their moments or order higher than 2. In that sense the method proposed in Jiao *et al.* (2007) uses simulated annealing to generate covariance-based indicator random fields which may lead to wider range of realisations than the method presented in this paper.

The question may be even harder to answer for GANs. Goodfellow (2016) has shown that so-called mode collapse can occur for GANs where the multi-modality of a probability distribution is not captured and only one mode of the dataset is represented. An effective measure against this is the addition of white Gaussian noise (zero mean and small variance) to the input of the discriminator. This imposes the challenge for the generator to explore the full domain of the probability distribution and allow multiple modes to be represented (Arjovsky and Bottou, 2017). This is an active research topic in the machine learning community (Goodfellow *et al.*, 2014).

5.3. *Which optimal combination of the two techniques*

Most of the initial GAN developments have been applied to the generation of two-dimensional images of human faces or landscapes. Therefore the main criterion for evaluating them has been their visual realism, that is their capacity to look like a real face or a real landscape to the casual observer. This is a perfectly valid approach for this objective. However, when working in three dimensions and with images which are of a more technical nature, objective criteria are needed to evaluate the quality of GAN-generated images. The covariance provides one such criterion.

Mosser *et al.* (2017) show that, even though statistics such as the mean or the covariance cannot be used as an input to GANs, they can, on the other hand be used as a quality control on the GAN representations. For example, Fig. 8.5 shows the covariances calculated on five images generated by GANs and, as expected, these covariances are close to the experimental images. This confirms that the specific surface area, the average chord lengths and the hole-effect (for Ketton and beadpack) of the GAN and training images are similar.

Figures 8.2 and 8.5 show that the CBS reproduces covariances more accurately than GANs. This results from a key difference between statistical and machine learning approaches. The former starts with a model inference and the realisations match the model. With the latter, there is no a priori statistical model and the parameter match can only be tested a posteriori.

6. Conclusion

CBS and GANs have been compared as examples of two methods used in the stochastic reconstruction of tomographic images for the case of a synthetic beadpack, an oolitic limestone and a sedimentary sandstone. While the CBS approach has the advantage of simplicity and of allowing a quantification of key statistics of the image, GANs are capable of generating three-dimensional images that are much closer to the real images than those obtained with CBS, which is the key objective of the approach.

Both techniques have been shown to be complementary by calculating the indicator covariances of GANs post-simulation rather than pre-simulation as is done with CBS. More work is needed to understand whether the GAN models, and in some ways the CBS models, span the whole spectrum of the implicit probability distribution of the training images.

Acknowledgements

Olivier Dubrule thanks Total for seconding him as a Visiting Professor at Imperial College London.

References

Arjovsky, M. and Bottou, L. (2017). Towards principled methods for training generative adversarial networks, preprint, arXiv:1701.04862.

Armstrong, M., Galli, A., Beucher, H., Loch, G. L., D., Doligez, D., Eschard, R. and Geffroy, M. (2011). *Pluri-Gaussian Simulations in Geosciences*, 2nd edn., Springer.

Chiles, J. P. and Delfiner, P. (2011). *Geostatistics: Modeling Spatial Uncertainty*, 2nd edn., Wiley.

Dubrule, O. (2017). Indicator variogram models: Do we have much choice? *Math. Geosci.* **49**, 4, doi:10.1007/s11004-017-9678-x.

Genz, A., Bretz, F., Miwa, T., Mi, X., Leisch, F., Scheipl, F. and Hothorn, T. (2017). *mvtnorm: Multivariate Normal and t Distributions*, r package version 1.0-6. https://cran.r-project.org/web/packages/mvtnorm/index.html.

Goodfellow, I. J. (2016). NIPS 2016 tutorial: Generative adversarial networks, preprint, arXiv:1701.00160v3.

Goodfellow, I. J., Pouget-Abadie, J., Mirza, M., Xu, B., Warde-Farley, D., Ozair, J. S., Courville, A. and Bengio, Y. (2014). Generative adversarial nets, *Adv. Neural Inform. Proces. Syst.* **27**, pp. 2672–2680.

Jiao, Y., Stillinger, F. and Torquato, S. (2007). Modeling heterogeneous materials via two-point correlation functions: Basic principles, *Phys. Rev. E* **76**, 3, p. 031110.

Lantuejoul, C. (2002). *Geostatistical Simulation, Models and Algorithms*, Springer.

Mosser, L., Dubrule, O. and Blunt, M. J. (2017). Reconstruction of three-dimensional porous media using generative adversarial neural networks, *Phys. Rev. E*, **96**, p. 043309.

Quiblier, J. A. (1984). A new 3-dimensional modeling technique for studying porous media, *J. Colloid Interface Sci.* **98**, 1, pp. 84–102.

Renard, D., Bez, N., Desassis, N., Beucher, H., Ors, F. and Laporte, F. (2015). *RGeostats: The Geostatistical Package*, version 11.0.1. http://rgeostats.free.fr.

Scholz, C., Wirner, F., Klatt, M. A., Hirneise, D., Schröder-Turk, G. E., Mecke, K. and Bechinger, C. (2015). Direct relations between morphology and transport in Boolean models, *Phys. Rev. E* **92**, 4, p. 043023.

Torquato, S. (2002). *Random Heterogeneous Materials. Microstructure and Macroscopic Properties*, Springer.

Yeong, C. L. Y. and Torquato, S. (1998). Reconstructing random media, *Phys. Rev. E* **57**, p. 495.

Chapter 9

Using Data-Driven Uncertainty Quantification to Support Decision Making

Charlie Vollmer[*], Matt Peterson[†], David J. Stracuzzi[‡] and Maximillian G. Chen[§]

Sandia National Laboratories, Albuquerque, NM, USA
[*]cvollme@sandia.gov
[†]mgpeter@sandia.gov
[‡]djstrac@sandia.gov
[§]mgchen@sandia.gov

As data collection and analysis methods become increasingly sophisticated, interpretation and use of results by end users become increasingly challenging. In this paper, we discuss the role of data-driven uncertainty quantification in supporting and improving decision making. We illustrate our argument with a case study in seismic onset detection, comparing statistically computed distributions over possible signal onset times to the onset times chosen by a set of domain analysts. Importantly, the uncertainty distributions sometimes identify subtle changes in the seismic waveform that are missed by both point estimate calculations and by domain analysts.

1. Introduction

Data science continues to emerge as an interdisciplinary field concerned with data acquisition, storage, curation, and analysis. In this paper, we take the view that data are collected and analyzed to provide new information to a decision-making process. We focus on cases in which ground truth or supervision are unavailable, precise judgements are important, and data do not easily yield to simple inspection or point estimate solutions.

To ground the discussion, we consider a case study in seismology in which the goal is to detect the onset of a signal, called the *pick*, in a single seismogram. Seismic picking is usually done by a combination of automated analysis, which identifies candidate onset times, and human analysts, who refine the pick using domain expertise. The precision with which the signal onset is identified can have a large impact on downstream analyses. For long-distance events such as earthquakes, changing the pick time by 0.1 seconds can move the estimated location by tens of kilometres, which can in turn impact the event's type classification and other characteristics (Ringdal and Husebye, 1982).

Although seismologists provide the gold standard for accuracy and precision, human error is a known problem in determining arrival times. Depending on experience level and training procedures, some analysts pick arrival times earlier than others. Zeiler and Velasco (2009) did extensive studies on analyst picks and found that not only do determinations vary among analysts, but also within a single analyst when presented with the same data multiple times.

The data science goal is therefore to extract arrival time information from the data in an effort to reduce the frequency and extent of disagreement among analysts. In this paper, we consider data-driven uncertainty quantification methods to extract additional insights into likely onset times from the available seismic waveforms. Importantly, fully characterising a distribution over onset times can also increase the statistical rigor of downstream analyses by opening the door to uncertainty propagation throughout the analytic sequence. Our proposed method works within the existing seismic analysis framework using the same data that is already collected and employs nonparametric modelling techniques to avoid strong distributional assumptions.

In the remainder of the paper, we first provide additional background on seismic waveform data and a review of existing analysis methods. We then describe our approach to estimating the seismic arrival times and associated uncertainty distribution. Next, we demonstrate our method using a subset of the SPEAR data initially studied by Zeiler and Velasco (2009). The paper concludes with a discussion of the decision-making implications of our statistical analysis, along with discussion of how these ideas apply to other analysis tasks and of future work required to prepare our methods for practical applications.

2. Background on Seismic Detection

Many events that occur on or within the earth's crust can be identified by analyzing seismic waveforms. Earthquakes (as in Trifunac and Brady (1975)), volcanic activity (as in Werner-Allen et al. (2005)), explosions such as from mining operations (as in Stump and Pearson (1996)), and ice events such as crevassing or iceberg calving (such as O'Neel et al. (2007)) can all be detected, geolocated, and identified using seismograms. Analytic process details may differ from one application to another, but in general the analysis proceeds in stages. Initial detection requires identifying precisely the onset of the signal, distinguishing it from background noise. A combination of multiple signals, typically from geospatially separate recording stations, is then used to determine source location, which in turn helps to inform the event type classification and magnitude estimations.

Seismic arrival time picking is an issue general to geologic and seismic monitoring sensors. The raw data consists of a multichannel time series that measures ground motion, for example in the x, y, and z directions. The time series may be perturbed by numerous sources, such as vehicle traffic, ocean waves, or wind in addition to phenomena of interest like earthquakes. Importantly, the perturbations can vary widely across measurement stations, with no two stations exhibiting the same characteristics.

Many error sources contribute to the uncertainty of a given arrival (Velasco et al., 2001), including the human errors described above. Measurement errors depend on external factors, such as the quality and location of the monitoring station, the strength of the source event, and the temporal properties of the signal, which may display a sudden (impulsive) onset or build slowly over time. Model errors refer to differences in predicted versus actual arrival times based on established models of wave propagation through the earth's crust and interior. These errors tend to influence tasks such as source location and magnitude estimation, and we do not address them further in this work. *Our goal is therefore to reduce human error by rigorously assessing and reporting measurement errors.*

The analysis task is to precisely identify the time at which background noise transitions to a seismic signal. Each channel is typically processed separately and standard practice includes preprocessing the data through bandpass filters, removing both high and low frequencies that experts believe to be irrelevant. Candidate arrivals are then identified in the filtered

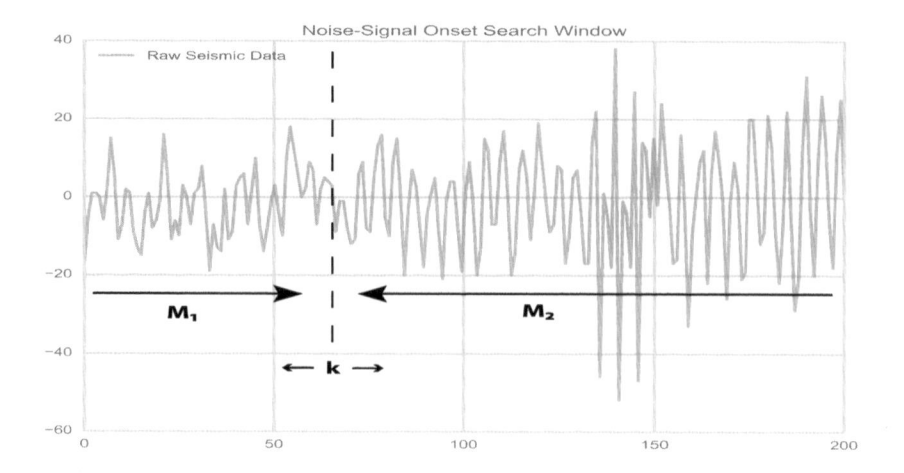

Fig. 9.1. Sliding window for estimating arrival time.

data, most commonly by computing the ratio of the short-term energy to the long-term energy (STA/LTA; see Rodriguez (2011)). A potential detection is identified when a predetermined threshold is exceeded for a specified number of channels (typically one). Output from the STA/LTA algorithm is a window containing the candidate arrival plus preceding noise and trailing noisy seismic waves.

In many cases, the window is further refined to a specific onset time by using a combination of autoregressive models and a model fitting metric, such as the Akaike information criterion (AIC). Two separate models, $\mathcal{M}_1$ and $\mathcal{M}_2$, are fit to the noise and signal portions of the window respectively, as shown in Fig. 9.1. AIC (Akaike, 1974) is then used to optimise the onset time as the point at which the two models meet. Several variations on this procedure are described by Kamigaichi (1992). Importantly, the uncertainty of the onset time is typically described only by a confidence interval calculated as a function of the signal-to-noise ratio.

3. Estimating Arrival Time

The following summarises our approach to refining the initial arrival time of the seismic signal. Our method is computationally efficient and relies on well-founded theory in statistical time series analysis. Note that the basic procedure corresponds to standard practice for automatic pick refinement in the seismology community as described above. Our approach differs in that we provide a complete *a posteriori* estimate of pick uncertainty.

3.1. *Time series models*

Assuming that $\mathcal{M}_1$ captures noise only, let each data point be an independent and identically distributed draw from a normal probability distribution with zero mean and finite variance whose parameters are estimated from the data at each individual station. $\mathcal{M}_1$ is specified in the following:

$$Y_t \sim N(0, \sigma_n^2), \qquad (1)$$

where $\sigma_n^2 < \infty$ for $t = 1, \ldots, k-1$.

$\mathcal{M}_2$ models the generative process of the seismic signal. The sensor will record a noisy signal measurement, so the model explicitly includes both noise and signal components. We assume a smooth functional form to the signal apart from the noise. Weak signals will be followed by weak signals, and strong signals should immediately be followed by strong signals. This implies an auto-regressive, moving-average (ARMA) model for $\mathcal{M}_2$ with auto-regressive terms of order p and moving average terms of order q:

$$Y_t = c + \sum_{i=1}^{p} \phi_i Y_{t-i} + \sum_{i=1}^{q} \theta_i \epsilon_{t-i} + \epsilon_t, \qquad (2)$$

where $\epsilon_t \sim N(0, \sigma_s^2)$ for $t = k, \ldots, T$, and σ_s^2 is the finite variance of the noise component of the signal model. The noise and signal distributions in Eqs. (1) and (2) provide likelihoods for our data which we can use to estimate both the arrival time and the associated uncertainty around it.

3.2. *Information theoretic arrival time refinement*

To refine the pick within the STA/LTA arrival time window requires evaluating the difference between models $\mathcal{M}_1$ and $\mathcal{M}_2$ and the observed statistics from our time series data. Model parameters are estimated from data in the onset search window. Following Kamigaichi (1992), we use the Akaike information criterion (AIC), a generalised entropy metric, to measure the differences between these specified prediction models and the observed time-series data. The general form for AIC is

$$\text{AIC}(\mathcal{M}) = -2 \log \mathcal{L}(\mathcal{M}) + 2\rho(\mathcal{M}), \qquad (3)$$

where $\mathcal{L}(\mathcal{M})$ is the likelihood of model $\mathcal{M}$, and $\rho(\mathcal{M})$ is the complexity of the model (e.g. degrees of freedom).

3.2.1. *Additive log-likelihood of noise-to-signal time series*

Suppose we observe T data points on a seismic sensor, Y_t, for $t = 1, \ldots, T$. We assume that there exists a time point $\alpha \in \{t : t = 1, \ldots, T\}$, such that for all time points $t \leq \alpha$ we record only noise. For all time points t after α, $\alpha < t \leq T$, we observe both a seismic signal and a noise component.

By independence, we have directly that

$$f(Y_1, \ldots, Y_T | \theta_1, \theta_2) = f(Y_1, \ldots, Y_k | \theta_1) f(Y_{k+1}, \ldots, Y_T | \theta_2). \tag{4}$$

Therefore, to find the MLE of the arrival time pick we need to find k that satisfies

$$\operatorname*{argmax}_{k} \{l(\theta_1 | Y_1, \ldots, Y_k) + l(\theta_2 | Y_{k+1}, \ldots, Y_T)\}. \tag{5}$$

By our definitions of $\mathcal{M}_1$ and $\mathcal{M}_2$ in Eqs. (1) and (2), their log-likelihoods are

$$l(\theta_1 | y_1, \ldots, y_k) = -\frac{k}{2} \ln(2\pi) - \frac{k}{2} \ln(\sigma_n^2) - \frac{1}{2\sigma_n^2} \sum_{t=1}^{k} y_t^2, \tag{6}$$

$$l(\theta_2 | y_{k+1}, \ldots, y_T) = -\frac{T-k-p}{2} \ln(2\pi)$$

$$-\frac{(T-k-p)}{2} \ln(\sigma_s^2) - \frac{1}{2\sigma_s^2} \sum_{t=k+p+1}^{T} \varepsilon_t^2, \tag{7}$$

where $\varepsilon_t = Y_t - c - \sum_{i=1}^{p} \phi_i Y_{t-i} - \sum_{j=1}^{q} \theta_j \varepsilon_{t-j}$ for $t = p+1, p+2, \ldots, T$. And we have the following Akaike information criterion to minimise for our arrival time estimation:

$$l(\mathcal{M}) = l(\theta_1 | Y_1, \ldots, Y_k) + l(\theta_2 | Y_{k+1}, \ldots, Y_T)$$

$$= -\frac{k}{2} \ln(2\pi) - \frac{k}{2} \ln(\sigma_n^2) - \frac{1}{2\sigma_n^2} \sum_{t=1}^{k} y_t^2 - \frac{T-k-p}{2} \ln(2\pi)$$

$$-\frac{(T-k-p)}{2} \ln(\sigma_s^2) - \frac{1}{2\sigma_s^2} \sum_{t=k+p+1}^{T} \varepsilon_t^2. \tag{8}$$

4. Estimating Arrival Time Uncertainty

By specifying a model form for both our noise and signal time series, $\mathcal{M}_1$ and $\mathcal{M}_2$ provide a basis for using Monte Carlo sampling to derive an a

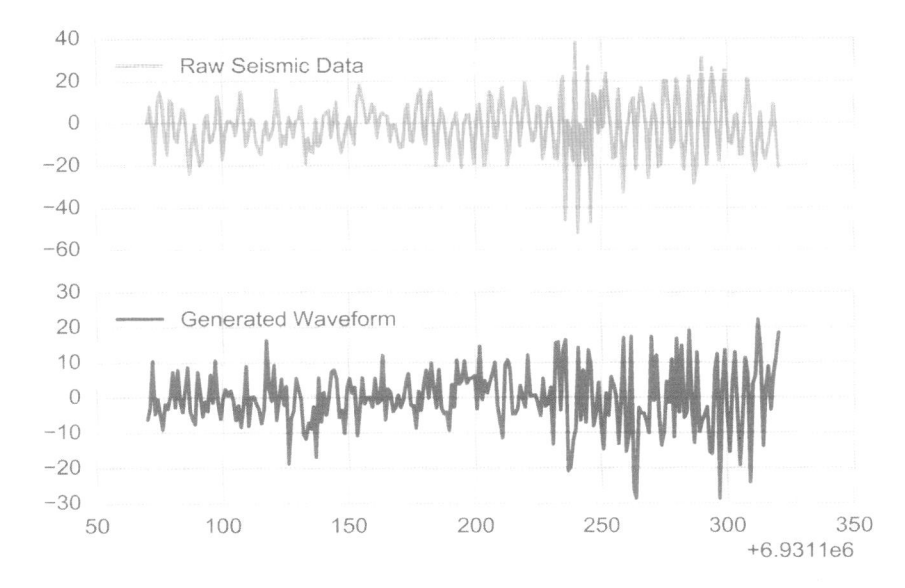

Fig. 9.2. Onset search window with samples drawn from $\mathcal{M}_1$ and $\mathcal{M}_2$.

posteriori distribution for the uncertainty of the onset time estimate. After fitting the models $\mathcal{M}_1$ and $\mathcal{M}_2$, as specified in Eqs. (1) and (2), we can now use them to randomly generate new time series from the models.

The top of Fig. 9.2 shows an original seismic waveform while the bottom shows data generated by random draws from $\mathcal{M}_1$ and $\mathcal{M}_2$, with the transition from $\mathcal{M}_1$ and $\mathcal{M}_2$ occurring at the identified onset point, k. Importantly, both the noise and signal models will be specific to the observed data for a particular station, sensor, and channel. Note that the noise process can also follow a functional form that captures dependence when appropriate. This would not cause any change to the algorithm itself, apart from swapping the likelihood of the white noise model for the dependence-capturing model in the estimation.

To estimate an *a posteriori* distribution of the arrival time estimate, we can now iterate. For each draw of the complete time series, we run the arrival time estimation algorithm detailed in Sec. 3 to get a new estimate, k', of the arrival time. As the two processes, noise and signal, become increasingly similar, the arrival time estimation algorithm will yield more varied estimates and produce heavier tailed distributions. As the two processes diverge, we will see less variation in our arrival time estimates giving a tighter distribution. Figure 9.3 shows a Kernel Density Estimate (KDE)

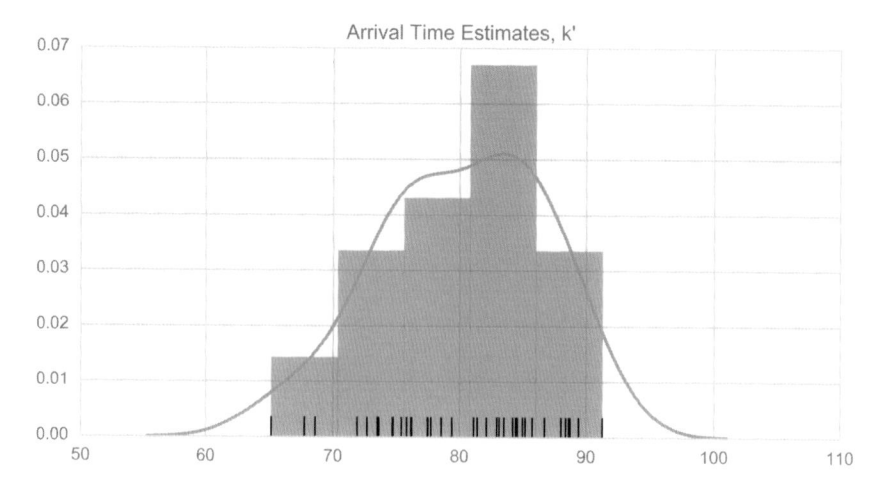

Fig. 9.3. Posterior density estimate of the arrival times, k'.

as an approximation of the complete arrival time posterior distribution for the data shown in Fig. 9.1.

5. Results and Discussion

To evaluate both the quality of our automated picks and their decision making value, we compared the output of our methods to picks made by human analysts using the data collected by Zeiler and Velasco (2009). Note that in the seismic domain, the complexity of the earth's subsurface and its impact on wave propagation makes providing ground truth for real events almost impossible. Synthetic waveform generation is also a challenge as it requires highly detailed models, extensive computation, and still may not accurately reflect real-world conditions.

Each waveform in the dataset had 5–18 analysts with varying degrees of seismic background knowledge pick the arrivals of seismic events. The original data included 26 examples. However, we discarded 11 because it was not clear how to set an appropriate bandpass filter to exclude extraneous frequencies, which has a large effect on the performance of the automated picks and associated uncertainty estimates. Future versions of this work will incorporate settings from domain experts. For most waveforms, the filter excluded frequencies outside of the 4–8 Hz range. We then created search windows centred around the first arrival, as determined by STA/LTA, with

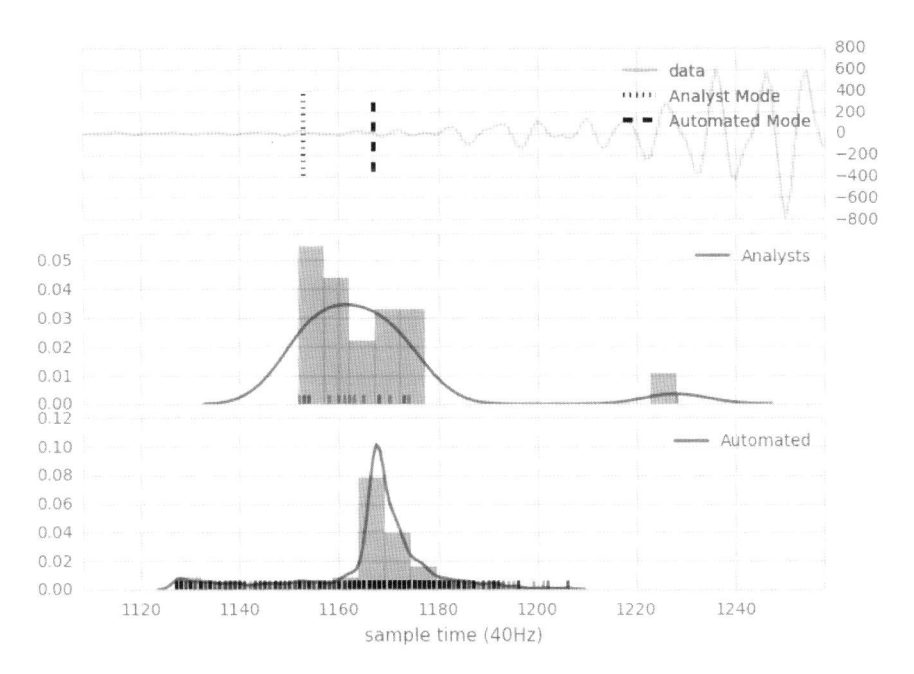

Using Data-Driven Uncertainty Quantification to Support Decision Making 149

Fig. 9.4. Sample filtered waveform (top) with the pick distributions from the analyst (middle) and automated picks (bottom). The rug marks at the bottom of the middle and lower plots indicate the specific pick times of individual analysts and individual runs of the Monte Carlo procedure respectively.

varying window sizes depending on variability in the data (more variability requires a larger window). The waveforms were sampled at 40 Hz.

We used AIC to simultaneously determine the order parameters, p and q, for the ARMA models and the optimal value of k. For each set, $\{p, q, k\}$, we used maximum likelihood to determine the model parameters $\sigma_n^2, \sigma_s^2, \theta$, and ϕ. The order parameters were universally small ($p, q \leq 4$).

Figure 9.4 shows the analysis results for one waveform. The top panel shows the filtered waveform along with indicators for the mode of the analysts' picks (dotted line) and the mode of the automated picks (dashed line). The middle panel shows the distribution created by 18 analyst picks, and the bottom subplot shows the distribution created by 1000 automated picks. The means of the analyst and automated pick distributions were exactly the same, at sample time 1166, while the modes are separated by approximately 0.5 seconds.

To understand the utility of the uncertainty distribution for decision making, consider the following points. First, the disagreement among the

18 analysts indicates that the initial change in the waveform is subtle in this case. Notice that the signal grows in strength gradually over the course of at least two seconds (80 samples). The true onset may therefore be buried in the noise. The mode of the automated pick distribution corresponds to the statistically most likely point at which the waveform changed. From a purely statistical standpoint, an analyst that moves the onset determination away from this point may be unjustified, though again, domain expertise can trump statistics. In this case, the mode falls close to the mean of the analyst picks, which is also the point that we would pick if we treated the set of analysts as an ensemble.

Note the minor mode in the automated distribution near sample time 1130. This small bump in probability indicates weak evidence that the onset may appear much earlier in the time series. Statistically, the true onset is unlikely to be near 1130, yet the result suggests that an analyst should examine the data in that area closely, to see if their domain expertise suggests a meaningful change in the data.

More generally, the distribution modes indicate points at which the statistical evidence suggests analysts should examine the data carefully. We view this as a potentially important guideline that focuses analyst attention and lead toward greater agreement and uniformity among analyst picks. As a simple example, consider whether the analyst that picked the onset on the far right, near 1225, might have reconsidered their selection if presented with such information. To be clear, the uncertainty distribution provides no definitive indication of the "correct" onset time. However, it does indicate the statistical likelihood of various possible solutions, and in this case, solutions near sample 1225 are very unlikely.

Other waveform examples, not shown here for space considerations, show similar results. Figure 9.5 shows a histogram of the difference between the means and modes of the analyst and automated pick distributions. The results suggest that the two tend to be similar, although in some cases they are very different. Interestingly, the modes tended to be more similar than the means, suggesting that the automated approach captured the consensus pick well, but showed different characteristics in variability (we have not run this test). Note that a positive value in the difference of modes (bottom panel) indicates that the analysts tended to pick the onset earlier than the automated system. We have not determined whether the difference is statistically or operationally significant. However, there tends to be more concern over picking onsets too late versus too early.

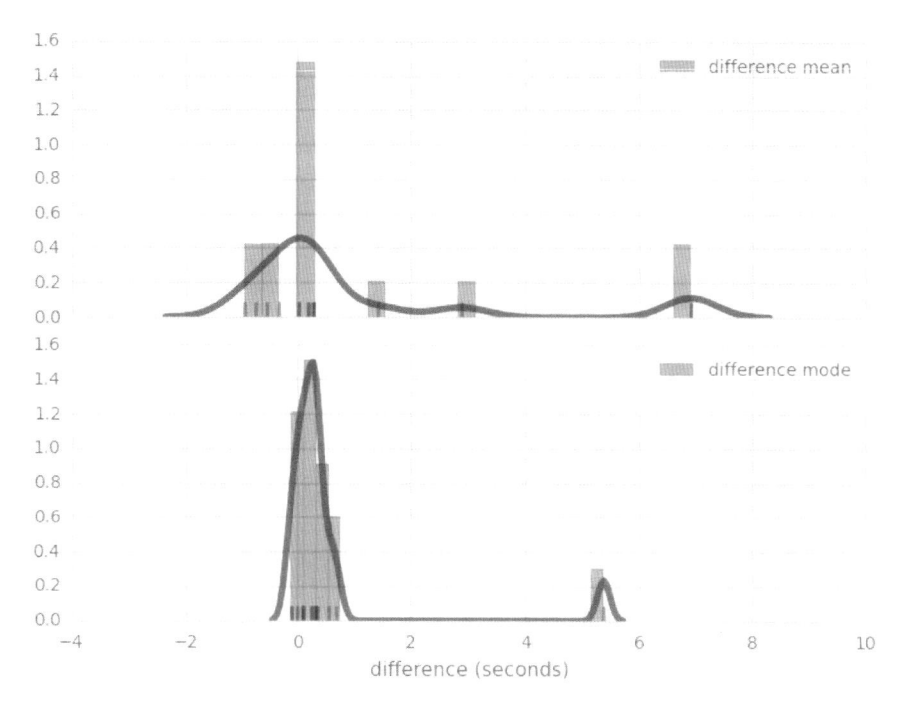

Using Data-Driven Uncertainty Quantification to Support Decision Making 151

Fig. 9.5. Histograms of the difference in the mean (top) and mode (bottom) pick times selected by the automated system and analysts.

A major component of future work focuses on extracting other sources of uncertainty. The work described above considers only uncertainty due to noise and measurement errors in the data. However, uncertainty also arises due to the form of the models for $\mathcal{M}_1$ and $\mathcal{M}_2$, such as the ARMA order parameters. Model sampling methods can quantify such uncertainties, but whether they will be substantially different from the data uncertainty is unclear. Likewise, the model fitting metrics, such as AIC, inject additional uncertainty, as different metrics will tend to select different models. In both cases, an open question concerns whether analysts gain anything in their decision making by viewing the different uncertainty sources separately versus together.

Many improvements are possible with respect to optimising and calibrating $\mathcal{M}_1$ and $\mathcal{M}_2$. While motivated by physical processes, the assumptions of white background noise and an auto-regressive signal both need to be validated. Noise could plausibly be of a functional form with a dependence structure and seismic signals may not be well-captured by an auto-regressive statistical model. Seismic signals can vary substantially depending on their source, such as ice sheets and man-made explosions, and measurement device, varying across station locations and equipment.

Automatic determination of ARMA order parameters raises questions related to model fit metrics, such as AIC, and whether they are capturing the correct change in the waveform, such as frequency versus amplitude. The question of model fit also influences the calculated uncertainty distribution. In the preceding discussion, we considered only uncertainty due to measurement errors, but model-form uncertainty, both due to the structure of the statistical models and the appropriateness of the fit criterion are equally important. As such, we need to capture these in our uncertainty estimates and get feedback from domain experts on whether any or all of the uncertainty sources provide useful input to the decision-making process.

6. Conclusion

Statistical analysis can play a much larger role in data-driven decision making than it currently does. We demonstrated how a rigorous analysis of the uncertainty in seismic arrival time estimates can provide valuable information to domain experts. The underlying lesson that uncertainty quantification can provide information not available from point estimates is general, and it applies to both other time series analysis problems, such as time series alignment and similarity, and to other data analysis problems, such as supervised and unsupervised classification. Future work should focus on providing uncertainty estimates for a variety of statistical and machine learning analyses, and using the results to improve associated decision making, whether automated or human.

Acknowledgements

The authors thank Chris Young and Cleat Zeiler for helpful discussion, and Michael Darling for technical support. Sandia National Laboratories is a multimission laboratory managed and operated by National Technology and Engineering Solutions of Sandia, LLC, a wholly owned subsidiary of Honeywell International, Inc., for the US Department of Energy's National Nuclear Security Administration under contract DE-NA0003525.

References

Akaike, H. (1974). A new look at statistical model identification, *IEEE Trans. Autom. Control* **19**, 6, pp. 716–723.

Kamigaichi, O. (1992). A fully automated method for determining the arrival times of seismic waves and its application to an on-line processing system, in *Proc. 34th GSE Session, GSE/RF/62*, G.S.E., Geneva, Italy.

O'Neel, S., Marshall, H., McNamara, D. and Pfeffer, W. T. (2007). Seismic detection and analysis of icequakes at Columbia Glacier, Alaska, *J. Geophys. Res.* **112**, F03S23, doi:10.1029/2006JF000595.

Ringdal, F. and Husebye, E. (1982). Application of arrays in the detection, location, and identification of seismic events, *Bull. Seismol. Soc. Amer.* **72**, 6B, pp. S201–S224.

Rodriguez, I. V. (2011). Automatic time-picking of microseismic data combining STA/LTA and the stationary discrete wavelet transform, in *CSPG CSEG CWLS Convention.* http://www.cspg.org/documents/Conventions/Archives/Annual/2011/078-Automatic_Time-picking_of_Microseismic_Data.pdf.

Stump, B. W. and Pearson, D. C. (1996). Regional observations of mining blasts by the GSETT-3 seismic monitoring system, Tech. Rep. LA-UR-96-3634, Los Alamos National Laboratories.

Trifunac, M. D. and Brady, A. G. (1975). A study on the duration of strong earthquake ground motion, *Bull. Seismol. Soc. Amer.* **65**, 3, pp. 581–626.

Velasco, A., Young, C. and Anderson, D. (2001). Uncertainty in phase arrival time picks for regional seismic events: An experimental design, Tech. Rep., US Department of Energy.

Werner-Allen, G., Johnson, J., Ruiz, M., Lees, J. and Welsh, M. (2005). Monitoring volcanic eruptions with a wireless sensor network, in *Proc. Second European Workshop on Wireless Sensor Networks*, pp. 108–120.

Zeiler, C. and Velasco, A. A. (2009). Seismogram picking error from analyst review (spear): Single-analyst and institution analysis, *Bull. Seismol. Soc. Amer.* **99**, 5, pp. 2759–2770.

Chapter 10

Blending Data Science and Statistics across Government

Owen Abbott[*,‡], Philip Lee[*], Matthew Upson[†], Matthew Gregory[†] and Dawn Duhaney[†]

[*]*Office for National Statistics, Government Buildings, Cardiff Road, Newport, Gwent, UK*

[†]*Government Digital Service, Kingsway, Holborn, London, UK*

[‡]*owen.abbott@ons.gov.uk*

Across government, departments are beginning to use data science techniques to realise the value of data and make more effective, data informed decisions. The Cabinet Office Government Digital Service, Office for National Statistics and Government Office for Science have collaborated to form the Government Data Science Partnership, to support departments to apply the potential of data science to their challenges. This paper outlines how data science and statistical practice are being blended across government. It explores this relationship via two case studies. The first case study is in the context of the production of official statistics, specifically the production of price indices. The second outlines how open source software is being used to reduce production time of official statistics whilst maintaining and improving the quality of the publications.

1. Introduction

Data science is growing as a discipline across government. In 2017, the Government Digital Service (GDS) published the Government Transformation Strategy (Cabinet Office, 2017c). This outlines core cross-government priorities for data; these include investing in data science capability and giving analysts who produce official statistics access to better and more diverse data. When government makes effective use of data, it makes better policy decisions and delivers improved services, tailored for users. For example, ensuring the right data is available when processing visa applications. The need to make better use of data was recognised by the Government Statistical Service in its 2014 "Better Statistics, Better Decisions" strategy (UK Statistics Authority, 2014). The strategy sets out an objective to innovate and exploit new methods and data sources in the production of official statistics, noting that it will blend statistical methods with data science to do so. This was reinforced by the Bean review of economic statistics (Bean, 2016) which called for more efforts in this area and the creation of a data science hub, resulting in the establishment of the Office for National Statistics (ONS) Data Science Campus launched in spring 2017. This paper showcases how these high level strategic aims are resulting in the blending of data science and statistical practice right across government. Firstly, we outline how the Government Data Science Partnership (GDSP) is driving forward cross-government initiatives to build capability. Secondly, we present two case studies which demonstrate how data science techniques and tools are being explored and blended with established statistical methodology. The first case study is in the context of the production of official statistics, specifically price indices. The second case study shows how we can more effectively produce statistics using open source software.

2. The Government Data Science Partnership

The Government Data Science Partnership (GDSP) supports departments in applying the potential of data science to their challenges. Its core focus has been on building data science capability and establishing a cross-government practitioner community. The Partnership has established the Data Science Accelerator (Cabinet Office, 2017a), a practical training program which gives analysts from across the public sector the opportunity to develop their data science skills by delivering a project of real business value. This training has been scaled across the UK to five sites; London, Newport, Bristol, Sheffield and Newcastle. Around 40 analysts have graduated. The GDSP has also established a new career path (Cabinet Office, 2017b) and recruitment process for data scientists in government after identifying a need to help departments and agencies recruit data scientists in a consistent way. There is currently a community of over 600 data scientists and analysts in government. GDSP is supporting the active Community of Interest through meetings and establishing a social media channel for the exchange of information and best practice. The GDSP hosted the first Government Data Science Conference on April 24th, 2017, bringing together over 250 data scientists, analysts and policymakers. The conference featured talks with departments sharing projects that use data science techniques to tackle policy problems. GDSP is now looking forward to enabling a wider data science network and bringing together and supporting training and development opportunities. Sections 3 and 4 outline the sorts of projects that the GDSP is encouraging and supporting in the statistical domain.

3. Case Study 1 — Statistical Production: Prices

ONS is researching alternative data sources for its statistical outputs. This case study outlines how data science techniques for collecting and processing the data can be used to supplement statistical outputs on prices. All work presented is in development and does not currently form part of the production of any official statistics.

3.1. *Background*

The Consumer Prices Index including owner occupiers housing costs (CPIH) (Office for National Statistics, 2016a) is the most comprehensive measure of inflation in the UK. The CPIH uses a fixed basket of approximately 700 representative goods and services (hereafter referred to as basket items). The data underpinning CPIH have always been gathered through sample surveys. Price quotes for the basket items are gathered on a specific day once each month, with much of the data coming from manual field collection. In the digital age, there are many alternative data sources which might be appropriate for the production of consumer price indices. Examples include point-of-sale transaction data (scanner data) and online data such as supermarket websites. Scanner data is arguably the superior source as it combines volume and price information, enabling a clearer view of the impact of changing prices on household expenditure. Unfortunately scanner data is also hard to acquire (Office for National Statistics, 2014). Whilst efforts continue to obtain scanner data, ONS has been exploring the collection of web scraped price data (Office for National Statistics, 2016b,c). Table 10.1 compares traditional and web scraped data collection methods for producing price indices to show that alternative data sources bring different challenges.

Table 10.1. Properties of different data sources (Office for National Statistics, 2016c).

Property	Traditional collection	Web scraped
Location	Multiple locations across the country from multiple retailers (small to large)	Prices from online retailers, generally only medium to large retailers
Timing	Prices collected around a single day of the month (index day)	Prices collected daily
Sample	Price collectors select representative products	Prices scraped for all products
Time series	Match products over time	High product churn
Timeliness	Publication takes place about a month after data collection	Price indices can in principal be calculated soon after collection

3.2. Project outline and ethical consideration

Beginning in 2014 this project has collected six million prices for 33 CPIH basket items from three major UK supermarket websites to produce experimental price indices. New ways of collecting data from alternative sources bring new challenges. In this case, web scraping brings with it legal and ethical considerations. Web site terms and conditions were obeyed for each of the supermarkets scraped. Practical measures were also taken to maintain a high ethical standard in the project, including avoiding scraping during peak hours and naming ONS as the requestor. Once raw data is collected, the scraped data is classified, passed through an anomaly detection process and used to calculate experimental indices. These are different to the standard processes that would be undertaken on survey data. Data science techniques which are highly automated were adopted as the data is large, could have many measurement errors and is collected daily. The steps are outlined below.

3.3. Classification of products

In the CPIH representative basket items are selected for categories of the international Classification of Individual Consumption according to Purpose (COICOP). In traditional collection products matching basket items are manually selected, for this project a data science solution was developed. For each basket item there are many supermarket products. For example there are many brands of 800 g loaves of white sliced bread. For each of the 33 scraped basket items, specific areas of the supermarket product hierarchy were manually identified as close matches. Supervised machine learning

Table 10.2. Example of manual verification data from price collectors.

CPI Basket Item	Item description	Manual verification
Apples, dessert, per kg	Pink Lady Apples 4s	Correct
Apples, dessert, per kg	Apple, Kiwi & Strawberry 160 g	Incorrect
Apples, dessert, per kg	Braeburn Apple 4 Pack 590 G	Correct

based on product names was used to remove any products which do not match the target basket item. The training data was manually verified by experienced price collectors, as shown in Table 10.2. A number of different machine learning models were evaluated, the most successful being a support vector machine (SVM) with radial basis function. The explanatory variables are a set of 1- and 2-word extracts from the product names. There is one model for each item, each using products which come from the matching area of the supermarket product hierarchy.

The model is not as accurate as a human price collector, but achieved a good balance between precision and recall. This means the machine learning model can make fairly robust predictions, important for large volumes of product items.

There are limitations in this classification process. For example, it requires manual intervention to add new basket items or to adapt to changes in the supermarket categorisation. New products, described with words not present during training, can cause classification errors. It is unknown whether retraining the model would be needed over a longer time frame or whether incremental corrections to the model would suffice to maintain performance. This is one of the drawbacks of using such an approach when the underlying data can change over time.

3.4. Anomaly detection

Data scraped from online sources will not always be reliable, contrasting with a carefully controlled survey data collection. To combat the potential for bias from either errors in the underlying source data or misclassifications, an anomaly detection algorithm is applied (Mayhew and Clews, 2016). This is a typical feature of alternative data sources, leading to a need to develop new approaches to deal with these data quality issues when the data is collected frequently (daily in this case). The anomaly detection algorithm handles situations such as the price for a product changing in an uncharacteristic manner. The approach taken in this case uses an unsupervised clustering algorithm, namely Density-Based Spatial Clustering of Applications with Noise (DBSCAN) (Ester et al., 1996). This makes very few assumptions about the distribution of the data. The results of the DBSCAN algorithm are used to validate the output of the classifiers in the previous stage. The approach taken depends on reliable data at the beginning of the time series, as the clusters discovered in the initial data are used for the whole time period. The anomaly detection method uses price data whereas the classification algorithm, described above, uses product description. This enables the filtering out of false positives which are sufficiently different to other valid data points.

3.5. *Clustering large datasets into price indices (CLIP)*

There are many ways that web scraped data could be compiled to form a price index. Traditional statistical methods can be applied, but the nature of the data in this case makes them extremely unstable over time due to product churn. A new index method, called CLIP (Office for National Statistics, 2016c), was developed. The approach aims to include products which are only temporarily or periodically available while also making use of all available clean data. It also attempts to satisfy a crucial statistical assumption that the indices calculated at the lowest level of aggregation are only based on groups of similar products. The CLIP methodology tracks the price of clusters of similar products rather than the individual products themselves. As products leave and rejoin the dataset (product churn) they also leave and rejoin the cluster, thus allowing the use of all available data. Experimental indices using this method have been published to seek user feedback. Work is on-going to understand the differences between online data and that collected through the survey, as there are some products and retailers that do not feature in online data. Methods for combining price data from different sources are being considered.

4. Case Study 2 — Reproducible Analytical Pipelines

Reproducibility is as important for government as it is for academia. A key function of Government statisticians is to produce and publish official statistics. Often these statistics have a direct impact on government policy, so it is imperative that they are accurate, timely, and importantly: reproducible.

All the steps required to produce a statistic should be reproducible, but manual processes (common in many publications) make this challenging. Open source tools and techniques used by software engineers and data scientists can greatly improve the speed and accuracy with which official statistics can be produced, whilst ensuring their reproducibility. This case study outlines the journey towards reproducibility that many departments are embarking upon, and explores how these techniques have been implemented using an open, transparent approach for statistics production for the first time in the UK Government.

4.1. Background

The production of official statistics typically involves extraction of data from a datastore, and manipulation in proprietary statistical or spreadsheet software. Formatted tables are often subsequently copied and pasted into a word processor, before being converted to PDF format, and finally published to GOV.UK. Statistical publications are usually produced by several people, so this process can happen many times in parallel. A key element in this process is quality assurance (QA). Each publication is meticulously checked to ensure the accuracy of the statistics being produced. This may occur multiple times throughout the production process or at the end, prior to publication. Traditionally, QA has been a manual process which can take up a significant portion of the overall production time.

4.2. Project outline

In 2016 GDS collaborated with a team in the Department for Culture, Media, and Sport (DCMS) who are responsible for the production of the Economic Estimates for DCMS Sectors Statistical First Release (SFR) (Department for Culture, Media and Sport, 2016). Currently this publication is produced with a mix of manual and semi-manual processes. The aim was to speed up production of the SFR, whilst maintaining the high standard of the publication and ensuring effective QA. By using open source tools, and a range of techniques from fields such as reproducible research and software engineering, part of the statistical release was recreated so that it can be easily reproduced, tested and audited. This was named a Reproducible Analytical Pipeline. The following outlines some of the key components.

4.2.1. Software tools and version control

Open source languages such as Python[a] and R[b] are increasing in popularity across government. One advantage of using these tools is the ability to reduce the number of manual data transfers from one program (or format) into another. This is in line with the principle of reproducibility, as the entire process can be represented as a single step in code, greatly reducing the likelihood of manual transcription errors. Version control tools like GitHub helps formalise quality assurance (QA) in an auditable way. GitHub[c] can be configured to require a code review by another person before the update to the code is accepted into the main workstream.

4.2.2. Writing generic functions and associated tests

Government analysts and statisticians rarely have a computer science background, and so the tendency is to write long scripts. To avoid 'copy and paste', and manual transcription errors, workflows should be composed of generic functions rather than bespoke scripts. For the DCMS publication individual functions were produced to extract, clean and produce final output tables and figures. As each function or group of functions (unit) is generic, it can be tested with a generic example, to ensure the unit of code works as expected. For identified cases where units do not perform as expected, these can be codified into new tests and used to drive work to fix the problem until the test passes.

4.2.3. Packaging code

Once code is written into generic functions with generic tests, the logical next step is to start to package them up along with accompanying documentation, and even data. Combined with version control, this allows for the creation of versions which might, for instance relate to publication years. Creating packages also aids knowledge transfer, as the logic and documentation can easily be shared across a large organisation, helping new team members to be brought up to speed quickly. A core problem that arises from working with open source software is a dependency on a series of open source packages which may be written by different people and updated

---

[a] https://en.wikipedia.org/wiki/Python_(programming_language)
[b] https://www.r-project.org/about.html
[c] https://github.com/

at different times. This may impede on the reproducibility of the process. Tools such as packrat,[d] which creates a cache of all the R packages used in the project which is then version controlled, avoids this problem.

4.2.4. *Automated testing*

Free online services such as Travis CI[e] can automatically test that a package of code builds correctly, and the unit tests are passed successfully. These tools integrate with services like GitHub, providing an easy way to view when a code update has failed one of the tests. It is also possible to run tests on the data. This can be useful as data for these publications are often received from a third party, and it is necessary to check for consistency with previous years. For example in the DCMS work a check for outliers was implemented by looking at the most recent values in comparison to values from previous years. These kinds of automated tests are repeated every time the data are loaded, reducing the burden of QA, and the scope for human error, freeing up statistician time for identifying more subtle data quality issues which might otherwise go unnoticed.

4.2.5. *Producing the publication*

There are tools to help preparation of the final publication. With DCMS Rmarkdown[f] was used to incorporate the R code into the same document as the text of the publication, so that all operations are contained in a single file, to ensure tables or figures are synchronised with the latest version of the text. This allows for the production of templates with boilerplate text like: this measure increased by $X\%$, where X is automatically populated with the correct value when the code runs.

4.3. *Getting the balance right*

The aim of this project was to achieve a high level of automation to demonstrate what is possible using the sorts of tools that data scientists are using. Whilst incredibly powerful, these approaches are not a panacea for all of the difficulties of statistics production. However, implementing even a few of these techniques can drive benefits in auditability, speed, quality, and

---

[d] https://rstudio.github.io/packrat/
[e] https://travis-ci.org/
[f] https://rmarkdown.rstudio.com/

knowledge transfer. There is a balance to be struck between ease of maintenance and the level of automation: this is likely to differ for every publication or team.

5. Discussion

Data science is growing and developing as a discipline across government. The role of GDSP is to support and encourage this growth and ensure that government is taking the opportunity to harness data science methods. Key to this has been the Accelerator Programme and the development of a strong community network. The two case studies show how data science techniques are being explored and blended with established statistical methodology to make better use of data and generate better outcomes. The second case study shows how some of these techniques can be used to streamline and reduce manual efforts in ensuring that statistical outputs are robust and presented clearly, as well as having reproducibility and a strong audit trail. This will help statistical production to become more efficient, freeing resource to focus on interpretation and developing better statistics rather than turning the handle. However, existing statistical methodologies will not be superseded by data science. Whilst there are many opportunities to make use of data science within statistical production, the future is likely to be a blend of the best of both. The prices example demonstrates this. Not all goods and services are sold online, and therefore a combination of the traditional survey methods and large scale online collection is likely to be the outcome. The challenge is to ensure that there are robust methods for blending, but also to recognise and manage expectations.

References

Bean, C. (2016). Independent review of UK economic statistics, https://www.gov.uk/government/publications/independent-review-of-uk-economic-statistics-final-report.

Cabinet Office (2017a). Data science accelerator now open for applications, https://data.blog.gov.uk/2017/05/05/data-science-accelerator-now-open-for-applications.

Cabinet Office (2017b). Data scientist: Role description, https://www.gov.uk/government/publications/data-scientist-role-description/data-scientist-role-description.

Cabinet Office (2017c). Government transformation strategy, https://www.gov.uk/government/publications/government-transformation-strategy-2017-to-2020.

Department for Culture, Media and Sport (2016). DCMS sectors economic estimates, https://www.gov.uk/government/statistics/dcms-sectors-economic-estimates-2016.

Ester, M., Kriegel, H.-P., Sander, J. and Xu, X. (1996). A density-based algorithm for discovering clusters in large spatial databases with noise, in *Proc. Second Int. Conf. Knowledge Discovery and Data Mining*, Vol. 96, pp. 226–231.

Mayhew, M. and Clews, G. (2016). Using machine learning techniques to clean web scraped price data via cluster analysis, *Survey Methodology Bull.* **75**, pp. 24–41.

Office for National Statistics (2014). Initial report on experiences with scanner data in ONS, http://www.ons.gov.uk/ons/rel/cpi/consumer-price-indices/initial-report-on-experiences-with-scanner-data-in-ons/index.html.

Office for National Statistics (2016a). CPIH compendium, https://www.ons.gov.uk/economy/inflationandpriceindices/articles/cpihcompendium/2016-10-13.

Office for National Statistics (2016b). Research indices using web scraped price data, https://www.ons.gov.uk/releases/researchindicesusingwebscrapedpricedatamay2016update.

Office for National Statistics (2016c). Research indices using web scraped price data: clustering large datasets into price indices (CLIP), https://www.ons.gov.uk/economy/inflationandpriceindices/articles/researchindicesusingwebscrapedpricedata/clusteringlargedatasetsintopriceindicesclip.

UK Statistics Authority (2014). Better statistics, better decisions, https://gss.civilservice.gov.uk/about/gss-strategy-better-statistics-better-decisions/.

Chapter 11

Dynamic Factor Modelling with Spatially Multi-scale Structures for Spatio-temporal Data

Takamitsu Araki* and Shotaro Akaho

Human Informatics Research Institute,
National Institute of Advanced Industrial Science and Technology,
Central 2, 1-1-1 Umezono, Tsukuba, Ibaraki 305-8568, Japan
*tk-araki@aist.go.jp

In spatio-temporal data analysis, dimension reduction is necessary to extract intrinsic structures. To reduce the dimension of spatio-temporal data, the spatially continuous dynamic factor model (SCDFM), a dynamic factor model for the spatio-temporal data, decomposes the data into a small number of spatial and temporal variations, where the spatial variation is represented by the factor loading (FL) functions. The FL functions estimated by maximum likelihood or maximum L_2 penalised likelihood can capture spatially global structures but cannot capture spatially local structures. We propose a method for estimating the parameters of the SCDFM using the maximum adaptive lasso (weighted L_1) penalised likelihood method. The method rejects redundant basis functions due to an adaptive lasso penalty, and thus the method provides the FL functions having spatially multi-scale structures, spatially global and localised structures. For the sparse estimation, we introduce the EM algorithm with coordinate descent that enables us to maximise the adaptive lasso penalised log-likelihood stably. Applications to ozone concentration data show that the proposed modelling procedure can extract not only the spatially global structures but also the spatially local structures, which the existing procedures cannot extract.

1. Introduction

In many scientific and industrial fields, spatio-temporal data, which depend on time and space, are often observed. The amount of spatio-temporal data are increasing as measurement devices continue to be developed, thereby increasing the importance of statistical modelling of the spatio-temporal data (Cressie and Wikle, 2011; Blangiardo and Cameletti, 2015). In spatio-temporal data analysis, when the time-series data at all observation sites are directly modelled by multivariate time series models such as the vector autoregression moving average model (Reinsel, 2003), the estimated models are complicated and difficult to interpret. Thus, dimension reduction for the spatio-temporal data is necessary to extract their inherent and essential structures.

To reduce dimension of the spatio-temporal data, a dynamic factor model (Geweke, 1977; Stock and Watson, 2011) has been extended to the spatial dynamic factor model (SDFM) that can capture spatial structures (Lopes et al., 2008; Takamitsu and Shotaro, 2017), and it has been applied in Strickland et al. (2011); Ippoliti et al. (2012). The SDFM that represents the spatial variations by vectors was further extended to the spatially continuous dynamic factor model (SCDFM; (Takamitsu and Shotaro, 2017)) that represents the spatial variations by continuous functions in order to allow it to apply more various kinds of data. The SCDFM is a general model that encompasses the SDFM as a special case. The SCDFM reduces the dimension of the spatio-temporal data by estimating a small number of spatial and temporal variations of the data. The spatial variations are represented by a few spatially smooth functions constructed by a basis expansion, in the form of factor loading (FL) functions. The temporal variation is represented by autoregressive processes of the factors, called factor processes, which are the stochastic processes corresponding to the FL functions. The estimated FL functions and factor processes reveal the spatial, temporal and spatio-temporal structures of the data.

The SCDFM has been estimated by the maximum penalised likelihood (MPL) method with an L_2 penalty or maximum likelihood (ML) method. The methods yield only the spatially global FL functions that take significant values over almost the entire observation region. Therefore, the SCDFM extracts only spatially global structures and temporal variation over the global regions, and cannot extract spatially local structures and temporal variation in local regions.

The important spatially local structures have been extracted through the dimension reduction of the data in scientific and industrial areas such as neuroscience, computer vision, meteorology and climatology. In computer vision, the sparse principal component analysis (sparse PCA; (Chennubhotla and Jepson, 2001; Zass and Shashua, 2007)) extracted the global and local structures from an image set, e.g. in human face images, from which the global and local structures indicate an entire face such as facial contours and parts of a face such as eyes, respectively. In meteorology and climatology, the rotated PCA (Horel, 1981; Dommenget and Latif, 2002) was applied to spatio-temporal data of sea level pressures and sea surface temperatures, and physically-meaningful local structures were extracted. The rotated PCA does not consider time dependency of data, and hardly captures the global structures.

We propose a sparse estimation method for the SCDFM that provides the spatially multi-scale FL functions comprising of global and localised FL functions. The method estimates the parameters in the SCDFM by the MPL method with an adaptive lasso (weighted L_1) penalty on the coefficient vectors in the FL functions (Tibshirani, 1996; Zou, 2006). The penalty rejects redundant basis functions and then leads us to the localised FL functions whose values are close to 0 over large areas and are significant over other areas, as well as the global FL functions. We derive an Expectation-Maximisation (EM) algorithm (Dempster et al., 1977) with coordinate descent (Friedman et al., 2007) that maximises the adaptive lasso penalised log-likelihood stably. Note that the proposed modelling procedure can also be directly applied to the SDFM. The maximum L_2 penalised likelihood estimation for the SCDFM and the proposed modelling procedure are applied to ozone concentration data. The applications show that the proposed method estimates the multi-scale FL functions which capture the spatially global and local structures and that the maximum L_2 penalised likelihood estimation does not provide such FL functions.

The rest of the paper is organised as follows. The SCDFM is described in Section 2. In Section 3, the MPL method with the adaptive lasso penalty for the SCDFM is introduced, and we derive the EM algorithm with coordinate descent for maximising the adaptive lasso penalised likelihood. In Section 4, the performance of our modelling procedure is evaluated through applications to ozone concentration data. Finally, we present conclusions in Section 5.

2. Spatially Continuous Dynamic Factor Modelling

The SCDFM consists of an observation model and a system model (Takamitsu and Shotaro, 2017). The observation model describes a relationship between the observation data and the factors via the FL functions. The system model describes the temporal evolution of the factors that represent temporal structures of the data.

Suppose that data $\mathbf{y}_t = (y_{1,t}, \ldots, y_{N_t,t})'$ are observed in $\mathbf{s}_t = (\mathbf{s}_{1,t}, \ldots, \mathbf{s}_{N_t,t})$ for each time $t = 1, \ldots, T$, where $\mathbf{s}_{it} \in \mathbf{S}$ and the observation sites $\mathbf{s}_t$ and its number N_t vary with time, e.g., the data containing missing values. The FL functions are constructed by the basis expansion as

$$\lambda_j(\mathbf{s}) = \sum_{i=1}^m b_i(\mathbf{s})\alpha_{ij} = \mathbf{b}(\mathbf{s})'\boldsymbol{\alpha}_j, \quad \mathbf{s} \in \mathbf{S}, \quad j = 1, \ldots, d,$$

where $\mathbf{b}(\mathbf{s}) = (b_1(\mathbf{s}), \ldots, b_m(\mathbf{s}))'$ is a vector of known spatially local basis functions, and $\boldsymbol{\alpha}_j = (\alpha_{1j}, \ldots, \alpha_{mj})'$ is a coefficient vector for the jth FL function. Then the observation model is expressed as

$$y_{it} = \boldsymbol{\lambda}(\mathbf{s}_{it})'\mathbf{f}_t + \epsilon_{it} = \mathbf{b}(\mathbf{s}_{it})'\mathbf{A}\mathbf{f}_t + \epsilon_{it}, \quad i = 1, \ldots, N_t, \quad (1)$$

where $\mathbf{f}_t = (f_{1t}, \ldots, f_{dt})'$ is a vector of factors, $\boldsymbol{\lambda}(\mathbf{s}) = (\lambda_1(\mathbf{s}), \ldots, \lambda_d(\mathbf{s}))'$, and $\mathbf{A} = (\boldsymbol{\alpha}_1, \ldots, \boldsymbol{\alpha}_d)$. A vectorised form of the observation model is

$$\mathbf{y}_t = \boldsymbol{\Lambda}(\mathbf{s}_t)\mathbf{f}_t + \boldsymbol{\epsilon}_t$$
$$\boldsymbol{\epsilon}_t \sim N(\mathbf{0}, \sigma_\epsilon^2 \mathbf{D}_{N_t}),$$
$$= \mathbf{B}_t \mathbf{A} \mathbf{f}_t + \boldsymbol{\epsilon}_t, \quad (2)$$

where $\boldsymbol{\Lambda}(\mathbf{s}_t) = (\boldsymbol{\lambda}(\mathbf{s}_{1t}), \ldots, \boldsymbol{\lambda}(\mathbf{s}_{N_t,t}))'$, $\mathbf{B}_t = (\mathbf{b}(\mathbf{s}_{1t}), \ldots, \mathbf{b}(\mathbf{s}_{N_t,t}))'$, $\boldsymbol{\epsilon}_t = (\epsilon_{1t}, \ldots, \epsilon_{N_t,t})'$, and $\mathbf{D}_{N_t}$ is a known N_t order positive definite matrix.

The system model that represents the time evolution of the factors is

$$\mathbf{f}_t = \boldsymbol{\Gamma}\mathbf{f}_{t-1} + \boldsymbol{\omega}_t, \quad \boldsymbol{\omega}_t \sim N(\mathbf{0}, \boldsymbol{\Sigma}_\omega), \quad (3)$$

where $\boldsymbol{\Gamma} = \mathrm{diag}(\boldsymbol{\gamma})$, $\boldsymbol{\gamma} = (\gamma_1, \ldots, \gamma_d)'$, and $\boldsymbol{\Sigma}_\omega$ is a positive diagonal matrix.

When the observation locations are invariant, that is, $\mathbf{s}_t = (\mathbf{s}_1, \ldots, \mathbf{s}_N)$, and $b_i(\mathbf{s}) = \mathbf{1}_{\{\mathbf{s}_i\}}(\mathbf{s})$, where $\mathbf{1}_{\{\cdot\}}(\mathbf{s})$ is an indicator function, we have $\mathbf{B}_t = I_N$ in (2), i.e., the observation model of the SCDFM is $\mathbf{y}_t = \mathbf{A}\mathbf{f}_t + \boldsymbol{\epsilon}_t$. Thus, the SCDFM is the same model as the SDFM (Lopes et al., 2008), and the proposed method for the SCDFM is directly applicable to the SDFM.

The SCDFM has a scaling indeterminacy in the coefficient vectors of the FL functions, so that we impose a constraint on $\boldsymbol{\Sigma}_\omega$, $\boldsymbol{\Sigma}_\omega = cI_d$, where c is a constant. After the estimation, the scales of the FL functions are adjusted to the same value in order to facilitate model interpretation. Accordingly the system noise variances $\boldsymbol{\Sigma}_\omega$ and covariances and means of $\mathbf{f}_0$ are also adjusted to maintain the same likelihood value. Note that the SCDFM does not have a rotational indeterminacy that lies in a traditional factor analysis model, because the factors in the SCDFM independently evolve according to different first autoregressive models (3).

The SCDFM has been estimated by the ML method, MPL method with the L_2 penalty (Takamitsu and Shotaro, 2017) and the SDFM has been estimated by the Bayes method with smooth prior distributions (Lopes et al., 2008, 2011). These existing estimation methods yield only the global FL functions, and thus the local structures and dynamical components on the local regions are not obtained. In order to estimate the multi-scale FL functions containing the global and localised FL functions, we introduce the MPL method with the adaptive lasso penalty for **A**.

3. Adaptive Lasso Estimation for Spatially Multi-scale Model

We estimate the parameters of the SCDFM $\boldsymbol{\theta} = (\mathbf{A}, \boldsymbol{\gamma}, \sigma_\epsilon^2)$ using the MPL method with the adaptive lasso penalty for **A**. To obtain the global and localised FL functions, we have to estimate dense and sparse coefficient vectors of the basis functions in the FL functions. The lasso estimation, an estimation with an L_1 penalty, is one of the most popular techniques for sparse estimation (Tibshirani, 1996), but the L_1 penalty tends to cause dense coefficient vectors for all FL functions value as reported in other models (Zou, 2006; Zhang et al., 2010). In order to enhance sparsity, we employ the adaptive lasso penalty (Zou, 2006), the weighted L_1 penalty.

For the observation data $\mathbf{y}_{1:T} = (\mathbf{y}_1, \ldots, \mathbf{y}_T)$, the penalised log-likelihood function with the adaptive lasso penalty for the SCDFM is expressed as

$$l_{\rho_\alpha}(\boldsymbol{\theta}) = \frac{1}{T} \log p(\mathbf{y}_{1:T}|\boldsymbol{\theta}) - \rho_\alpha \sum_{j=1}^{d} \sum_{i=1}^{m} \frac{|\alpha_{ij}|}{|\bar{\alpha}_{ij}|^\nu}, \qquad (4)$$

where p denotes a probability density function, $\nu > 0$, $\rho_\alpha (> 0)$ is a regularisation parameter that controls the sparsity of the basis functions in the estimated FL functions, and $\bar{\alpha}_{ij}$ is an $\sqrt{n}$-consistent estimator. We maximise the penalised log-likelihood function using the EM algorithm.

3.1. *Estimation algorithm*

Since the adaptive lasso penalty term in the penalised log-likelihood function is nondifferentiable, its maximisation is difficult. For example, gradient-based optimum algorithms such as a quasi-Newton method cannot be applied to maximise the function. In the lasso estimation of linear regression model, the coordinate descent algorithm *coordinate descent algorithm* updates the parameters quite fast using simple explicit formulae (Friedman et al., 2007, 2010). Since the log-likelihood of the linear regression model is a quadratic function of the parameters, the updates of the coordinate descent algorithm are given by explicit expressions.

The EM algorithm is suitable for the SCDFM because the update formulae of the EM algorithm are explicit and the algorithm is stable and not sensitive to an initial value. In the MPL estimation with the adaptive lasso penalty of the SCDFM, the EM algorithm maximises a Q-function of the SCDFM with the penalty term iteratively to maximise the penalised log-likelihood function. The Q-function with respect to $\boldsymbol{\alpha}_j$ is nondifferentiable, but the Q-function except for the penalty term with respect to $\boldsymbol{\alpha}_j$ is also the quadratic function. Thus, the Q-function with respect to $\boldsymbol{\alpha}_j$ can be maximised via the explicit update of $\boldsymbol{\alpha}_j$ by applying the coordinate descent algorithm.

The Q-function at iteration n, $Q_{\rho_\alpha}(\boldsymbol{\theta}|\boldsymbol{\theta}^{(n-1)})$, is defined by $\frac{1}{T}E\,[\log p(\mathbf{y}_{1:T},\mathbf{f}_{0:T},\boldsymbol{\theta})|\mathbf{y}_{1:T},\boldsymbol{\theta}^{(n-1)}] - \rho_\alpha \sum_{j=1}^{d}\sum_{i=1}^{m}\frac{|\alpha_{ij}|}{|\tilde{\alpha}_{ij}|^\nu}$, where $E[\cdot|\mathbf{y}_{1:T},\boldsymbol{\theta}^{(n-1)}]$ denotes a conditional expectation with respect to $\mathbf{f}_{0:T}$ given $\mathbf{y}_{1:T}$ with the parameters $\boldsymbol{\theta}^{(n-1)}$.

The Q-function is maximised with respect to $\mathbf{A}$ by applying the coordinate descent algorithm. In the coordinate descent algorithm, the function is maximised with respect to every element of $\mathbf{A}$ and the maximisations are expressed by the explicit updates as follows:

$$\alpha_{ij}^{(n)} = \arg\min_{\alpha_{ij}}\left\{\frac{1}{2}(\alpha_{ij} - \tilde{\alpha}_{ij}^{(n-1)})^2 + \tilde{\rho}_\alpha^{(n-1)}|\alpha_{ij}|\right\}$$
$$= \mathrm{sgn}(\tilde{\alpha}_{ij}^{(n-1)})(\tilde{\alpha}_{ij}^{(n-1)} - \tilde{\rho}_\alpha^{(n-1)})_+, \tag{5}$$

where

$$\tilde{\alpha}_{ij}^{(n-1)} = \frac{r_i^{(n-1)} - (\boldsymbol{\alpha}_j^{(n-1)})'_{-i}(\mathbf{u}_i^{(n-1)})_{-i}}{u_{ii}^{(n-1)}},$$

$$\tilde{\rho}_\alpha^{(n-1)} = \frac{\rho_\alpha}{u_{ii}^{(n-1)}|\tilde{\alpha}_{ij}|^\nu},$$

where $r_i^{(n-1)}$ is the ith element of $\mathbf{r}^{(n-1)}$, $\mathbf{u}_i^{(n-1)}$ is the ith column of $\mathbf{U}^{(n-1)}$, $u_{ki}^{(n-1)}$ is the kth element of $\mathbf{u}_i^{(n-1)}$, $(\boldsymbol{\alpha}_j^{(n-1)})_{-i} = (\alpha_{1j}^{(n)},\ldots,\alpha_{i-1,j}^{(n)},\alpha_{i+1,j}^{(n-1)},\ldots,\alpha_{mj}^{(n-1)})'$, and $(\mathbf{u}_i^{(n-1)})_{-j}$ denotes the vector of all elements of $\mathbf{u}_i^{(n-1)}$ except $u_{ji}^{(n-1)}$, where

$$\mathbf{U}^{(n-1)} = \frac{1}{T\sigma_\epsilon^{2(n-1)}} \sum_{t=1}^{T} \langle f_{jt}^2 \rangle^{(n-1)} \mathbf{B}_t' \mathbf{D}_{N_t}^{-1} \mathbf{B}_t,$$

$$\mathbf{r}^{(n-1)} = \frac{1}{T\sigma_\epsilon^{2(n-1)}} \sum_{t=1}^{T} \mathbf{B}_t' \mathbf{D}_{N_t}^{-1} (\langle f_{jt} \rangle^{(n-1)} \mathbf{y}_t - \mathbf{B}_t \mathbf{A}_{-j}^{(n-1)} \langle f_{jt}(\mathbf{f}_t)_{-j} \rangle^{(n-1)}),$$

where $\mathbf{A}_{-j}^{(n-1)} = (\boldsymbol{\alpha}_1^{(n)}, \ldots, \boldsymbol{\alpha}_{j-1}^{(n)}, \boldsymbol{\alpha}_{j+1}^{(n-1)}, \ldots, \boldsymbol{\alpha}_d^{(n-1)})$, and $\langle \cdot \rangle^{(n-1)} = E[\cdot | \mathbf{y}_{1:T}, \boldsymbol{\theta}^{(n-1)}]$, which is calculated by applying Kalman smoothing.

In the maximisation of $Q_{\rho_\alpha}(\boldsymbol{\theta}|\boldsymbol{\theta}^{(n-1)})$ with respect to $\boldsymbol{\gamma}, \sigma_\epsilon^2$, the updates of $\boldsymbol{\gamma}, \sigma_\epsilon^2$ are obtained from $\frac{\partial Q_{\rho_\alpha}(\boldsymbol{\theta}|\boldsymbol{\theta}^{(n-1)})}{\partial(\boldsymbol{\gamma},\sigma_\epsilon^2)} = \mathbf{0}$, as follows:

$$\boldsymbol{\gamma}^{(n)} = \text{diag} \left\{ \sum_{t=1}^{T} \langle \mathbf{f}_{t-1}^2 \rangle^{(n-1)} \right\}^{-1} \left(\sum_{t=1}^{T} \langle \mathbf{f}_t \circ \mathbf{f}_{t-1} \rangle^{(n-1)} \right),$$

$$\sigma_\epsilon^{2(n)} = \frac{1}{\sum_{t=1}^{T} N_t} \left\{ \sum_{t=1}^{T} \mathbf{y}_t' \mathbf{D}_{N_t}^{-1} \mathbf{y}_t - 2 \sum_{t=1}^{T} \langle \mathbf{f}_t \rangle^{(n-1)'} \mathbf{A}^{(n)'} \mathbf{B}_t' \mathbf{D}_{N_t}^{-1} \mathbf{y}_t \right.$$
$$\left. + \text{tr} \left(\sum_{t=1}^{T} \langle \mathbf{f}_t \mathbf{f}_t' \rangle^{(n-1)} \mathbf{A}^{(n)'} \mathbf{B}_t' \mathbf{D}_{N_t}^{-1} \mathbf{B}_t \mathbf{A}^{(n)} \right) \right\},$$

where $\circ$ denotes an element-wise product.

Before the MPL estimation with the adaptive lasso penalty, the parameters of the SCDFM are estimated by the MPL method with the L_2 penalty for $\mathbf{A}$ or the ML method. We set the estimated parameters as initial values of the EM algorithm for the MPL estimation with the adaptive lasso penalty as well as constants of the weight of the adaptive lasso penalty, $\bar{\alpha}_{ij}$ in (4).

When we update the system noise variance σ_ω^2 only for the initial iterations in the EM algorithm, the parameters converge faster. Thus, in the EM algorithm we update σ_ω^2 until M iterations, e.g., $M = 50$, and fix it from the iteration $M + 1$.

3.2. Regularisation parameter selection

In the MPL estimation with the adaptive lasso penalty, it is crucial to appropriately select the regularisation parameter ρ_α, because the regularisation parameter controls the sparsity of the basis in the estimated FL functions, i.e., the localisation of the estimated FL functions. In Efron (2004) and Zou et al. (2007), the degree of freedom of a linear regression model obtained by the L_1 sparse estimation was derived as the number of nonzero coefficients, and the AIC and BIC for the model (Akaike, 1973; Schwarz, 1978) were derived by introducing the degree of freedom. We introduce a model selection criterion that incorporate the degree of freedom as

$$-2\log p(\mathbf{y}_{1:T}|\hat{\boldsymbol{\theta}}) + w(T)(df(\rho_\alpha) + d),$$

where $df(d, \rho_\alpha)$ denotes the number of estimated nonzero basis coefficients, $w(T) = 2$ for the AIC and $w(T) = \log(T)$ for the BIC. We select the regularisation parameter ρ_α that minimises the criteria.

4. Applications to Ozone Concentration Data

The proposed modelling procedure and the maximum L_2 likelihood estimation for the SCDFM were applied to ozone concentration data. Ozone (O_3) is an air pollutant near the ground, and the O_3 concentration data were observed at 26 sites on the ground in New York state (Fig. 11.1). The data were observed daily for 46 days (Fig. 11.2), and contain 15 missing

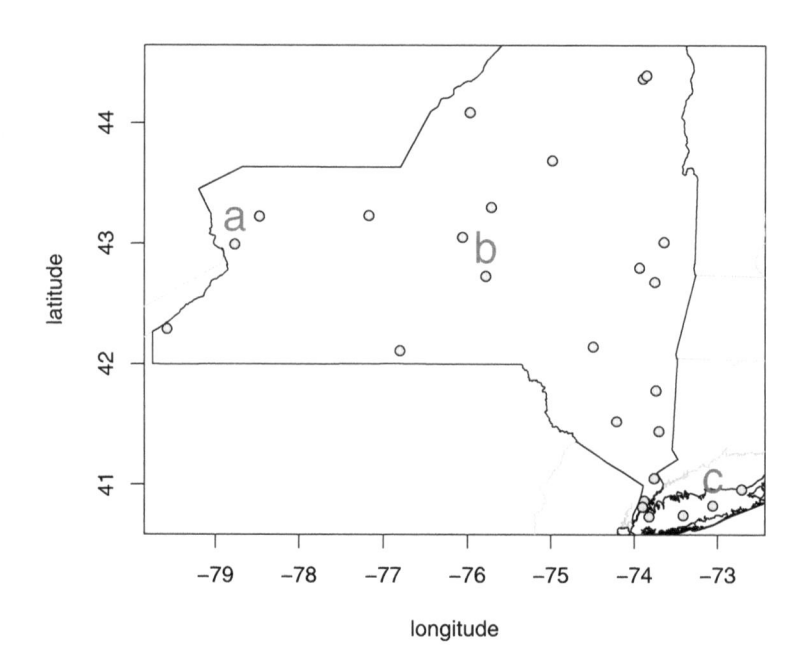

Fig. 11.1. The map of New York state, the boundary of which is denoted by black lines. Open circles show the observation sites of the O_3 concentrations.

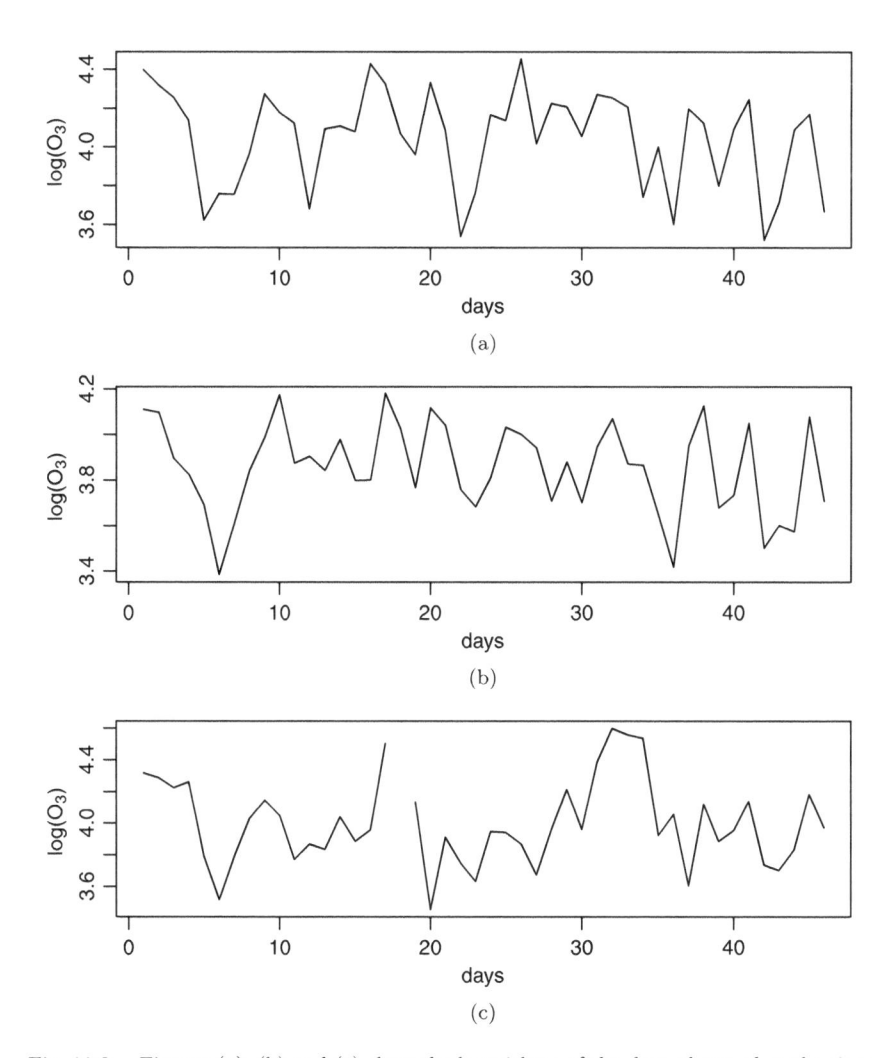

Fig. 11.2. Figures (a), (b) and (c) show the logarithms of the data observed at the sites "a", "b" and "c" in Fig. 11.1, respectively. The blank at the 18th day in the site "c" shows a missing value.

values. The data were also log-transformed to normalise them. The coordinates of the locations were converted from their latitudes and longitudes to orthogonal coordinates, measured in kilometres.

We estimated the SCDFM with five factors using the MPL methods with the L_2 penalty and the adaptive lasso penalty from the dataset. In the adaptive lasso MPL estimation, the parameters were preliminarily estimated by the L_2 penalised likelihood estimation. We introduced the estimates into the weights of the adaptive lasso penalty and set them as initial values of the EM algorithm. The EM algorithm was run for 10^4 iterations. We selected the regularisation parameter by the BIC defined in Section 3.2, because the BIC selects the parameter giving more sparse and clearer FL functions than those chosen by the AIC. The estimated coefficients in each of the FL functions, $\hat{\alpha}_j$, were scaled so that the average of absolute values of the FL function on the observation sites was 0.5.

We used the Gaussian basis functions whose number was the same as that of the observation sites, 26. The centres of the basis functions are the observation sites, and each of their spatial extents, ν_i, is the mean of the distances between the centre of the basis function, $\boldsymbol{\mu}_i$, and the centres of its three nearest-neighbour basis functions.

The estimated FL functions are plotted in Fig. 11.3. In both the MPL estimations with the adaptive lasso penalty and the L_2 penalty, the first FL function takes positive values all over the observation region (Fig. 11.3(a)(1), (b)(1)), so that the temporal variation of the corresponding first factor represents common temporal variation over the region. The signs of the other FL functions vary by site, and the difference in the signs is considered to represent directions of migrations of O_3. For example, the second FL function estimated by the both MPL methods takes positive values in the west area and negative values in the east (Fig. 11.3(a)(2), (b)(2)). Since the rise in the second factor increases the second component $f_{2t}\lambda_2$ on the west area and decreases that on the east area, the rise in the second factor is considered to represent a migration of O_3 from the east area to the west. We can find out the spatio-temporal structure of the migration of O_3 from the estimated factor processes and the structures of the corresponding estimated global FL functions.

The FL functions estimated by the adaptive lasso MPL method captures global structures (Fig. 11.3(b)(1)–(3)) and local structures (Fig. 11.3(b)(4)–(5)). The fourth and fifth estimated FL functions take high absolute values only in and around the City of New York, a heavily-populated area, and thus the functions are considered to capture the variation of O_3 not by a meteorological factor but a human factor. On the other hand, the FL functions estimated by the L_2 MPL method capture only the global structures. The FL functions estimated by the adaptive lasso MPL method were simpler and clearer than those by the L_2 MPL method, but the log-likelihood of the model estimated by the adaptive lasso MPL method is 99.1% of that by the L_2 MPL method nonetheless.

Dynamic Factor Modelling with Spatially Multi-scale Structures 177

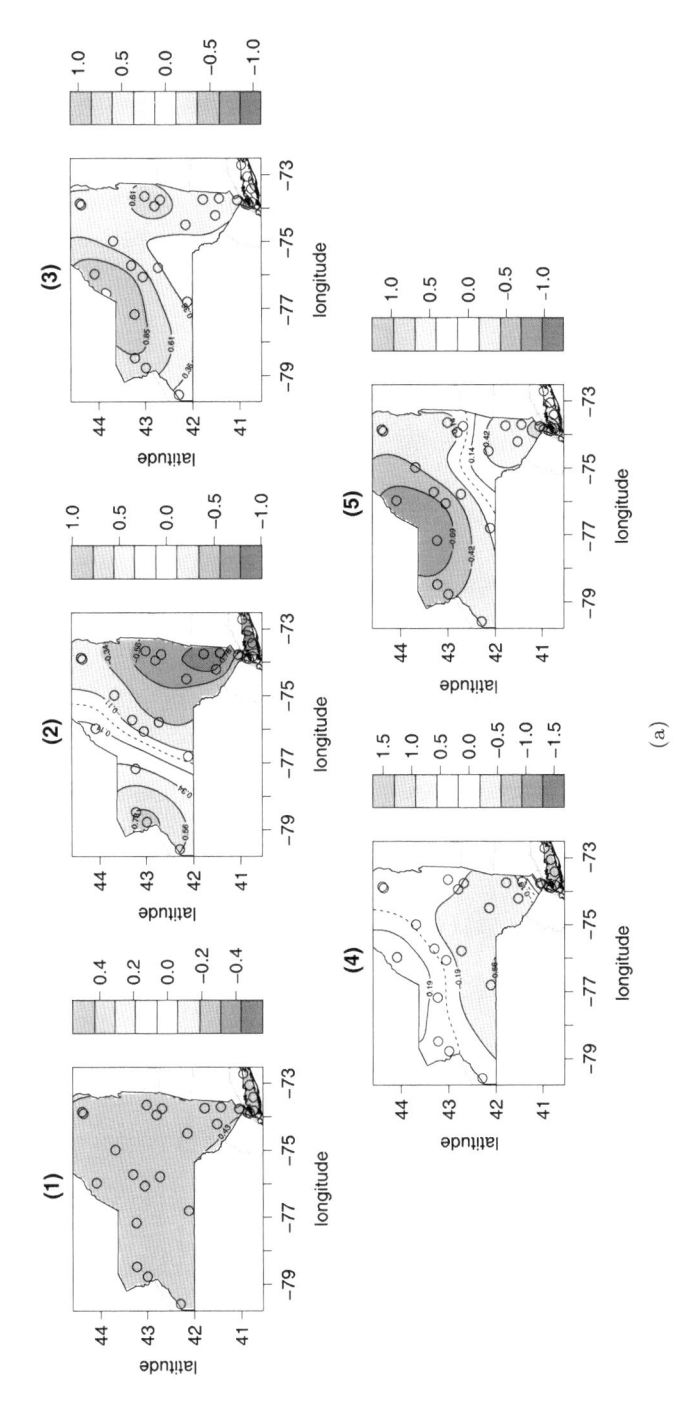

Fig. 11.3. The FL functions estimated by the MPL methods with the adaptive lasso penalty (a) and the L_2 penalty (b). Open circles denote the centres of the Gaussian basis functions incorporated in the estimated model, and cross marks denote the centres of the Gaussian basis functions rejected through the adaptive lasso MPL estimation. Dotted lines denote contour lines of 0.

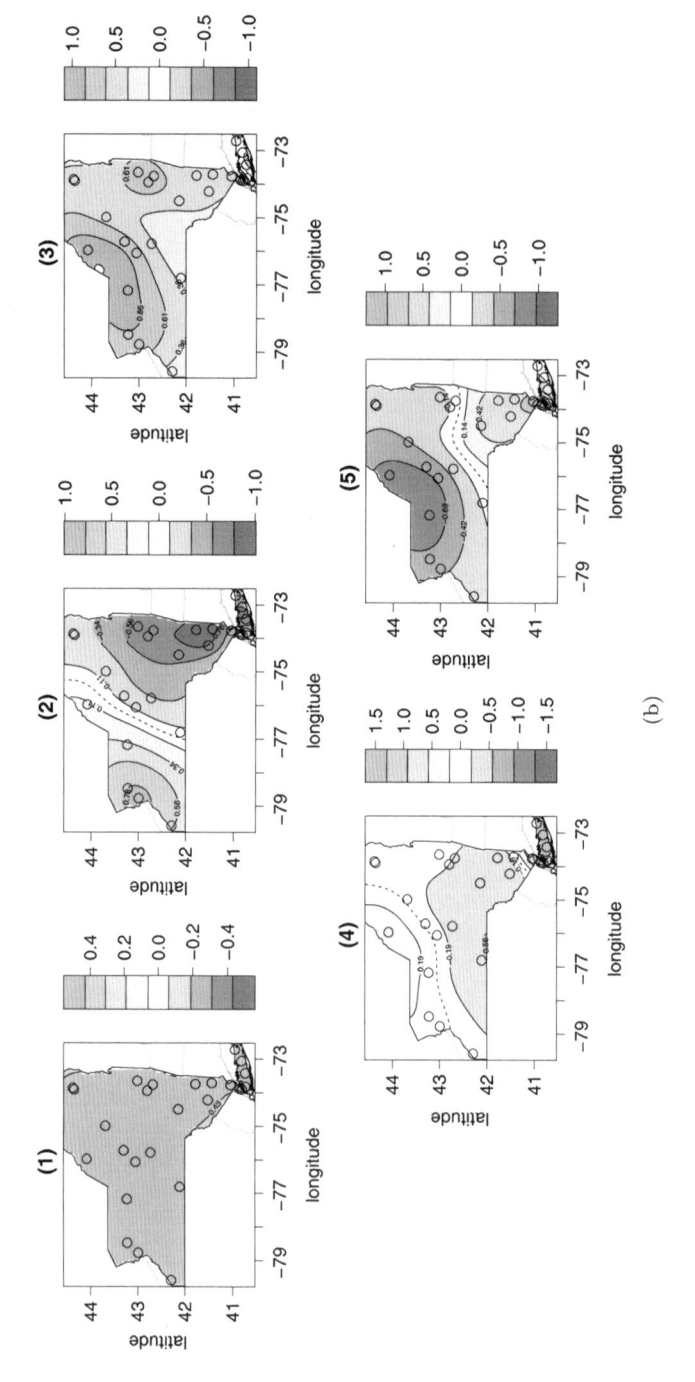

Fig. 11.3. (*Continued*)

5. Conclusion

We proposed a method for estimating the SCDFM having the spatially multi-scale FL functions that capture the spatially global and localised structures. The method estimates the coefficients in the FL functions by the MPL method with the adaptive lasso penalty. We derived the EM algorithm for maximising the adaptive lasso penalised likelihood stably by introducing the coordinate descent algorithm. Since the SCDFM contains the SDFM, the proposed modelling procedure can be applied to the SDFM and may estimate the SDFM that has multi-scale FL structures.

The applications to ozone concentration data showed that the proposed modelling procedure could estimate the spatially multi-scale FL functions and that the FL functions estimated by our procedure were simpler and easier to interpret their structures than those by the MPL method with the L_2 penalty.

Our modelling procedure can be applied to various kinds of spatio-temporal datasets, such as those arising in neuroscience and meteorology, and can extract the significant spatially multi-scale structures from such datasets.

Acknowledgements

This study was supported by MEXT KAKENHI Grant Number 25120011.

References

Akaike, H. (1973). Information theory and an extension of the maximum likelihood principle, in *Second Int. Symp. Information Theory*, pp. 267–281.

Blangiardo, M. and Cameletti, M. (2015). *Spatial and Spatio-temporal Bayesian Models with R-INLA*, John Wiley & Sons.

Chennubhotla, C. and Jepson, A. (2001). Sparse PCA. Extracting multi-scale structure from data, in *Proc. Eighth IEEE Int. Conf. Computer Vision, 2001. ICCV 2001*, Vol. 1, pp. 641–647.

Cressie, N. and Wikle, C. K. (2011). *Statistics for Spatio-temporal Data*, John Wiley & Sons.

Dempster, A. P., Laird, N. M. and Rubin, D. B. (1977). Maximum likelihood from incomplete data via the EM algorithm, *J. Roy. Statist. Soc. Ser. B (Methodological)* **39**, 1, pp. 1–38.

Dommenget, D. and Latif, M. (2002). A cautionary note on the interpretation of EOFs, *J. Climate* **15**, 2, pp. 216–225.

Efron, B. (2004). The estimation of prediction error: Covariance penalties and cross-validation, *J. Amer. Statist. Assoc.* **99**, 467, pp. 619–632.

Friedman, J. et al. (2007). Pathwise coordinate optimization, *Ann. Appl. Statist.* **1**, 2, pp. 302–332.

Friedman, J., Hastie, T. and Tibshirani, R. (2010). Regularization paths for generalized linear models via coordinate descent, *J. Statist. Softw.* **33**, 1, p. 1.

Geweke, J. (1977). The dynamic factor analysis of economic time series, *Latent Variables in Socio-economic Models* **1**.

Horel, J. D. (1981). A rotated principal component analysis of the interannual variability of the Northern Hemisphere 500 MB height field, *Monthly Weather Rev.* **109**, 10, pp. 2080–2092.

Ippoliti, L., Valentini, P. and Gamerman, D. (2012). Space–time modelling of coupled spatiotemporal environmental variables, *J. Roy. Statist. Soc.: Ser. C Appl. Statist.* **61**, 2, pp. 175–200.

Lopes, F., Hedibert, Salazar, E. and Gamerman, D. (2008). Spatial dynamic factor analysis, *Bayesian Anal.* **3**, 4, pp. 759–792.

Lopes, H. F., Gamerman, D. and Salazar, E. (2011). Generalized spatial dynamic factor models, *Comput. Statist. Data Anal.* **55**, 3, pp. 1319–1330.

Reinsel, G. C. (2003). *Elements of Multivariate Time Series Analysis*, Springer Science & Business Media.

Schwarz, G. (1978). Estimating the dimension of a model, *Ann. Statist.* **6**, 2, pp. 461–464.

Stock, J. H. and Watson, M. (2011). Dynamic factor models, in *Oxford Handbook on Economic Forecasting*, Oxford University Press.

Strickland, C., Simpson, D., Turner, I., Denham, R. and Mengersen, K. (2011). Fast Bayesian analysis of spatial dynamic factor models for multitemporal remotely sensed imagery, *J. Roy. Statist. Soc.: Ser. C Appl. Statist.* **60**, 1, pp. 109–124.

Takamitsu, A. and Shotaro, A. (2017). Spatially continuous dynamic factor modeling with basis expansion using l_2 penalized likelihood, submitted for publication.

Tibshirani, R. (1996). Regression shrinkage and selection via the lasso, *J. Roy. Statist. Soc. Ser. B (Methodological)*, pp. 267–288.

Zass, R. and Shashua, A. (2007). Nonnegative sparse PCA, *Adv. Neural Inform. Proces. Syst.* **19**, p. 1561.

Zhang, C.-H. et al. (2010). Nearly unbiased variable selection under minimax concave penalty, *Ann. Statist.* **38**, 2, pp. 894–942.

Zou, H. (2006). The adaptive lasso and its oracle properties, *J. Amer. Statist Assoc.* **101**, 476, pp. 1418–1429.

Zou, H. et al. (2007). On the degrees of freedom of the lasso, *Ann. Statist.* **35**, 5, pp. 2173–2192.

Index

A

AIC, 145, 174
anomaly detection, 159
ARMA model, 145

B

Bayesian quadrature, 104
BIC, 174
bioacoustics, 111

C

clustering large datasets into price indices (CLIP), 160
Conditionality Principle, 23
Consumer Prices Index, 157
covariance-based simulation, 126, 128
CT imaging, 126
cyber security, 4

D

data sets
    bat echolocation, 111
    SPEAR, 142
    galaxy, 93
    LANL, 6
    MNIST, 10

Density-Based Spatial Clustering of Applications with Noise (DBSCAN), 160
density estimation, 82

E

EM algorithm, 17, 172

F

F-measure, 45
File Drawer Effect, 26
Fourier transform, 113, 131

G

Gaffer, 4
Gaussian process, 105, 115
General Click Model, 59
GitHub, 162
Government Data Science Partnership, 156

H

H-measure, 47
hidden Markov model, 12

I

image reconstruction, 132

K

kernel density estimate, 148
Kolmogorov–Smirnov statistic, 44

L

label switching, 92
lasso, 31, 34, 171
logistic regression, 10, 37

M

map reduce, 4
Markov Chain Monte Carlo, 34, 69
mixture modelling, 90
model selection, 34, 82, 88, 174

N

neural network, 7, 10, 38
    deep networks, 15, 101
    generative adversarial networks, 15, 126, 132
    recurrent, 12

O

Office for National Statistics, 156–157
Ornstein–Uhlenbeck process, 117
OSI-communication model, 3

P

phylogenetic tree, 113
post-selection inference, 26

precision, 42, 159
Probabilistic Click Model, 58
probabilistic numerics, 103
probability calibration, 11, 40

R

R package
    sdsBAT, 122
    mvtnorm, 130
    packrat, 163
    RGeostats, 131
recall, 42, 159
recommender systems, 56
ROC curve, 12, 47
    AUC, 12, 48

S

saturated model, 30
seismology, 142
sequential algorithm, 62
sequential Monte Carlo, 80
submodularity, 60
support vector machine, 159

T

Threshold Click Model, 58
time series, 6, 143, 160, 168

U

uncertainty quantification, 99, 102, 126, 136, 142

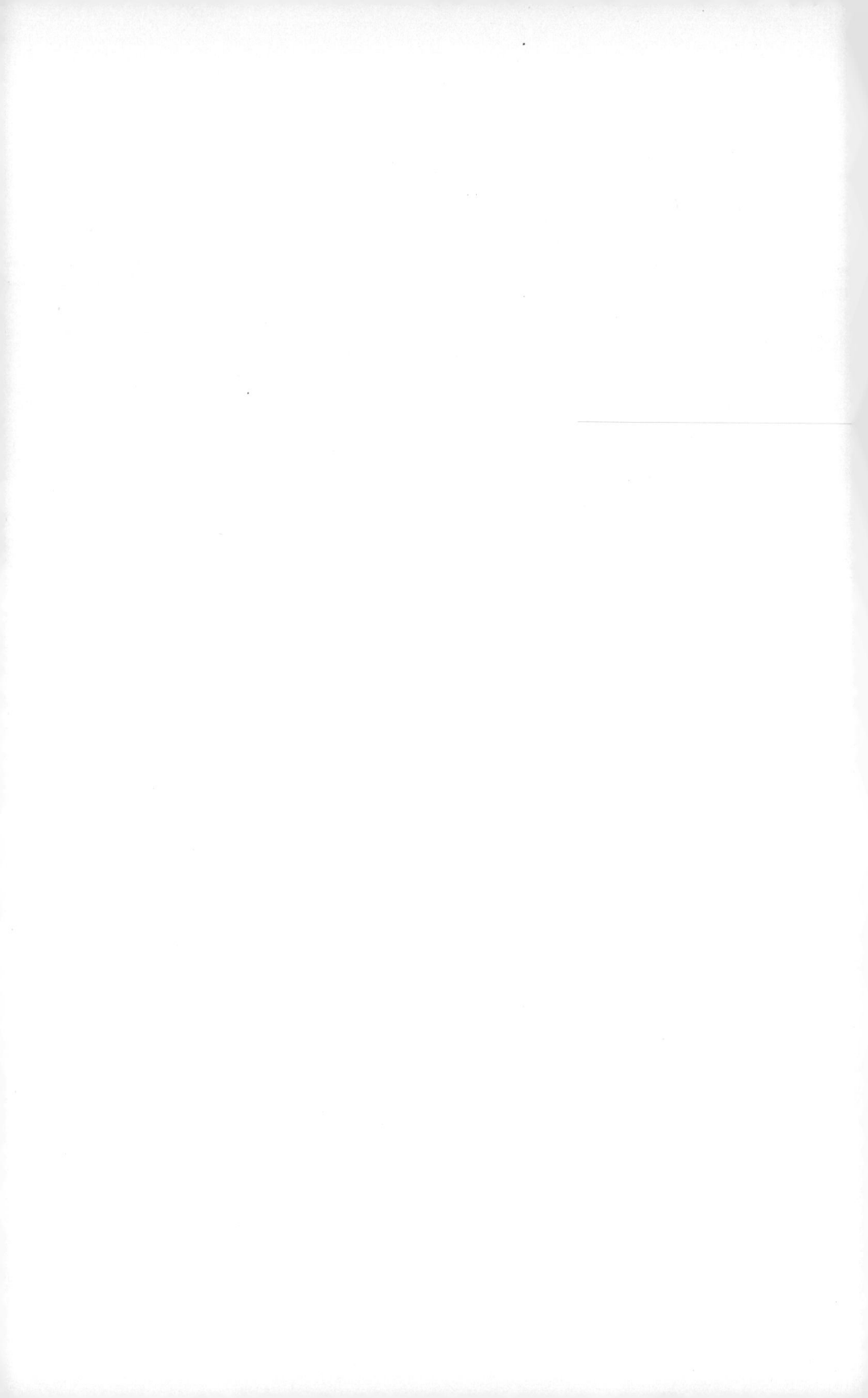